Sport and Peace-Building in Divided Societies

Sport is a cultural institution that stands at the interface between political and civil society. In divided communities, sport has been an agent of separation, sectarian hatred and violence, but also a highly effective tool for conflict resolution, reconciliation and peace-building.

In this important study, John Sugden and Alan Tomlinson draw on their extensive international experience of working with divided communities to develop a methodological and theoretical model for peace-building in sport. The book showcases original case studies from three regions of the world in which sport has played a prominent role in social deconstruction and reconstruction: Northern Ireland, Israel/Palestine and South Africa. Combining a wealth of primary and secondary data, the authors chart the rise of the contemporary Sport for Development and Peace movement (SDP) and outline an important new practice-based framework for understanding, researching and working to achieve positive social change in the SDP sector.

This is essential reading for any student, researcher or practitioner with an interest in the sociology of sport, sport development, international development, peace studies or conflict resolution.

John Sugden is Professor of the Sociology of Sport at the University of Brighton, UK. He is well known for his work on the sociology of boxing; sport and peace-building in divided societies; his studies – with Alan Tomlinson – of the world governing body for football, FIFA; and for his investigative research into football's underground economy. Currently, John is a leading member of the Sport and Leisure Cultures research network at Brighton, and Director of the University of Brighton's flagship worldwide community relations project, Football 4 Peace.

Alan Tomlinson is Professor of Leisure Studies, School of Humanities, at the University of Brighton, UK. He is a renowned scholar and researcher on the social history and sociology of sport, leisure and popular culture. Alan has researched the history and politics of FIFA since the mid-1980s, alongside studies on the political economy of the Olympics and the IOC. He is the author/editor of numerous books on sport, leisure and consumption, including *Consumption, Identity and Style* and *FIFA: The Men, the Myths and the Money*, and a long-term contributor to the soccer periodical *When Saturday Comes*.

Routledge Research in Sport, Culture and Society

For a full list of titles in this series, please visit www.routledge.com/sport/series/RRSCS

82 Transgender Athletes in Competitive Sport
Edited by Eric Anderson and Ann Travers

83 Sport and Militarism
Contemporary Global Perspectives
Edited by Michael L. Butterworth

84 Sport, Community Regeneration, Governance and Development
A Comparative Global Perspective
Rory Shand

85 Women Sport Fans
Identification, Participation, Representation
Kim Toffoletti

86 Sport in Korea
History, Development, Management
Edited by Dae Hee Kwak, Yong Jae Ko, Inkyu Kang and Mark Rosentraub

87 Sport and National Identities
Globalization and Conflict
Edited by Paddy Dolan and John Connolly

88 Sport and Contested Identities
Contemporary Issues and Debates
Edited by David Hassan and Ciaran Acton

89 Sport and Peace-Building in Divided Societies
Playing with Enemies
John Sugden with Alan Tomlinson

Sport and Peace-Building in Divided Societies

Playing with Enemies

John Sugden with Alan Tomlinson

LONDON AND NEW YORK

First published 2018 by Routledge

2 Park Square, Milton Park, Abingdon, Oxfordshire OX14 4RN

52 Vanderbilt Avenue, New York, NY 10017

Routledge is an imprint of the Taylor & Francis Group, an informa business

First issued in paperback 2019

Copyright © 2018 John Sugden and Alan Tomlinson

The right of John Sugden and Alan Tomlinson to be identified as authors of this work has been asserted by them in accordance with sections 77 and 78 of the Copyright, Designs and Patents Act 1988.

All rights reserved. No part of this book may be reprinted or reproduced or utilised in any form or by any electronic, mechanical, or other means, now known or hereafter invented, including photocopying and recording, or in any information storage or retrieval system, without permission in writing from the publishers.

Notice:
Product or corporate names may be trademarks or registered trademarks, and are used only for identification and explanation without intent to infringe.

British Library Cataloguing-in-Publication Data
A catalogue record for this book is available from the British Library

Library of Congress Cataloging-in-Publication Data
A catalog reference for this book has been requested

ISBN: 978-0-415-53268-6 (hbk)
ISBN: 978-0-367-34001-8 (pbk)

Typeset in Sabon
by Apex CoVantage, LLC

Contents

Foreword vi
Acknowledgements xii

1 The question? 1

2 SDP in never-never land – sport and peace-building in Northern Ireland 15

3 SDP in the promised land – sport and peace-building in Israel 33

4 SDP over the rainbow – sport and peace-building in South Africa 64

5 Can sport save the world? – SDP in cloud cuckoo land 92

6 SDP back down to earth – epistemological foundations of critical pragmatism 113

7 Critical pro-activism and the ripple effect 123

Appendixes A–E: materials underpinning the Football 4 Peace (F4P) project 135
Index 163

Foreword

'You should see me on the inside'. How Beachy Head and Sepp Blatter saved my life![1]

This book is considerably different to the one I had originally envisaged writing and believed I would be close to finishing by the beginning of June 2013. How wrong could I have been? It was a late Sunday evening in May of that year when, hurriedly packing my bags in preparation to go on an outdoor education field-trip to Cornwall in the west of England with a group of students the following day, I made sure my laptop was safely tucked away hoping that I would be able to find some time while the students were playing in the surf to do a little more work on the first draft of this book. I had planned to have completed the manuscript before heading off the following week to speak at an international conference in Canada. As I was preparing for bed in anticipation of an early start the following day, I began to feel unwell and found myself stumbling around the bedroom before eventually banging my head on the door jamb, prompting me to stagger to my bed which I managed to lay on the top of before sliding off onto the floor. Fortunately for me my wife, Christine, realised that this was more than a case of me having had a few too many Sunday afternoon beers. Instead she recognised that I was betraying the first symptoms of a stroke, and fortunately she had the presence of mind to call an ambulance. In doing so, between them my wife and the NHS emergency services team that attended my collapse almost certainly saved my life. When several days later I awoke finding myself in Eastbourne's DGH (District General Hospital) I had no idea what had happened to me when, rather drowsily, I came round finding myself not in my bedroom at home but tucked up in a hospital bed. Feeling more than a little bewildered, when I was able to I asked one of the nurses what had happened to me; "You've had a stroke sir" she replied. Although at the time I wasn't really sure what a stroke was – other than it was something serious that would probably put me on the side-lines for a few days – my total ignorance of the seriousness of my situation is the only explanation I can offer for my naive response to the nurse: "I can't have had a stroke I'm too busy – I'm going to Vancouver next week, where I'm due to give a lecture" (at ISSA's International Sociology of Sport Association Annual Conference). The nurse gave me a kind smile before saying words that chilled me to the bone: "I'm sorry sir you'll not be going anywhere in the foreseeable future, not at least until you've learned to walk again".

To say I was terrified would be the grossest of understatements. It would take some time before the catastrophic scale of what had happened to me would sink in. This came only later when I was informed by a neurological consultant that I had experienced a significant right-sided brain haemorrhage, a major stroke following which I was "lucky to still be alive". Although I did not feel particularly lucky at the time, I would learn later that in the UK one out of three of the one hundred and fifty thousand people who have a major stroke dies within 24 hours of the event. Even if they do survive, victims do so with serious cognitive and physical impairments and/or combinations thereof. Fortunately for me, though to begin with my stroke did leave me with some relatively minor physical problems with some marginal paralysis on my left side, I experienced no immediately obvious cognitive impediments, insomuch as my memory and speaking capacities were relatively unimpaired. Thanks to the dedicated work of the National Health Service (NHS) professionals who were assigned to aid my recovery, several weeks after my stroke I was able to take my first tentative steps around the ward and was eventually by the middle of June mobile enough to be discharged and allowed home to continue my recuperation.

Once out of hospital, supported and encouraged by an excellent team of NHS stroke specialists and related therapists I became determined that I would become the world champion of stroke-recovery. I was spurred on in this mission by an unquenchable thirst for living and an indefatigable self-determination that bordered on a pig-headedness cultivated and honed hitherto through a challenging, adventurous and sometimes perilous life at the centre of which was my passion for and participation in sports of many and varied kinds: hitherto 'the riskier the better' had been my rule of thumb. Thus it was with grim determination that I set about devising and operationalising an uncompromising personal recovery plan the foundation of which, drawing on my own experiences as a sportsman, was the classical mantra, *'mens sana in corpore sano'*: the belief that having a fit and healthy body is the key to having a strong and agile mind. This is a phrase from the works of the Roman satirist Juvenal, from his Satire X entitled 'The Futility of Aspirations', which warned against the follies of the pursuit of political or military power, and good looks to boot.[2] Thinking about my post-stroke future I was in no danger of falling into these vanity traps, but desperately wanted my life back and the re-integration of a healthy mind and a healthy body. Alongside the various individual and team competitive sports that I had played throughout my childhood and adult life I had always been a runner/jogger, and I became determined to use running as the lynch-pin of my post-stroke recovery plan. This led me as soon as I could to increasing the pace and distance of my slow walking until my balance and gait were steady and sturdy enough to facilitate a slow jog and eventually by mid-July I was able to undertake a moderate run. As a veteran participant in 12 full-marathons and scores of half-marathons prior to the stroke I felt I needed to set myself a target that would require me to incrementally progress my physical restoration.

Having competed in it several years before, I was familiar with one of the UK's toughest hill races in Britain, the Beachy Head Marathon, scheduled to be run at the end of October 2013. This was the event that I targeted. Entering for this race only a few weeks after coming out of hospital seemed to confirm to many of my friends and acquaintances that in having a stroke I had indeed lost my mind. But there was method in my madness. Registering was no act of foolhardy bravado; in entering a race that was scheduled to take place across the South Downs National Park very close to where I live, I knew that once I had registered my intent to take part in the race, in order to prepare properly I would have to get up every morning to train. Thus it was, accompanied by my faithful and now very fit retriever dog Che, we'd run, jog and walk for several miles each day in order to prepare for the ordeal ahead. Throughout the summer and autumn of 2013 this is exactly what I did, enabling me to complete the 26-mile hill marathon not much less than four months after experiencing a near-lethal stoke. As I staggered across the finish line in Meads village on the edge of Eastbourne I was able to say to myself "if I can do this, I can do anything so let's put the stroke in the past and move on!" It is not without irony that Beachy Head the cliff-top beauty spot that lends its name to the marathon which I used to accelerate my physical recovery is also the UK's most frequently used launch pad for people intent on committing suicide. It has been associated since the early nineteenth century, in early depictions of Romanticism and in the lexicon of climbers, with a persisting sense of 'mortal terror'.[3] I was determined to imbue the Beachy Head story with a dose of optimistic symbolic meaning in my personal theme of restoration.

Subsequently while my physical recovery continued to progress, as the journalist and publisher Robert McCrum (2008) explains in *My Year Off*, his excellent auto-ethnographic account of his own experiences of suffering and recovering from a stroke, the needs of body and mind are related and are essential components of any post-stroke rehabilitative and therapeutic regime. Recovering one's intellectual faculties after what amounts to a catastrophic attack on the brain is much more challenging and time-consuming than getting your body back in shape.[4] Hence the prefix to this book's foreword: "You should see me on the inside". If I had a pound for every time someone has come up to me and said, "you look really well", I'd be a wealthy man. I usually respond to this type of comment somewhat flippantly by saying, "You should see me on the inside". By this I mean that the presentation of the physical-self may mask the more insidious and longer-term impact of brain damage on the inner-self or 'spirit' which is a projection of the body's most vital organ, the mind. In recovery, I was living testimony to the brilliant sociological work of George Mead and Erving Goffman; Mead taught a generation and more of international sociologists and social psychologists to understand the distinction between the "I" and the "me" of interpersonal and interactive life; Goffman's brilliant blend of ethnographic study and interpretive thinking has enabled us to understand the distinction between the "front-stage" and the "back-stage" of social life in the presentation of ourselves in everyday life.[5] Training for and running a marathon might contribute to healing both the body and the mind, but for full intellectual restoration – in effect, to completely recover one's mind – one has to use it and if you are wondering how I set about achieving this task, this book is testimony to that process of recovery. And in case you might be wondering, re-training my mind to engage with the re-drafting of this book has been much harder than running any or indeed all of the 13 marathons I've completed. Alongside the completion of my final running marathon, in ways that I had never anticipated, I was also soon to become engaged in a "media marathon" that would require me to reconnect and re-engage with my intellectual self, in relation to long-term work on the politics and sociology of an increasingly corruptible FIFA, the world governing body of association football.

Kick-starting my damaged and comparatively slothful brain would be the most difficult part of the intellectual dimension of my recovery. To say I was suffering from writer's block is an understatement, but as I foundered and struggled for the fluency of word and turn of phrase that used to come so easily, salvation came from the unlikeliest of quarters. In the middle of 2015 FIFA suffered an escalating series of political and financial scandals and serious administrative failings that would eventually lead to the premature exit in disgrace of the organisation's long-serving president, Joseph 'Sepp' Blatter. The affairs of FIFA and its leadership is a subject about which along with my friend and colleague Alan Tomlinson I am considered to be one of the world's leading authorities. It was therefore not entirely surprising when as FIFA's crisis deepened, becoming headline news throughout the world, along with Alan I received countless requests from national and global media organisations to provide contextual detail and informed views on FIFA's trials and tribulations and speculate over the role played in this farrago by Sepp Blatter – a media marathon in which national and global media approached both of us in a blitz of global media coverage of the scandals. Whilst, before his stroke John's attention had been prominently focused upon the sport and peace-building work that is the focus of this book, Alan had stayed on the FIFA trail, logging the scandals throughout Blatter's tarnished tenures.[6] In the light of this media blitz, we began to work together again on the FIFA story, leading to an update of the FIFA narrative, revisiting and reframing earlier texts.[7] I believe it was this as much as anything else that injected much needed new electricity into my recovering brain as I prepared myself in anticipation of having to give authoritative live radio and television interviews to listening and watching audiences numbering thousands or potentially even millions, and we began together to produce *Football, Corruption and Lies*. Having felt to have been intellectually left for dead after my stroke, because of Herr Blatter and his cronies who starred in the epic narrative of the FIFA scandals, I suddenly realised that my dormant ideas were, in the maelstrom of worldwide publicity, in wide demand, and the reinvigorated partnership with Alan convinced me that with his support we could not only complete the update of the FIFA narrative, but could go on to revive and enhance the comparative cultural analysis on sport and peace in divided societies that I had been unable to continue and complete due to the stroke. The FIFA scandals were a rallying call and an opportunity. I had felt that there was no option but to step up to the microphone and give my views when the media requests flooded in; and to do so I had to force my mind to reconnect some of the neurological pathways that had become disconnected and/or blocked when my brain had been damaged by the 2013 stroke. The reconnections would also be sustained by the revival of the work underpinning this book.

Having achieved the update of the FIFA work, I finally felt willing and able, in sustained collaboration with Alan, to pick up the pieces of this manuscript. In his spellbinding study *Awakenings* (1973), the writer, psychoanalyst and surgeon Oliver Sacks described how the adventurous use of the drug L-DOPA brought to life, however transiently, a group of patients who had been suffering for up to 40 years from a purportedly hopeless "sleeping sickness" and mental illness;[8] Blatter was my drug, the FIFA scandals my awakening, an unanticipated source of inspiration that brought me back more fully to intellectual life and a resumption of individual and collective endeavour geared to establishing and consolidating a critical sociology of sport suited to the generation of an understanding of sport's place and potential in a complex and challenging global social order. Alan and I were up and running together again, going on to focus, in this book, upon a more positive side of football, the capacity – potential and actual – of the sport to bring benefits to diverse cultures and divided societies. Our study begins in a first-person voice, and here and there – we hope without clumsiness or pomposity – slips into a contextualising third-person. As the book develops, and particularly from Chapter 3 onwards, the narrative voice is increasingly the plural 'we'. In the narrative of the book our voices therefore progressively blend in a synthesis of theory and practice; the fieldwork for the earlier case studies has, as will be seen, linked extensively with my lived experiences in Northern Ireland and later in Israel, though by the latter case the two of us had been collaborating closely on the FIFA-based research, and were by then also working together and building a research culture for the critical sociology of sport at the University of Brighton.

Notes

1 An earlier draft of this Foreword provided the basis of a research article, jointly authored by Jayne C. Caudwell and John Sugden, published in 2016. See Jayne C. Caudwell and John Sugden, "'You should see me on the inside': Researching the post-stroke mental health of a male professor of sport", *Sociology of Sport Journal*, May 2016, online, ahead of print.
2 *Juvenal: The Satires,* trans. Nial Rudd with introduction and notes by William Barr (Oxford: Oxford University Press, 1992). For a contextual summary see Alan Tomlinson, *A Dictionary of Sports Studies* (Oxford: Oxford University Press, 2010): 267.
3 Paul Gilchrist, "Beyond the brink: Beachy Head as a climbing landscape", *The International Journal of the History of Sport*, 29/10, 2012: 1383–1404.
4 Robert McCrum, *My Year Off* (London: Picador, 1998).
5 Erving Goffman, *The Presentation of Self in Everyday Life* (London: Allen Lane The Penguin Press, 1969), see especially his third chapter on 'Regions and region behaviour' for extensive discussions on the distinction between social relations in front regions, or frontstage, and those in back regions, or backstage, in the broader context of a dramaturgical model in which all of us act out performances that contribute to everyday life. Goffman's study, first published in 1959, remains a brilliant application of a particular case – much of what he calls his 'report' stems from ethnographic work in the Shetland Islands, Scotland, conducted for his University of Chicago doctoral study – to the generalities of everyday life and social relationships. On the "I" and the "me", see George Herbert Mead's *Mind, Self and Society* (Chicago: The University of Chicago Press, 1934) for influential discussions of how the concept of the self comprises what one might call an individual's inner "I", in endless interplay with the individual's "more social 'me'"; and this "me" is constantly in the making.
6 Alan Tomlinson, *FIFA: The Men, the Myths and the Money* (London and New York: Routledge, 2014).
7 John Sugden and Alan Tomlinson, *Football, Corruption and Lies: Revisiting "Badfellas", the Book FIFA Tried to Ban* (London and New York: Routledge, 2016).
8 Oliver Sacks, *Awakenings* (New York: Summit Books, 1973).

Acknowledgements

The Foreword to this book explains why my deepest gratitude for helping me finish the book must go to my wife Christine whose vigilance and prompt actions probably saved my life when in 2013 she recognised that I was having a stroke and contacted the NHS emergency services who rapidly deployed an ambulance and in so doing undoubtedly contributed to my survival and subsequent recovery. In this regard I'd also like to thank my other family members; particularly my children Alexandra and Jack and my son-in-law Neil whose unflinching support helped me overcome this traumatic episode in my life. Likewise I'd like to pay tribute to my close work colleagues, none more so than Gary Stidder and Graham Spacey. More generally I'd like to recognise the University of Brighton's School of Sport and Service Management for standing by me in this the most difficult period of my academic career. In a similar vein I'd like to thank the University of Brighton's occupational health and Human Resources teams who likewise have been steadfast in their support for me during these difficult times. Alan and I are also grateful to the University of Brighton which from a variety of sources has provided support and funding for much of the research which underpins this book, including periods of sabbatical leave supported by a research budget. Finally I'd like to thank myself, without whose help, Alan Tomlinson would not have been able to finish this book.

John Sugden
Eastbourne, East Sussex, UK,
May 2017

Many thanks for stalwart support from my partner Bernie Kirrane, and our four daughters Alys, Rowan, Jo and Sinead, who have all been understanding and supportive of the work involved in producing *Playing with Enemies*. I very much appreciate how John has trusted me to help him, after his stroke and its consequences, resume work on the manuscript of this book. This has provided us both with an opportunity to place ourselves in the narrative of accumulating research studies over an unusually long period, and in some senses to review our academic and intellectual trajectories as we have worked together in a developing field of social science-based sport studies. It is, as I write, 31 years since John provided, with a colleague, a chapter on football and politics in Northern Ireland for my book, co-edited with Garry Whannel, *Off the Ball: The Football World Cup* (London: Pluto Press, 1986). I did not anticipate then that we would join forces on so many research adventures that have helped us shape our critical sociological approach to the study of sport, linked to our conviction that critique alone is merely one-dimensional unless it is conceived itself as a form of praxis. So I am very pleased to have been able to join John in completing this book, and helping retrieve a narrative, a project, and a vision for a relevant and useful critical sociology of sport. We have worked extensively together on the shady side of big-time sport, exposing FIFA's corrupt core; here we consider the other side of sport, its capacity to deliver worthwhile, progressive, even humanitarian, goals – in the right time, and the right place, but only if based in sociologically sensitive and properly informed actions and interventions.

I would also like to thank our publisher, Routledge, and especially Simon Whitmore, for continuing to support our work; and the University of Brighton for awarding a sabbatical that allowed me, in 2010, to undertake research in South Africa preceding and during the FIFA men's World Cup in South Africa.

Alan Tomlinson
Brighton, East Sussex, UK; and
Campillergues, L'Hérault, Languedoc, France,
May 2017

Chapter 1

The question?

It can sometimes be hard to identify exactly where and when the inspiration for a book comes from. Not so in this case. While the data that feed into the following pages have been gleaned from a wide range of experiences and informed by a multitude of primary and secondary sources, the idea for the book itself derives from a simple question that was asked by Dominic Malcolm, fellow sport sociologist, during a staff and graduate seminar at the University of Loughborough in 2006, in which John Sugden reflected upon the role that he had played in establishing and developing the sub-field of Sport for Development and Peace (SDP). At the end of the presentation, a familiar range of questions was asked, particularly concerned with technical/logistical, funding, safety and related security issues. Once the research students had finished their interrogations, Dr. Malcolm raised his hand and asked, "What difference does the fact that you are a sociologist make to your leadership and development of projects like this?"

'What an outstanding question'! I thought, as I then *ad libbed*, stumbling and stuttering through what, on reflection, was at best a vague and incomplete answer; but at the same time, replying: "Of course it makes a difference, in as much as being a sociologist isn't just a job, it's more a vocation, a way of life, and as such as a sociologist everything you see and do stimulates and is filtered through and activated by your trained sociological imagination". This was an implicit acknowledgement of the significant influence that the American sociologist C. Wright Mills had on my own development as a sociologist and activist.[1] This being the case, inevitably the evolution of our approaches to SDP and interpretation of that experience has been and continues to be heavily influenced by a particular model of the "sociological imagination". While at the time this answer seemed to satisfy the audience, on reflection later it became clear that the simple questions demand the most complex answers. In the intervening years since the Loughborough seminar seeking a satisfactory answer to Dr. Malcolm's question has been a recurrent concern. What follows in this book provides the more complete – both evidenced and theorised – answer that his perceptive and challenging question deserves.

Having said this, the original answer was by no means completely off-the-mark, and was in fact a compass point for what follows: that all of the sport-based, community activism over more than three decades has been influenced by a particular sociological gaze, one framed not just by the corpus of sociological knowledge absorbed during an intellectual journey through Higher Education as both student and academic, but equally importantly by the places where as a sociologist one has lived, by the experiences encountered in the world of SDP and beyond, and by the many influential people (both academic and lay) engaged with along the way. This book is based on the interpretive juxtaposition between the lived and theoretical hemispheres of the SDP globe as dwelt in and scrutinised for the past three decades. For reasons made clear in the foreword this is not exactly the book that was originally planned. While neither an auto-ethnography nor a biography, John's near-death experience and subsequent convalescence has led us to produce a professional narrative spiced by memoir, lived experience and interpretive immersion in the subject contexts. This has produced both a much more self-reflective account, and a more grounded theoretical analysis, than might have otherwise been the case.

Nonetheless in adopting such an approach, one must be very conscious of the need to guard against allowing self-reflection to turn into self-indulgence. With this in mind the 'telling of tales' has been restricted to events and circumstances shaping and defining a direction towards the study of sport, conflict-resolution and peace-building, a field that became one of the domain concerns of the Brighton research agenda, constituting a founding contribution to the creation of SDP as a sub-field within the sociology of sport. In this comparatively new area of academic inquiry this contribution, as the narrative in the following pages reaffirms, has been to take as a lead the 'P' component of the acronym, that is to give priority to the conflict-resolution and peace-building dimensions of SDP.[2] At the heart of this contribution, too, has been a concern with practical and intellectual/philosophical objectives and outcomes. While there have been more generic development goals and outcomes associated with the work in sport and peace-building it is the use of sport to promote conflict-resolution and co-existence that we believe to be the most distinctive and significant contribution to the field. In doing this, bringing the researcher's phenomenological presence into play alongside the critical sociological gaze has been a means of recognising the agency of the researcher, and this has consistently informed the developing work concerning the relationships and tensions between the practice-based and theoretically orientated dimensions of the personal SDP expedition.

As such, this is not a definitive and comprehensive text that reviews and synthesises all that is known and has been written about SDP, nor is this book a wholly conventional research monograph, but it is purposely designed to be of interest and use to the academic community. Even more importantly, it is designed to be accessible to a wider audience, particularly those activists and policy makers who are practically engaged at different levels of the SDP world. Which is why, with the publisher's indulgence, the book is written and presented as a narrative, with footnoted attributions limited to the most relevant sources and those whose work directly informs the telling of this tale. In doing this a life in SDP is shown to have consistently interacted with a maturing sociological imagination, so informing a distinctive approach to civil society activism in the world of sport for development and peace. The primary aim of the book remains, though, to produce a plausible theory and method for SDP work that can be easily understood, implemented and further developed in a multitude of different settings around the world.

The book articulates an answer to 'The Question' by comparing and contrasting case studies in three regions which have long histories of deep social division and socio-political violence, and which are or have been experiencing, at different stages of progress, so-called 'peace processes': Northern Ireland, the Middle East and South Africa. These regions have been selected for a number of overlapping reasons: with the possible exception of the Balkan countries that used to be part of the former Yugoslavia, not only are they the sites of the most high-profile and enduring racial/ethno-religious conflicts of the modern era, they are also all societies within which peace processes feature prominently and in which, to borrow Eric Dunning's phrase, 'sport matters'.[3] They have also been singled out because they are all places where we have either lived or spent extended periods of time. I lived and worked in Northern Ireland from 1983 until 1996 and from 2001–2012 spent extended periods of time engaged in sport-focused co-existence projects and programmes in Israel, Jordan and Palestine. While I have spent less time in South Africa, in 1996 shortly after the fall of apartheid Alan Tomlinson and I were in Johannesburg and Durban for the duration of association football's African Cup of Nations and we have visited the country on numerous occasions since, including nine weeks in the field gathering material for *FIFA: The Men, the Myths and the* Money (Tomlinson, 2014) and for this book, in 2010 and 2012 respectively.[4] Furthermore, given the role played by sport in the dis-establishment and reformation of the 'Rainbow Nation', to write a book about sport and peace-building that did not feature South Africa would have been an unjustifiable omission.

These case studies form Chapters 2, 3 and 4 and, alongside our parallel intellectual trajectories, provide the experiential core of the book. The later chapters review the wider context of the field, considering critically the key features of the SDP 'movement' and arguing that its recent growth has suggested a journey towards institutionalisation and ossification; and they reflect back on the case studies to outline the most prominent lessons that have been learned in journeying through the world of SDP. We argue how, under carefully constructed and managed circumstances, with modest, pragmatic and incremental goals, sport can be used as a vehicle to carry and inculcate the values upon which better lives can be built. The main features of 'the ripple effect' model, a praxis-based heuristic designed to help guide political engagement and civil society activism in this sphere, are evaluated in the final chapter. But to begin with we need to go in search of the roots of the sociological imagination that we believe is best fitted to the journey that has framed and informed this book's narrative.

'When I was in the Sudan . . .': a quest for the sociological imagination

Before 'gap years' had become the flavour of the day, John was in the Sudan as a volunteer teacher in a postgraduate year after leaving the University of Essex with a modest degree result in Government and Sociology and a stellar triple honours in political protest, socialising and sport (not necessarily in that order). Graduate jobs were scarce then, in the mid-1970s, particularly for those of us with degrees in the social sciences and the humanities. As a default, after university many graduates opted for careers in secondary education, social services or the prison and probation services. I felt that the world had more to offer than *Please Sir?* or *Porridge* and I was determined not to follow any of the default options.[5] After three months working as a full-time barman in the *Royal Oak*, a pub in Harlesden, north London, serving pints of Guinness to thirsty London-Irish labourers, my resolve faltered and I was about to begin work as a rookie social worker in the London Borough of Tower Hamlets; but three weeks before I was scheduled to start my new job I was browsing through the situation vacant pages of *The Guardian* newspaper when my eye was caught by a small, almost deliberately vague, advertisement for volunteer teachers to work, for local wages only, teaching English for the Ministry for Education in the Sudan.[6] Except that it was somewhere in Africa, I was not even sure where the Sudan was. I decided to apply anyway and against all odds, or so it seemed, after a hurried interview somewhere in West London was offered a position. Three weeks later, with little or no time to think through the consequences of this career move and post-colonial adventure, I found myself alongside a dozen or so fellow volunteers sweltering on the baking tarmac at Khartoum's International Airport.

Sudan has a classic post-colonial shape, its boundaries having been drawn more or less in straight lines during the nineteenth-century's "scramble for Africa".[7] At that time, regardless of traditional tribal and ethnic regional distinctions and power relations, geographic borders would often be set in smoke-filled rooms in London, Brussels, Paris or Berlin when the armies of one European power would bump into those of another as they sought to extend the boundaries of their African Empires. Which is why, since its independence in 1956, the Republic of Sudan, has been blighted by internal tribal conflicts and protracted civil war between the Arab-dominated North and the African South. This conflict seemed to be finally resolved in 2011 when the Southern part of the country was granted independence, although tensions between the Sudan (North) and its nearest and newest neighbour remained high, particularly in the districts closest to the border where the region's copious oil reserves can be found, while in Darfur, in the North, rebels and Government-sponsored militia continue to fight it out, bringing devastation and death to local populations; and, as we write, civil war continues to rage in the South.

But all that was still in the future when a group of hopeful though apprehensive young volunteers was led through the airport and onto a waiting bus which took us all to the Ministry of Education where we would be assigned to our different schools. After the briefest of inductions I was deployed to an ex-colonial boarding school in a town called El Obeid in the west of the sprawling country. It was the rainy season and in the absence of any useable roads, this involved another flight in a small plane to cover the 300 miles between Khartoum and El Obeid. This was hardly a journey to the dreaming spires or to a cloistered idyll of a college campus comprising welcoming quads, gothic spires and green fields. The School, *Khor Taggart*, was a barracks-like relic of the British Empire, by whom the country had been ruled in association with Egypt until 1958. It was one of only a handful of boys' secondary schools in the whole country. The school that was to be a home and place of work for ten months sat in an area of scrub-land and semi-desert surrounded by a scattering of mud-hut villages about five miles away from the main town. At this time I had never taught a day in my life and was naïvely expecting a period of training and induction, not just a cursory briefing at the airport. I was wrong, as it turned out the next day when greeted by a regal, olive-skinned headmaster, dressed in a flowing starched-white *jelabia*, – the preferred, cooling, shift-like robe of Arab men in the ferocious heat of North Africa – "Welcome", he boomed, thrusting a time-table into the hands of this pedagogic neophyte, wishing him luck as he was sent straight in to a debut teaching lesson.

Minutes later, I found myself standing nervously in front of a classroom of 30 or more 16-year-old boys dressed in battleship-grey short-sleeve shirts and shorts eagerly awaiting me to lead them through an English GCE O Level literature syllabus that included Charles Dickens's *Oliver Twist*, Oscar Wilde's *A Woman of No Importance* and Alan Paton's *Cry, the Beloved Country*. I could speak no Arabic and my pupils could speak very little English. We, the pupils and I, and the family of huge, double-bodied, Nile wasps that had nests in the corner of my classroom, got on famously. Suffice to say the days ahead were extremely challenging but I managed to survive without doing too much damage to the intellectual development of my charges. I even might have taught one or two of them how to write and speak English a little better – albeit with a Liverpool twang. In my spare time, helped by local teachers, I was able to explore the surrounding villages and during brief periods of leave venture further afield to explore what at the time, and right up to the 2011 partition, was Africa's largest and poorest country. My travels took me deep into the war-torn and lawless south of the country where I came face-to-face with dignified nomadic tribespeople, living amid grinding poverty, exacerbated by the terror tactics wielded by rebel and government forces.

The whole experience was quite a shock for the recent hedonistic undergraduate. To help the months of relative isolation pass, at the school I got involved with the boys' extracurricular sporting activities. The Empire had left behind a pair of rusting goalposts bestriding a dirt football pitch and an open-air basketball court with a dim floodlight and two naked basketball hoops. Here in the late afternoons and early evenings I'd join in with the boys, helping them with their football technique when I could, but more often, particularly in the case of basketball, picking up tips from them.

Before leaving London, hurriedly packing more in hope than expectation, I had thrust a pair of training shoes and a brand-new pair of football boots into my backpack. This later turned me into a celebrity among the schoolboys as most played barefoot and only the better senior boys, who played for the school team in the very occasional interscholastic football match, had boots. These tended to be imperial antiques, the stiff leather, high-ankle, studs-nailed-in kind that I remember my father playing in when I was a primary schoolboy in the early-to-mid 1950s. My moulded sole, soft leather *Mitres* became the talk of the town where I would go to train with and play once a week for one of the local teams, *Al Hilal* (crescent moon) in the city of El Obeid. Each time I made the journey into town, bouncing along the dirt track on a bench in the back of the school's old army truck, I would stop off at an open-air cafe on the main street for a cooling iced-lemon drink. A hoard of ragged, impoverished, shoe-shine boys would descend on the truck, competing noisily for the honour of cleaning my envied and glorified football boots. The normal rate for a shoeshine was a Sudanese penny, but I would give a shilling to the one anointed for the task. No wonder I almost caused a riot every time I came to town! I have never had cleaner boots before or since. When it came time for me to leave my post, I offered my gleaming boots to Khalifa, the captain of the school's senior boys' football team. The way he looked at those boots, the way his hands trembled as he held them, you might have thought they contained a contract to play for Manchester United.

I did not think of it at the time but the experiences in the Sudan and that departing gesture could be interpreted as part of the long colonial and neo-colonial legacy of British rule in the Sudan, famously referred to by the historian J. A. Mangan as a country of "blacks ruled by blues".[8] This was reference to the fact that many of the officials recruited into the Sudan Political Service, the British colonial administration that ruled the country in the late nineteenth and much of the twentieth century, were Oxford or Cambridge (Oxbridge) graduates, many of whom had earned their sporting colours (blues) – often at the expense of any credible academic qualification – before moving on to serve the empire. H. C. Jackson, arriving in the Sudan in 1907, recalled in his memoir that it was the "emphasis on physical fitness which gave rise to the aphorism that the Sudan was a country of *Blacks* and *Browns* administered by *Blues*".[9] Before they left, just like me, they had made sure that their cricket bats, tennis rackets, rugby balls and yes, football boots were safely packed into their luggage.

Did they know that by so doing they were offering themselves as peddlers of 'soft power': a continuation of the British Empire's strategy of using home-grown sports to help spread and sustain the impact of the imperial bootprint, through means of persuasion rather than outright force or coercion?[10] Or were they simply relatively privileged if naïve adventurers like me, who were bringing with them the few things from home that they anticipated might make their 'exotic' sojourns in 'darkest Africa' a little more bearable? If in the process they could lend a helping hand to needy locals, to improve valued second-language skills, while at the same time teaching them how to better head a ball or do a step-over to beat a defender, and gift a few pairs of football boots on their departure, then in my view, in a postcolonial world this speaks more of development than despotism.[11]

That I can remember the Sudanese episode in my life so vividly is because it had such a profound impact on my own personal development. These reminiscences have been helped by the fact that throughout the nine months in a personal log I recounted and reflected upon my everyday experiences, and wrote detailed descriptive letters to family and friends in tiny script on thin blue aerogrammes. Though I did not know it at the time, thus began my career as an ethnographer, a skill that has been the bedrock of my research endeavours ever since. It had been a watershed year during which my view of the world and my privileged place in it had been turned upside down. It made me aware of the ethnocentric parochialism that can stifle any developed understanding of societies and cultures across the world; perhaps implicitly, but pivotally, a sociological imagination was taking shape and finding its voice. I vowed when I returned home never again to take anything for granted or at face-value; this Damascene realisation would fuel a sociological vocation.

But then what? In 1976 when I arrived back in the UK attractive graduate careers remained hard to find and I found myself back where I had been a year earlier, exchanging a bar job for labour on a London building site. As a holding measure, I managed to squeeze onto a one-year programme at the University of Liverpool that would qualify me as a Physical Education teacher.[12] While I thoroughly enjoyed this course, I harboured no serious ambitions to become a PE teacher. Fortunately, at the time the PGCE Senior Course Tutor at Liverpool was Ian Ward, a former British stiff-pole vault champion. He had led seminars in which, accompanied by the groans of my fellow students, most of my observations and interjections were prefaced with, "When I was in the Sudan . . .". Ward perhaps sensed in me a level of intellectual curiosity and appetite for adventure that would be ill-suited to a career in the gym. Mid-way through the course he encouraged me to consider applying to go to the United Sates to study for a Master's degree under Andrew Yiannakis. Like Wade himself, Yiannakis was a graduate of Madeley College of Physical Education in the UK (long since incorporated into the North Staffs Polytechnic, now Staffordshire University). Both men had been among the first to go to North America to take up postgraduate academic scholarships in sport-related subjects. After completing his Master's degree Ward had returned to Great Britain, but his contemporary Yiannakis had stayed in the US, eventually earning his doctorate and securing a faculty position at the University of Connecticut (UConn) where he devised a pioneering postgraduate programme in the sociology of sport.

My application was accepted and I was one of the first students to undertake this programme. At the time my ambition went no further than being paid a small stipend to spend 12 months abroad, living in America, getting a bit of university teaching experience, before, like Ward, returning home with a Master's degree. The longer I stayed, however, the more I began to see this fledgling sub-discipline as an area within which I could thrive and prosper. While by no means a high-flying undergraduate, I had always had high levels of intellectual curiosity, but this was not matched by scholarly application. In other worlds I was lazy. At UConn I found a refreshing new dimension to satisfy this curiosity and the unusual juxtaposition, sociology and sport, motivated me to put more effort into my scholarship. To my great surprise I discovered that when I focused my efforts I was quite good at producing academic essays and related assessments, going through Graduate School, to use an Americanism, with 'straight As'.

Equally importantly, I still considered myself a political radical and activist. In its earliest days an activist branch of the sociology of sport in North America grew up around an investigative and campaigning spirit, the goal of which was to expose some of the greatest excesses and injustices then prevalent in sport in the USA and further afield. Back then, the graduate student rubbed shoulders with figures like Jack Scott and Harry Edwards who were preeminent in a field of scholars whose prime goals were not then tied to questions of promotion and tenure, but were more concerned with what was wrong with American sport and what needed to be done to fix it. In short, these early pioneers were public intellectuals who used academia as a base from which to launch their attacks on the American sports establishment, particularly with regard to issues such as race relations, women's rights and exploitation and corruption in professional and intercollegiate sports.[13] In the formative years of my academic career I was immediately at home and thrived in this campaigning-activist approach and it is something that has routinely characterised subsequent research trails and directions.

Connecticut offered the opportunity to seriously formulate a distinctive sociological imagination. Back in the early 1970s the University of Essex had a reputation for left-wing radicalism and the Marxist-oriented content there would bear this out. The UConn Sociology Department provided an expanded and enhancing understanding of critical sociology and theory in elective graduate courses given by world-leading scholars on topics such as critical criminology, social stratification, the sociology of law. Among them and key to my formative development was a class taught by Professor Ken Neubeck on the critical sociology of C. Wright Mills. This came at a time when I was beginning to get disillusioned by the direction being taken by sociology in general, and branches of Marxism in particular, wherein theoretical refinement was given priority over empirically based interpretation and critically informed engagement. With Neubeck's help I rediscovered Wright Mills and in his work found the beginnings of a recipe through which critical theoretical reflection and empirical observation could be brought together to write the script of public intellectuals and inform the practice of social and political activists.

Courses were also available in qualitative methodologies and ethnography. Fulfilling an assessment in the latter required me to gain some field experience, necessitating the negotiation of access to a ghetto boxing club in nearby Hartford, Connecticut. The moment I entered the exotic subculture that inhabited that stifling basement gymnasium I realised I'd discovered the focus for my PhD thesis. I would spend two years as a participant observer trying to make sense of the relationship between the social world of the boxing club and the abrasive youth cultures that swirled around it in the surrounding urban ghetto. While a full interpretation of this mysterious world can be read in my book *Boxing and Society*, one key characteristic that I observed of this boxing subculture is worth mentioning here because it is central to understanding the values-based approach to sport interventionism presented in the case studies and advocated in Chapter 7: "Continued membership of the boxing subculture necessitates the acceptance of a value system which emphasises respect for oneself and for others: not just physical respect, but equally respect for one's own and an opponent's character. . . . In short, boxing inculcates in its adherents the value system and behavioural trappings of a 'civilised' society".[14]

Leaving Connecticut in 1982 with all of the ingredients needed to cook up a distinctive, critical sociological imagination, the young sociologist was hungry for sociological action. As I packed my bags to head for yet another uncertain future in London, if I had been asked to make a list of where in the world I would least like to go, given political currents prevailing in the early 1980s, with little doubt Northern Ireland, South Africa and Israel would have been bunched at the top of that list. That I would end up spending a considerable amount of time in all of these places could not have been predicted, but that is what happened, and along the way I was provided with and honed the kitchens and utensils that, working with close collaborators and colleagues, have enabled me to cook this sociological and vocational dish. *Bon appetit*.

Meanwhile, the stirrings of a critical sociology of sport were becoming increasingly visible in the UK and Canada. Networks of scholars emerged through the conferences of the North American Society for the Sociology of Sport (NASSS); and publishing initiatives in Canada, stimulated by Richard Gruneau and Hart Cantelon, and in the UK via the Leisure Studies Association (LSA) and the British Sociological Association (BSA) Study Group, made influential interventions in the emerging field.[15] I had, as a graduate student, attended the inaugural conference of NASSS in Denver, Colorado, in 1980, speaking on "Sport and the dialectics of freedom in capitalist society"; and at the NASSS conferences of 1981 (Fort Worth, Texas) and 1982 (Toronto, Ontario) Alan Tomlinson, whose interdisciplinary education had straddled the humanities and the social sciences at the University of Kent and the University of Sussex, culminating in his doctoral study reviewing and critiquing cultural and critical theory in the context of selected comparative cultural analyses of the novel, presented papers on theory and methods and debates within the sociology of culture that were also germane to the sociological study of sport. This included a chapter in the book of the 1981 conference on the sociological imagination and its application to sport and sport cultures.

In 1982 Alan spent time at the Queen's University Centre for Sport and Leisure Studies, Kingston, Ontario, where his "stint as the Centre's first Visiting Scholar initiated a broad-ranging debate about theory, history and analysis of sports and leisure in working-class cultures".[16] A workshop took place at the Queen's Centre the following year, and in the UK the British Sociological Association/Leisure Studies Association's Leisure and Recreation Joint Study Group generated working papers and publications and conference volumes that established new and engaged networks of critical and interdisciplinary scholars. In many respects the Queen's Centre, with Rick Gruneau and Hart Cantelon alongside a group of young colleagues and graduate students, was cultivating a blend of critical sociology and cultural studies that was also informing much of the emergent British work, and in 1992 a special theme issue of the *Sociology of Sport Journal*, drawing upon presentations made at the Leisure Studies Association's 1988 International Conference in Brighton, UK, featured "British Cultural Studies".[17] Confluences of critical work were increasingly marked, and the cross-currents of debate and theory were escalating across the USA, Canada and the UK.

The chapter by Alan in Peter Donnelly and Nancy Theberge's edited book emanating from the 1982 NASSS conference, *Sport and the Sociological Imagination*,[18] had urged the application of Wright Mills's framework to the critical study of sport, including his insights on the relationship between personal troubles and public issues, and the necessity to connect history and biography in any adequate sociological analysis. This piece also, novelly, alerted the sociological constituency to the relevance of political and cultural commentary (by the likes of George Orwell and C.L.R. James) for the sociological project, and gave examples of the social scientific insights generated by new journalistic writers combining mediated ethnographies (or bouts of participant observation) with literary techniques of *reportage*. Rick Gruneau had also for some time highlighted the importance of Wright Mills's work for an emerging sociology of sport, stressing the centrality of his public issues/personal troubles, and history/biography couplets for any adequate alternative sociological model to the current North American orthodoxy: this latter Gruneau called a "mechanistic application of the natural scientific model of inquiry to sporting situations"; and his call to sociological arms concluded with the observation that any understanding preceding action "lies in the reflexivity and critical 'consciousness' of the sociological perspective".[19] In his bold and brilliant combination of sociological and cultural theory and analysis, *Class, Sports and Social Development*, published in 1983, Gruneau again praised and paraphrased Mills's core connection between personal troubles and public issues.[20] In the period from the late 1970s and throughout the 1980s, in our different ways but in the context of increasingly reciprocally informed and enjoined academic and intellectual work, Alan and I were converging to contribute to a postfunctionalist blend of critical theory and qualitative methodology, anchored too in a sense of history and Wright Mills's core concerns: first, with the relationship between "personal troubles" and "public issues"; second, with the connection between history and biography. We both believed that the rigorous study of such connections and relationships was essential for the cultivation of a critically informed, and historically and politically sensitive, sociological approach to understanding sport's place in the contemporary world.

We might have started in different kitchens and canteens but we recognised each other's ingredients and elements, as well as utensils. Two decades and a series of collaborations later, the edited book *Power Games: A Critical Sociology of Sport* further articulated our epistemological framework, and a cluster of University of Brighton-based scholars was turning its attention to myriad issues and contexts in which troubles and issues were calling out for serious analysis and interpretation and, wherever possible, intervention.[21] One of these contexts was the deep-rooted political and cultural setting of the Israel-Palestine question, the focus of Chapter 3. But first, an extended stint of academic duty in Northern Ireland would lay some foundations for this deepening concern with sport in divided societies, and with the power of sport to challenge cultural stereotypes, not blindly reproduce them, and so to foster potential and actual forms of conflict-resolution. In the subsequent pages of this book, we draw on the case studies to present the evolution of a praxis-based model for undertaking such analysis. This model and its sociological pedigree – which we believe constitute a distinctive answer to Dr. Malcolm's question – are articulated and elaborated in the book's final chapter.

Notes

1 The book to which we frequently refer throughout this study is C. Wright Mills, *The Sociological Imagination* (Harmondsworh: Penguin, 1970), first published 1959.
2 See John Sugden, "Putting the 'P' in SDP: Sport and peace-building in divided societies", *Alan Sack Honorary Lecture*, University of New Haven, New Haven, MA, USA, Tuesday 4 May 2017. See too for complementary and further contextual detail, John Sugden, Keynote Address on the history and development of SDP, presented at *Forming Partnerships and Linkages in Sport for Development and Peace: Considerations, Tensions, and Strategies*, University of Illinois at Urbana-Champaign, Symposium, 7–8 March 2017. See too John Sugden "SDP partnerships and the government sector: Mana from heaven or Faustian pacts?" (with Graham Spacey), also presented at the symposium.
3 Eric Dunning, *Sport Matters: Sociological Studies of Sport, Violence and Civilization* (London and New York: Routledge, 2002).
4 Alan Tomlinson, *FIFA: The Men, the Myths and the Money* (London and New York: Routledge, 2014).
5 These were popular television situation comedies: *Please Sir?* (London Weekend Television, 1968–1972) depicted the hapless adventures of a young teacher in London's East End; *Porridge* (BBC 1, 1974–1977) featured life in a London prison. Both series were hugely popular and spawned feature films of the same name.
6 The very terms of this advertisement, particularly in retrospect, appear embarrassingly patronising. Why should it be presumed that an inexperienced young Englishman, a naïve Essex undergraduate supremely under-qualified (as yet) for teaching of any kind, should be entitled to anything more than local wages?
7 The term "scramble for Africa" refers to the process throughout the final decades of the nineteenth century and in the first years of the twentieth century (from, it is widely agreed, the 1870s to 1902) when European nations competed to acquire African territory in the colonization and partition of almost 90% of the continent. It is a British term, coined in 1884. See Henry Louis Gates Jr. and Kwame Anthony Appiah eds., *Encyclopedia of Africa* (Oxford: Oxford University Press, 2010). De-colonisation in the second half of the twentieth century was often fuelled by political protest movements that could use football as a means of mobilising nationalist passions and fuelling the independence movement. We interviewed the physician and sport politician Dr. Abdel Halim Mohamed of Sudan on this theme, in London, on 12 June 1997, and he confirmed that in the 1950s he and other members of the radical indigenous elite "started football clubs as social clubs where we could talk the principles of civics to the masses – that this is their country and they have the right to independence". See John Sugden and Alan Tomlinson, *FIFA and the Contest for World Football: Who Rules the Peoples' Game?* (Cambridge: Polity Press, 1998): 129.
8 J.A. Mangan, "The education of an elite Imperial administration: The Sudan Political Service and the British Public School system", *The Journal of African Historical Studies*, 15/4, 1982: 671–699. See too J.A. Mangan, *The Games Ethic and Imperialism: Aspects of the Diffusion of an Ideal* (New York: Viking, 1986), which demonstrates incontrovertibly that "the successful athlete was favoured"

(p. 85) in the selection for the Sudan Political Service (whether or not one was actually the holder of a "blue" from Oxford or Cambridge). A blue could be held by an individual who might have played just once in the annual fixture between Oxford and Cambridge; a small injury could deprive a top player of the blue. But the symbolic significance of the "blue" was immense, providing a shorthand for the sterling qualities of an individual whose athleticist qualities could equip him to become one of the "manly chaps in control" (Mangan, Chapter 3) of British imperial assets.
9 Mangan, *The Games Ethic*: 83.
10 On 'soft power', see Joseph S. Nye Jr., *Soft Power: The Means to Succeed in World Politics* (New York: Public Affairs, 2004). Nye first developed the concept in the late 1980s and published *Bound to Lead: The Changing Nature of American Power* (New York: Basic Books, 1990).
11 On sport and the British Empire more generally, including a fuller discussion of sport and British colonial rule, see Richard Holt, *Sport and the British* (Oxford: Oxford University Press, 1990), particularly Chapter 4, "Empire and Nation", pp. 203–261; and Harold Perkin, "Teaching the nations how to play: Sport and society in the British Empire and Commonwealth", *The International Journal of the History of Sport*, 6/2, 1989: 145–155.
12 Back then any undergraduate degree coupled with a record of practical sporting achievement could get a person onto a PGCE PE course. This is far from the case today when a good undergraduate degree (2.1 or better) in a sport-related subject is the minimum requirement.
13 For the best examples of this type of work see Harry Edwards, *The Revolt of the Black Athlete* (New York: Free Press, 1969); and Jack Scott, *The Athletic Revolution* (New York: Free Press, 1971).
14 John Sugden, *Boxing and Society: An International Analysis* (Manchester: Manchester University Press, 1997): 183.
15 Alan Tomlinson was the convenor of the British Sociological Association's Leisure & Recreation Study Group for much of this period, and also Publications Officer of the Leisure Studies Association for many years. We are grateful to these associations' officers and members for support throughout an intellectually exciting and formative phase of growth.
16 Hart Cantelon and Robert Hollands eds., *Leisure, Sport and Working-Class Cultures* (Toronto: Garamond Press, 1988): 9. This book had appeared earlier in 1985, circulated as part of the Centre's *Working Papers* series.
17 In retrospect, the "British Cultural Studies" issue of *Sociology of Sport Journal* 9/2 appears somewhat preoccupied, though we would argue justifiably so, with class, nationalism and the media. An earlier collection of articles, in *Sport, Leisure and Social Relations*, eds. John Horne, David Jary, and Alan Tomlinson (London: Routledge & Kegan Paul Ltd., 1987), several of which also emanated from BSA/LSA workshops and events, placed gender and the body more centrally onto the sociology of sport agenda. Also hugely influential in this shaping of the critical field were Jennifer Hargreaves, ed., *Sport, Culture and Ideology* (London: Routledge & Kegan Paul, 1982); and John Hargreaves, *Sport, Power and Culture: A Social and Historical Analysis of Popular Sports in Britain* (Cambridge: Polity Press, 1986).
18 Alan Tomlinson, "The sociological imagination, the New Journalism and sport", in *Sport and the Sociological Imagination*, eds. Nancy Theberge and Peter Donnelly (Fort Worth: Texas Christian University Press, 1984).
19 Richard S. Gruneau, "Sport as an area of sociological study: An introduction to major themes and perspectives", in *Canadian Sport: Sociological Perspectives*, eds.

Richard S. Gruneau and John S. Albinson (Don Mills, Ontario: Addison-Wesley [Canada] Limited, 1976): 37. Jean Harvey and Hart Cantelon also saw Wright Mills as an inspiration, quoting his observation that "all sociology worthy of the name is 'historical sociology'" or an attempt (in the words of Paul Sweezy) to write "the present as history". See Jean Harvey and Hart Cantelon's influential edited book, *Not Just a Game: Essays in Canadian Sport Sociology* (Ottawa: University of Ottawa Press, 1988), which "in postulating that sport is at once the product of contingent historical conditions and of the actions of social agents . . . explains the dialectical relations that exist between constraint and freedom, between structure and action, and between production and reproduction of society", p. 5.

20 Richard S. Gruneau, *Class, Sports and Social Development* (Amherst: The University of Massachusetts Press, 1983): 15–16.

21 The collaborations included John Sugden and Alan Tomlinson eds., *Hosts and Champions: Soccer Cultures, National Identities and the USA World Cup* (Aldershot, UK: Arena, 1994); and John Sugden and Alan Bairner eds., *Sport in Divided Societies* (Oxford: Meyer & Meyer Sport, 1999), a Chelsea School Research Centre Edition Volume 4, stemming from a workshop supported by the University of Brighton and held at Sussex Arts Centre, Brighton, in May 1997. *Power Games: A Critical Sociology of Sport* (London and New York: Routledge) appeared in 2002. The workshop/sessions at which contributors presented their draft chapters took place at the NASSS annual meeting in Colorado Springs, USA, November 2000, where Professor Peter Donnelly and Dr Jim McKay provided full and frank critical responses to the chapter drafts and outlines. The shell of the book had emerged in 1997 when we were invited to the University of Buenos Aires, Argentina, to talk about what our Argentinean hosts had described as the distinctive nature of our sociological work on sport. Also stimulated by our exchanges with Pablo Alabarces and his Argentinean colleagues was our joint article "Digging the dirt and staying clean: Retrieving the investigative tradition for a critical sociology of sport", *International Review for the Sociology of Sport*, 34/4, 1999: 385–397. We cannot stress too highly the importance of such networks and exchanges for a critical comparative sociology of sport.

Chapter 2

SDP in never-never land – sport and peace-building in Northern Ireland

Introduction

Living in Northern Ireland on the outskirts of Belfast from the early 1980s until the mid-1990s was to live close to some of the worst manifestations of the modern 'Troubles'. 'The Troubles' is a term widely used to refer to the vicious and often murderous sectarian conflicts that blighted the Irish Province of Ulster in the later decades of the twentieth century. These conflicts were themselves deeply rooted in older colonial and post-colonial Anglo-Irish ethno-sectarian political struggles and conflicts. Not long after my arrival in Northern Ireland in September 1982, to take up an academic position at the Ulster Polytechnic, I had my first meeting with the Senior Course Tutor who overviewed the sports studies programme on which I would be teaching. At that meeting he offered two memorable pieces of advice: firstly, do not get too close to the students (the sub-text of which was not to get involved physically or romantically with any of them); secondly, he counselled, never bring local politics into the classroom or in other words 'don't mention the war'. One was expected in the academic haven to avoid talking about 'the Troubles'. Such authority of local knowledge, initially unavailable to the newcomer, was premised on the view that in any cohort of students made up of a mixture of Protestants and Catholics, talking about 'the Troubles' might raise uncomfortable feelings and tensions in the classroom.

As a somewhat naïve newcomer to the region it had come as a surprise to learn that it was only if they were part of the relatively small minority who at that time made it into Higher Education that the two different ethno-national and religious groups would share an educational and social environment. Otherwise, following the physical and social sectarian patterning of the Province's religiously divided demographic, they would live in separate neighbourhoods having gone to separate state or faith-based primary and secondary schools, attended separate churches and, as I would soon come to learn in both academic and practitioner roles, played different sports and games. As such, Higher Education was possibly the only shared space wherein Northern Irish students might sit together to engage with anything like a common curriculum. But it was not the norm; and the realities of cultural and political conflict, and the sedimented practical difficulties of cultural co-existence, constrained the possibility of open discussion of the Troubles in everyday life. But the Course Tutor's advice regarding the avoidance of politics in the classroom was to be dramatically challenged.

The fourth of November 1983 changed everything because of an event that not only shocked me to the core but also stimulated a quest to acquire more understanding regarding Ulster's violent sectarian make-up and the role played by sport in this tragic and horribly tangled story. That autumn day I was scheduled to be lecturing to a group of about 30 undergraduate students. The planned theme of the lecture was 'the relationship between sport and politics'. I had heeded the warning not to introduce local political issues into the classroom, even though in my relatively short experience of living in Northern Ireland I had begun to realise that far from being a neutral cultural enclave, sport was implicated in and in part contributed to the sectarian topography of the Province. Rather than lecture about and discuss these potentially controversial interpretations, though, South Africa provided a proxy illustration of another deeply divided society, where sport was thoroughly implicated in and contributed to the fissures and conflicts in the socio-political landscape. Mid-way through the lecture, 'BOOM!' – my voice was drowned by a deafening detonation, a massive explosion generating a rumbling roar that caused the blast-proof landscape windows of the classroom to vibrate violently. The students scattered and huddled against the far wall of the classroom. Looking out of the still shuddering windows towards the adjacent teaching block, smoke and fire was still bellowing from a top-floor classroom, the decimated remains of which were cascading down from the sky. Somewhat inappropriately, and certainly nervously, asking nobody in particular, I uttered "I don't suppose that was the Chemistry Department?"

And this was no laboratory experiment gone wrong. It was in fact just another general teaching room much like the one I was in, but as we would all learn later instead of standard students that morning it was full of RUC (Royal Ulster Constabulary) police officers who were there for a lecture as part of their professional training. The PIRA (Provisional Irish Republican Army) had 'discovered' this gathering would be taking place and decided that the police-filled classroom constituted a 'legitimate target', managing to conceal a number of anti-personnel bombs in the classroom ceiling. Once the room was full these were detonated to devastating effect. Two police officers were killed on the spot, a third died nine months later, and 33 more officers were seriously wounded, as well as a course tutor and lecturer, Paul Maidement. Until that fateful day he had been an accomplished Olympic race-walker, but after this incident he would never walk properly again, let alone race-walk. So, despite my attempt to adhere to the wise counsel of not bringing the war into the classroom, uninvited the war had gate-crashed its way into my institution, my professional life and my sociological consciousness. From that day forward my sociological curiosity was redirected towards and focused upon the sectarian environment that now framed my new living and working life.

A living laboratory

No longer something to be ignored, the sectarian context provided a research and professional focus, a sociological problem that needed to be mapped, interpreted, understood in informed ways, and learned from and talked about among those for whom it was a lived and everyday reality. I can see now the classroom bombing as a major awakening and although I did not realise it at the time it was one of two events that stimulated and helped to launch what was to become a pioneering voyage of discovery through the largely uncharted waters and unknown regions of SDP in an endeavour to find and/or invent ways of using sport in the service of conflict-resolution and peace-building: first in Northern Ireland; and subsequently in other divided, ethno-religiously distressed and socio-politically fractured countries across the world.

As discussed in the introductory chapter, a sociological consciousness is not generated solely by bodies of theory and abstract conceptualisation; sociological agendas can emerge from individual experience, generating research questions and lines of enquiry from observation, from direct encounters and lived experiences. As such, so long as I was living in Northern Ireland it was inevitable that the seismic social and political events that characterised the 14 years I would dwell there (1982–1996) would shape both my identity as a scholar and practitioner/activist, and the accompanying research agenda. An early attraction to and immersion in the sociology of the Chicago School fuelled a sociological commitment to take the city of Belfast as a living sociological laboratory.[1] After the classroom bombing, a critical sociological imagination was combined with an ethnographer's eyes and ears to map and interpret the city's sectarian geography, particularly in relation to the Province's sports cultures. I had studied the political sociology of Northern Ireland on a final year undergraduate course at the University of Essex where, as discussed in the introduction, I had also been introduced to the critical sociology of C. Wright Mills. Combined with the theoretical and methodological grounding gained in graduate school at the University of Connecticut, this furnished me with intellectual and interpretative tools suited to analysing and understanding the transcending social-political context that framed 'the Troubles'.

A key source would soon emerge: the lived experiences of the people alongside whom I lived and worked, in particular my students. Interactions and conversations with them in the classrooms and on the sports fields cultivated a rich harvest of information. They taught me as much if not more than I taught them. Not long after bedding into my lecturing role I also got involved with the students' sport activities, taking on the dual role of the Polytechnic's men's association football coach and manager, a role I fulfilled successfully for several years; it was a form of apprenticeship for taking on the position of manager/coach of the men's Northern Ireland combined universities representative team. Here, on the sports field, sport implicitly challenged sectarian divides, as the players in the squads and teams were drawn from a variety of universities and colleges across the Province, coming from an ethno-religious mixture of Catholic and Protestant, Unionist and Nationalist backgrounds. On the training field or during down-time on the numerous trips and playing tours shared with them, I got to know these students well and listened fascinated by their accounts of growing up on different sides of the 'barricades' during the Troubles. Over the years I watched with considerable satisfaction as firm friendships took root and flourished, often across sectarian barriers. And these were not just fleeting encounters; in many cases the friendships endured far beyond their university sporting days.

It was partially in fulfilment of aspects of my soccer coaching responsibilities that the second 'Troubles'-related event took place that was to catapult me into the unexplored world of sport and peace-building. The PIRA bomb had undoubtedly triggered and accelerated my quest to understand more about the relationship between sport and sectarianism in Northern Ireland. This second event, tit-for-tat killings on the streets and in a sports stadium, spurred me to get involved with hands-on cross-community sport and conflict-resolution work. On 16 March 1988, in charge of the combined Northern Ireland Universities Football Team, I was driving a mixed group of Catholic and Protestant student footballers to a training session that I was scheduled to hold at Queen's University's playing fields in South Belfast. And even for Belfast, there was an unusually high level of tension in the air.

The city was on high alert after a series of sectarian atrocities, and even in our vehicle the atmosphere was unusually subdued and tense. Outside on the streets, though – and this was unusual – we saw little sign of police or army activity. Just a week before in Gibraltar, while reportedly preparing an attack on a Royal Marines ceremonial marching band, a PIRA active service unit was intercepted and eliminated by members of the British Army's elite special forces regiment, the SAS. The bodies of the three dead PIRA members had been returned to Belfast for burial, scheduled for the same day as the training session at Queen's. The drive that morning to the practice ground took us close to Milltown Cemetery in West Belfast where the funerals of the Gibraltar PIRA dead were underway. In a failed attempt to avoid inflaming an already incendiary gathering, the security forces had decided not to police the funeral march, which explained the absence of police and army from the surrounding roads and streets.

Driving off the roundabout that fed onto the M1 motorway heading south out of the city the cars in front of us juddered to a halt. Suddenly, as if from nowhere, dozens of heavily-armed British soldiers and RUC officers appeared in the middle of the road waving their arms and gesturing motorists to get off the motorway. Looking further down the motorway we could see what appeared to be a crowd chasing a fugitive who came running towards us. The fugitive as we would learn later was Michael Stone, an infamous Loyalist paramilitary terrorist, UDA (Ulster Defence Association) leader and 'hit-man' who had infiltrated the nationalists' funeral cortège allowing him to throw a number of hand grenades and unleash a hail of automatic gunfire into the graveside throng. Three mourners were killed, more than 50 injured. Although the students and I did not realise it at the time, we were witnessing Stone's attempted escape from the enraged – nationalist – group of mourners who had chased him from the cemetery on the hill above onto the motorway along which he hopelessly attempted to make his escape. Not having to be asked twice, quickly responding to the urging of the rapidly arriving security forces, I spun the vehicle round, exiting the Belfast ring-road and sped off via an improvised route through the grounds of the City Hospital, eventually arriving breathless at the Queen's University playing fields.

In those pre-mobile-phone days, as confirmation of what had happened eventually trickled down to us, we sat numbed and stunned in silence in the changing room, a mixed group of young Catholic and Protestant footballers and friends; and me, an outsider learning fast. We were all struggling to come to terms with what we had just witnessed. In the ensuing days the sectarian violence erupting in the city around us would spiral upwards caught in an escalating tit-for-tat dynamic of attacks and revenge, following a well-worn pattern characteristic of the worst days of the Troubles. Then only days after Stone's outrageous attack, as the funeral cortège of Caoimhín Mac Brádaigh, one of Stone's victims, made its way through Andersonstown, a Catholic neighbourhood in West Belfast, two plain-clothes British security personnel drove perilously close to the funeral precession before being halted by an angry crowd. As the world's media looked on, the British were dragged from their vehicle to be brutally beaten and killed in the grounds of Casement Park, a nearby Gaelic football stadium.

In that Queen's University changing room after the Milltown Cemetery killings, my emotions swung between a sense of helplessness and anger, but also moved towards a conviction that access to sociological understanding should, wherever possible, be mobilised for the public good, should speak to the possibility of a different future. From that point forward, rather than just observing and criticising from the academic side-lines the role played by sport in the Province's fractured community structure, my sociological commitment and vocation would be geared towards developing a contextual understanding of the damaging impact of the Troubles on community relations in the Province. And here was the chance to combine that sociological perspective and expertise with what had been learned in coaching football to players from conflict-soaked backgrounds. A formula was emerging that would identify and inform ways of inflecting sport and its positive qualities towards making an active contribution to peace-building.

The coaching roles at the Polytechnic – from 1984, the University of Ulster – and for the combined universities team were pivotal to the commitment to channel sport's values in particular ways, and I absorbed a huge amount from these experiences. The teams I coached, and also played for myself, were a mixture of Catholic and Protestant players and as I participated at these different levels, it was reaffirmed that the dynamics and ethos of team-building were essential to success. Any good coach strives to establish forms of team spirit that are manifest as collective endeavour and achievement; the development of strong, cross-sectarian interpersonal bonds and friendships was a major priority. It became completely clear that sport could be organised and delivered in appropriate ways so that sporting encounters could be contested within a culture of anti-sectarian principles and values, in ways that could make a positive contribution to inter-personal and inter-community relations. And if this could work at a university level, could it also be achieved outside of Higher Education, in ways that could expose less privileged sectors of the population to sport's positive potential for stimulating inter-community relations? This question would lead to the birth of what has been acknowledged as the world's first formally researched and documented sport-based peace-building programme, namely 'Belfast United'.[2]

I had learned firstly as a player and later as a coach that notwithstanding extrinsic socio-political and cultural factors, given a common cause and goals, a shared set of values and dedicated mentors, a sport team was an excellent crucible within which to fan the flames of intimacy and nurture friendship, mutual understanding and reciprocal respect. In this post-traumatic moment of critical reflection I became convinced that access to and experience of the cross-community *camaraderie* of an integrated sport team should not be limited to the relative few in Northern Ireland who made it into Higher Education and played sport there. To this end, in cooperation with friends in local secondary schools and supported by visiting scholars from the University of Rhode Island (URI) USA, the first Belfast United programme was designed and instigated, in 1989.[3]

Beginning with soccer, and later adding basketball, this was to become a multi-sport programme that targeted Catholic and Protestant teenage boys recruited from some of Belfast's most ethno-religiously divided, entrenched and mutually hostile neighbourhoods.[4] We used our contacts within a network of physical education teachers and soccer coaches working in the city's divided school system to identify and recruit the boys. An interesting feature of this recruitment process was that at first it was much easier to recruit Catholic participants to the programme than it was to draw in their Protestant counterparts. This was a common problem with inter-community cultural relations programmes as, according to representatives on Northern Ireland's Community Relations Council (CRC), the Protestant constituency viewed community relations initiatives as a threat to their pre-eminence. On the contrary for the minority Catholic population such enterprises offered opportunities that otherwise were not widely available to them. This was a time when the wider politics of the Troubles was still being played out as a zero-sum game: that is, if one side was gaining the other must be proportionately losing. Thus, if Catholics saw projects like Belfast United as being good for them, by definition they must be bad for the Protestant community. As detailed in the following chapter, this was a pattern we would see repeated when we began working with Jewish and Arab communities in Israel.

Nevertheless to begin with in Northern Ireland enough Protestant boys were recruited into the Belfast United programme to facilitate ethno-religiously balanced projects. In the beginning the structure and processes associated with the programme were relatively simple, based loosely on Gordon Allport's 'contact hypothesis', a theory that had considerable currency in the early years of the cross-community relations movement in Northern Ireland: the theory postulated that the facilitation of cross-community interpersonal contact between Protestants and Catholics would eventually lead to the fostering of increased mutual understanding and co-respect.[5] To this formula Belfast United added the dynamic of sport team-building: Catholic and Protestant children were recruited and allocated to ethno-religiously mixed coaching groups and shaped into teams at what was perceived to be the unaffiliated and neutral setting of a university campus. Subsequent to recruitment the boys were required to meet regularly to share and undertake technical coaching and physical training, thus in the process getting to know one another, and so melding as a team before embarking on playing and coaching tours of New England in the USA. Undoubtedly the prospect of the US tour acted as a great incentive in the recruitment of the participants in the first place, and contributed towards keeping them in the programme as the team-building progressed. For the duration of the USA tours the boys were hosted in mixed pairs (Catholic and Protestant) by local American families. This strategy in part was based on something that I had observed when encountering people from Northern Ireland holidaying outside of the Province in continental Europe. Once away from their home region's divisive sectarian environment, and ensconced in a mutually unfamiliar cultural environment, Catholics and Protestants tended to, at least temporarily, suspend their separate sectarian identities and affiliations, preferring to see themselves collectively as Northern Irish. It was hypothesised that this tendency would likewise prevail for the Belfast United boys once they were away from Belfast's stifling sectarian atmosphere. Five years living in New England informed my intuition that the east coast of the USA could be conducive to co-habiting and playing together; in such circumstances, the boys could essentially experiment in the process of co-operative co-existence.

Sectarian issues notwithstanding it was not always easy to handle these groups of teenage boys who were at that predacious stage of development when pecking-order rivalries and related peer-group conflicts could be expected to bubble to the surface from time to time, as indeed they did. Our evaluations suggested that while small fights and squabbles did occasionally break out none of these was obviously caused by the boy's separate ethno-religious affiliations. Indications that the team dynamic was in fact pushing in a contrary direction were well illustrated by a remarkable incident that took place on one of the early Belfast United tours which featured a 'friendly' match between the young Belfast United boys and an older all-star varsity XI, played at the University of Rhode Island in front of a crowd of about 200 people. It was literally men against boys as Belfast's 15- and 16-year-olds bravely went head-to-head with young adult URI athletes up to four or five years older than themselves. Trailing 1–0 with five minutes to go, Belfast United's 5'8" right back made a lung-bursting run which found him one-on-one with the 6' 2" URI goalkeeper. He slightly overran the ball and the big keeper scooped it up only to find himself barged to the ground by the onrushing full back who himself was upended by the out-rushing and now furious custodian. The two players squared up. Punches were thrown and then all hell broke loose as both teams - including occupants of both teams' benches - converged on the URI penalty box to fight in support of their respective players. I looked on feeling a mixture of horror and pride as Protestant and Catholic boys from East and West Belfast fought side by side against their Yankee hosts. As the melee subsided, URI's head soccer coach ambled over to me and after having observed the Belfast lads sticking up for one another, said, "well John, whatever else, I guess this shows that your project's working!" Several weeks later when I was back in Belfast I got a call from the same coach who told me that he was interested in offering the transgressing Belfast full back a scholarship to study at URI and play soccer for the URI team. The lad in question took up that offer and played with distinction for the University for four years. After graduating he went on to complete his Master's degree at the same institution. Many years later, I was back in Belfast for the wedding of a former student. At the reception there were no less than four young men, crossing the sectarian divide, who had been part of the Belfast United programme more than two decades earlier. It was notable how much detail of their experiences they could still remember, as they spoke fondly of their Belfast United days. It was heart-warming and humbling that after all this time they were still firm friends. Perhaps the most outstanding example of Belfast's United's lasting interpersonal legacy came when I met up with Belfast United's first-ever goal-keeper who had gone on to have a decent career in semi-professional and professional football in Northern Ireland and later England. At the pinnacle of his career he was selected to play for the Northern Ireland international team. I met him in again in 1995 when I travelled away with the international team when it played Armenia in Yerevan in a World Cup qualifier, and he played in goal. After the game he came up to me and told me, "notwithstanding the success he went on to achieve" in his career his best football memories were associated with the relatively short time he had "within the embrace of Belfast United"; with that he stripped off his still sweaty shirt and gave it to me as a token of his thanks and respect. This shirt still has a prime spot among the sport trophies and memorabilia in my study.

In addition to anecdotes such as these, accompanying research and evaluation, using diaries, interviews and participant observation, demonstrated that Belfast United did have a measurable, positive impact on the young people who participated. Although initially small in scale, Belfast United also helped to inspire larger and much more ambitious cross-community residential sport festivals both in Northern Ireland and the USA. This was also reflective of a broader shift in the mood of the people of Northern Ireland who by the late 1980s had become weary of being passive spectators to the ever-upward spiral of sectarian violence that was blighting their communities, and so the initiative occurred at an historical and political moment receptive to such an intervention. In increasing numbers the people of the Province wanted to do something to stop the conflict. For some, this might mean getting more involved in political protest, but for others it meant discovering local cultural resources that could be harnessed in the service of peace-building. Belfast United was one such programme and it might in its own modest legacy have helped pioneer what would come to be known as the Sport for Development and Peace (SDP) movement. It is a big leap from a community achievement on a local level to the aspiration of SDP initiatives to have the effect of a 'movement', with all that this entails in terms of social change and cultural and political transformation. And as noted earlier, many community initiatives of the day were then sparked by a psychological contact theory model that encouraged a form of learning through experience; the gains of the contacts and the communication with others generated by the contact were frequently, in such an approach, constrained and undermined by the reassertion of structural and ideological processes – class, religion, institutionalised political power – in the everyday life and familiar and framing culture to which people returned. But what the Belfast United model showed was that sport and the collective culture that it could stimulate in positive circumstances could offer more than a glimpse of a possible future; it could shift perspectives, change horizons, cultivate aspirations. You could imagine a community and culture that was a world away from the shackled upbringing of a rigid and walled-in sectarian world. The key was to relate the cultural and community initiatives more explicitly to policy debate and practice; and to make more explicit the values that would underpin initiatives seeking to make a difference in the long rather than the short or medium term.

Theory, practice and intervention and their influence on the policy community for sport in Northern Ireland

Belfast United did not develop in an intellectual vacuum. On the contrary, using the lens of a critical sociological imagination, knowledge gained from researching and learning about the structure, processes and sectarian politics that framed the practice and culture of sport in Northern Ireland was used to inform and shape the character of the Belfast United project, as well as related grass-roots peace-building interventions, in cultural spheres especially, such as dance, music and theatre.[6] At the same time, data gleaned from researching and evaluating these interventions fed into a growing corpus of critical scholarship that in turn began to have an impact upon the embryonic policy community for sport in the Province. This community comprised the cluster of government, private and voluntary stakeholders as well as non-affiliated pressure groups that shaped the wider institutional agenda for sport in a particular locale. A community of this kind needs to find ways of cultivating common cause and shared goals; otherwise it can stall, even ossify, as a well-intentioned but loose network. Importantly, then, forms of practical intervention such as Belfast United should not be considered in isolation from other avenues of research, critical scholarship and related expressions of public intellectualism and debate.

For example, in June 1989 working with colleagues from the University of Ulster, Queen's University Belfast and the University of Rhode Island we organised what was then a ground-breaking symposium that questioned the relationship between sport and politics both locally and in the international sphere. For the first day of the symposium the focus was on the big international sporting controversies of the day and featured keynote addresses by Soviet sport specialist the late Jim Riordan, to be followed by a moving speech by exiled South African intellectual Kader Asmal, a professor of human rights, who was a leading spokesperson for the anti-apartheid sports movement. A decade later he would go on to become Minister for Education in the national government of Thabo Mbeki (1999–2004). For the second day of the conference the focus switched to local sport-related political and community relations and that is when the fireworks started. We had invited representatives from the GAA (Gaelic Athletic Association), the IFA (Irish Football Association) and the IRFU (Irish Rugby Football Union) as well as the director of the Sports Council for Northern Ireland (SCNI) to make presentations. They were asked to respond to a paper co-authored by Alan Bairner and myself, and presented in summary as a keynote address at the conference, that provocatively argued that those who occupied the commanding heights of the institutional order of sport in the Province were implicated in augmenting the region's sectarian-fuelled turmoil. This public statement met with hostility from Ulster's sporting patriarchs; one after the other, these well-intentioned but delusional men stepped up to the conference podium, and in defiance of the evidence that we had provided condemned us as heretics. In so doing, they were repeating the long-since exposed, and threadbare and fallacious, proposition that politics and sport existed in separate spheres. The representatives of the opposite poles of Ulster's sectarian sporting spectrum – Jimmy Davidson, then the manager of the Irish Rugby international team, and Peter Quinn, the President of Ulster's GAA Council – were most vociferous in their protests and condemnations. But there was no turning back, and whether Ulster's sport tsars liked it or not, the sport and sectarianism *djinni* was out of the bottle and the debate concerning the role played by sport in the 'Troubles' was now being aired in the public domain. This debate was amplified when not long after the Queen's symposium I collaborated in the production of a BBC Northern Ireland television documentary entitled *Sport the Healer*, the opening credits of which were set against a backdrop of clips of bruising sporting encounters in the Province's various codes of football, accompanied by Frankie Goes to Hollywood's pulsating rendition of their hit record, *Two Tribes Go to War*. This was followed by a series of talking heads who argued positions similar to those articulated during the symposium at Queen's. The programme was aired during primetime viewing and attracted widespread comment throughout Northern Ireland. This challenge to the received wisdom that sport was some kind of antidote to the Troubles and should be left alone, required a more systematic response from the Province's sport mandarins who began to see the tide turning against them.[7]

Following this watershed conference and the documentary, the research into the history, culture and politics of sport, in collaboration with Alan Bairner, deepened and intensified, leading to the first book-length research monograph on the subject: *Sport, Sectarianism, and Society in a Divided Ireland* became the key resource for not only our own postgraduate students, but also other academics and commentators in the UK and Ireland, and increasingly, as the innately political character of institutionalised sport became more and more recognised in both academic and policy-making networks and communities, throughout the rest of the world.[8]

At this time other civil society organisations and initiatives taking shape throughout Northern Ireland were, as aforementioned, using sports and other cultural activities such as drama, dance and music to promote improvements in cross-community relations. This emerging community relations movement was driven in part by DENI (Department of Education Northern Ireland) which helped to energise the EMU (Education for Mutual Understanding) agenda and gave support to the 'integrate schools' movement.[9] Alongside DENI, at a time when direct rule from Westminster was still in place, the Northern Ireland Office based at Stormont set up the Community Relations Unit (CRU) with a brief to investigate and support an expansion in community relations activities. In turn, in 1990 the CRU helped to set up and fund the Community Relations Council (CRC), an organisation that was to play a significant role as the momentum built in the peace process in the early 1990s and beyond the signing of the Good Friday Agreement in 1998.

In 1993 the University was commissioned by the CRU to lead a research project that looked in detail at the community relations dimensions of the different sectors that made up Northern Ireland's sports order. Working alongside researcher Scott Harvie, we probed the community representativeness of all the major governing bodies as well as the composition and working practices of the SCNI, while at the same time looking at the cross-community texture of sports provision in the Province's 26 local authorities.[10] Published in 1995, the findings confirmed that Northern Ireland's existing institutional order for sport supported an informal system of sporting apartheid whereby separate Protestant and Catholic identities were confirmed and reinforced through differential patterns of association and socialisation around sports choice and participation. In the conclusions and recommendations it was argued that, despite the prevailing sectarian attitudes and practices of the day, if positive steps were taken to reform sport, it was one obvious area where the Community Relations agenda could be revitalised and moved forward.

The publication of this report sparked a further series of debates and conferences on the subject involving a wide variety of government bodies and civil society organisations. Out of this a consensus was emerging that something more systematic needed to be done if the community relations potential of sport in Northern Ireland was to be unlocked and realised. This established the basis of an emergent policy consensus consolidating an emerging policy community.[11] With this in mind, SCNI was brought together with the CRC to set up a task-force, the remit of which was to develop a community relations policy for sport in Northern Ireland. This 'think tank' was a mixture of civil servants, academics, community activists and sports administrators and practitioners. Wearing at least two of these hats, I was invited to take part and given a key role in helping to frame this adventurous new policy which, when adopted, would initiate widespread, sustained, and long-lasting changes in the culture of community sport in the region.

Conclusion: never say never

By the time I left Northern Ireland in 1996, the Sports Council (subsequently re-branded as Sport NI) had developed and introduced a full-blown Community Relations Policy for Sport, while most local councils and sport governing bodies had recruited dedicated Sport and Community Relations workers. This was all part of a complex set of interactions among social, economic, political and civil society actors and organisations that was contributing and giving momentum to a peace process in the region that has since gone from strength to strength. While it is impossible to say precisely how much the combined critical interventions in sport in Northern Ireland emanating from the initiatives discussed in this chapter have contributed to the peace process there, without doubt a more progressive, proactive and politically sensitive approach to sport development and provision has contributed – however indirectly – to making Northern Ireland a more peaceful and prosperous place to live, work and play.

It was that most belligerent of Unionist politicians, the Reverend Ian Paisley, who on the day that British Prime Minister, Margret Thatcher, signed the Anglo-Irish agreement with her Irish counterpart, Taoiseach Garret Fitzgerald, at Hillsborough Castle, thumped his fist on the lectern from which he was addressing a mass gathering of Loyalists and roared, "Never, never, never!", screaming his and his followers' opposition to any paving of the way for the government of the Irish Republic to have any say in the governance of Northern Ireland. Paisley's bellowing phrase was to become one of the signature mantras for both him and elements of Ulster's Loyalist community, as they sought to undermine prospects of a peaceful settlement to the Irish question. The Paisley mantra came to mind during one of several return visits to the Province in 2012, as Visiting Professor at the University of Ulster. Scanning the newspapers on the short flight from London to Belfast's George Best International Airport, the dominant headline was about the historic handshake that was scheduled to take place during the Royal Jubilee visit of Her Majesty, Queen Elizabeth the Second, sovereign Monarch of Great Britain and Ireland, and Martin McGuiness, Deputy First Minister of Northern Ireland. McGuiness was a Sinn Fein MP who had formerly been a senior figure in the Provisional IRA. Supported in no small measure by the momentum building up in civil society institutions and organisations, the 1985 Anglo-Irish Agreement had provided a framework for the ensuing political dimensions of a peace process that, after a lot of blood had flowed under the bridge, culminated in the signing of the Good Friday Agreement in 1998. This paved the way for the return of devolved government from Westminster to Northern Ireland's mothballed parliament at Stormont. The terms of this devolution required a form of Consociationalism: a power-sharing arrangement between the Province's main Unionists and Nationalist parties which effectively brought together Ian Paisley's DUP (Democratic Unionist Party) and Gerry Adams's Republican Sinn Fein. It had seemed impossible that these two men would sit in government together, as First and First Deputy Ministers in the Northern Ireland assembly at Stormont, for the first time in March 2007. This eventuality which most observers would have disregarded as a utopian fantasy had it been predicted ten years earlier was widely viewed as a signal that the Troubles were indeed well on the way to being over.

This view had seemed to be confirmed too the previous year when on that June 2012 the Queen made an historic visit to Croke Park, Dublin, becoming the first serving UK Sovereign to set foot on Republic of Ireland soil since Partition in 1921. When in 2008 Paisley and in 2010 Adams stepped down from their leadership roles in the Northern Ireland assembly these positions were occupied by Peter Robinson of the DUP and Sinn Fein's Martin McGuiness respectively. Thus it was that the Queen's Golden Jubilee visit in 2012 coincided with McGuiness's tenure as First Deputy Minister. Through a smiling handshake between the Queen and McGuiness in a private room in Belfast's Lyric Theatre this provided a further opportunity to make a very powerful symbolic statement that from the perspective of the British Government and republican Sinn Fein, the armed struggle was indeed over, to be replaced once and for all by democratic, constitutional political mechanisms of negotiation.

But it was another handshake that confirmed for me that the Troubles were indeed over. When I had lived in the Province and the green shoots of the peace process were first poking through the barren political soil, during a run in Belfast in the early 1990s along the side of the Lagan, the river that bisects the city, my running partner Eamonn McCartan and I passed the time by breathlessly debating about how, if it ever happened, we would know when the Troubles were over. I can no longer remember which of us came up with the formula, but between us we drew the conclusion that we'd know the Troubles were over the day the RUC played Gaelic Football against the *Garda Siochanna* (police force of the Irish Republic) at the headquarters of Gaelic games, Croke Park. As things stood at that time there would have been battalions of Northern Irish sports people chanting the Paisley mantra: "Never, never, never!".

A decade and a half later, on November 25, 2011 Dave Moynihan and Senan Fenucane, captains of the Gaelic Football teams of the *Garda Siochanna* and the PSNI (Police Service of Northern Ireland) shook hands at the centre of Croke Park, Dublin, at the commencement of their McCarthy Cup fixture. This was the location of the Queen's visit just months before. Admittedly the PSNI was a new and more inclusive police force reconfigured as part of the peace process and made more open to members of the nationalist community north of the border. Nonetheless, given the GAA's founding political mission, in particular the endurance of the century-long ban that had prohibited the police in Northern Ireland joining GAA clubs and playing the game, this encounter was an historical watershed. Taking place in the shadow of the Hogan Stand – named after Michael Hogan, one of the 14 people killed by the members of the Royal Irish Constabulary (RIC) and Black and Tans (British Auxiliary Army reservists) during a Gaelic Football match in 1920 – this symbolic moment was a huge milestone in the normalisation of relations between North and South on the island of Ireland.

Not long after this I was sat in a meeting in a room not far away from the spot where I had delivered the lecture on sport and politics in South Africa when the PIRA bomb was exploded back in November 1983. A key person at this meeting was Dr. Deidre Brennan, who had been one of the undergraduate students in that class. She would go on to get involved with the Belfast United programme and a variety of other sport-related community relations initiatives.[12] This time, almost 30 years later, I was there to discuss with her and other colleagues at the University of Ulster how we could draw upon subsequent initiatives in the Middle East to further collaborate to help to strengthen the sport-related community relations initiatives that Dr. Brennan and her colleagues had been driving forward in support of the peace process.

Things had come full circle, and it was gratifying to see Dr. Brennan, now Professor of Physical and Education and Sport at the University and Director of the award-winning Ulster Sports Outreach Unit, continuing the work that began to be shaped as a response to such trying and troubling times and circumstances. In the next chapter the emergence of the Football 4 Peace (F4P) programme in Israel, Palestine and Jordan is considered in detail, and it is the model that emerged from that project, as it was developed and matured, that helped to nourish a complementary peace-building project on either side of the border between the Irish Republic and Northern Ireland. This programme is now called F4P Ireland and the meeting at the University of Ulster was designed to discuss how the University could link up with F4P Ireland to add value to the endeavours of both the organisations in the field of sport-related peace work. It was agreed that, as in the F4P model in the Middle East, the delivery of training for local volunteers using a bespoke, values-based, co-existence/conflict resolution curriculum would be adopted as a central element of the F4P Ireland initiative. In 2013, F4P Ireland's project manager Damien McColgan observed that "without the Brighton-based links and international recognition of the credibility of the programme and model", wider peace-building support and funding could not have been forthcoming; and Michael Boyd, Director of Football Development at the Irish Football Association (Northern Ireland) recalled his experience of the F4P model, when experiencing the project in Israel in 2005, as eye-opening, a stimulus to the adoption of values-based coaching in his association's developmental mission. Their statements, presented more fully in Appendix D at the end of this book, are gratifying testimony to the influence of the long narrative of research that had laid foundations in the Belfast United project and later informed the work that was initiated and developed in Israel.

After finishing meetings with University colleagues in Belfast I travelled North West for meetings with representatives of Derry City Council. Up for discussion was how we could work together to provide Good Relations (the vogue, if vague, term used to describe what used to be referred to as community relations) training for all of their community coaches by adapting pedagogical models that we already had in place for F4P Ireland. Next we moved onto the meeting that was a personal milestone. It was with Maura Kelly, a Community Development Officer with the Ulster branch of the GAA. We got together to discuss the development of a dedicated Good Relations module for Ulster's GAA coaches along lines discussed with Derry City Council. Maura explained that there was increasing demand for the Ulster GAA to get involved in school and community-based initiatives that had clear community relations aims and objectives. She recognised that involvement in such programmes required different skill sets to more standard performance-focused coach education courses. They did not have those skills but we did, and the GAA was becoming interested in accessing this kind of learning. During this meeting I began to smile as the memory of the Ulster GAA president's rant in response to critical and informed argument during the 1989 Queen's University conference came flooding back. Never say never. What the Belfast United story demonstrates is that to achieve significant shifts in policy direction requires a combination of actors, activists and practices across political, academic and related professional constituencies. This model of collaborative praxis provided a template for future work in peace-building in other divided societies.

Notes

1 There are hundreds of books and articles dedicated to the Chicago School. An excellent *resumé* of this work can be found in M.J. Deegan, "The Chicago School of ethnography", in *The Handbook of Ethnography*, eds. Paul Atkinson, Amanda Coffey, Sara Delamont, Jon Lofland, and Lyn Lofland (London: Sage, 2007): 11–22.
2 See John Sugden, "Belfast United: Encouraging cross-community relations through sport in Northern Ireland", *Journal of Sport & Social Issues*, 15/1, 1991: 59–80. This has been acknowledged as a ground-breaking intervention in the emergence of SDP work. See Alexis Lyras and Jon Welty Peachey, "Integrating sport-for-development theory and praxis", *Sport Management Review*, 14, 2011: 311–326, which acknowledged the Belfast United initiative as a field-shaping work for the understanding of sport's contribution to "fostering intercultural exchange and conflict resolution" p. 311. Lyras has also commented, in his doctoral thesis, that Sugden's "pioneer work" has made it "possible to identify several additional components that are considered as fundamental building blocks for the development of a new theoretical framework in this new line of inquiry. The qualitative results of Sugden's work indicate that: Transformational leadership and international contacts provided the opportunity to design and implement the Belfast United project" and that cultural bonds were strengthened by collective experience of difference. See Alexis Lyras, *Characteristics and Psycho-Social Impacts of an Inter-Ethnic Educational Sport Initiative on Greek and Turkish Cypriot Youth*, unpublished PhD thesis, University of Connecticut, 2007: 42.
3 The visiting scholars were interns at the Institute for International Sport at URI. The executive director of the Institute was Dan Doyle, and the Institute's funding supported this pioneering initiative. Many years later, in December 2016, Doyle

was convicted, in the state of Rhode Island, on multiple charges of embezzlement and fraud, and the Institute was closed down. See *Providence Journal*, 5 December 2016 (online at providencejournal.com).
4 Soccer was the obvious sport to choose to launch the programme because it was popular with and widely played in both Catholic and Protestant communities. The programme began with boys as at the time girls' and women's soccer was not so widely played.
5 See Gordon W. Allport's widely influential, *The Nature of Prejudice* (Reading, MA: Addison-Wesley, 1979, first published 1954) for the genesis of the contact hypothesis. Research drawing upon the Belfast United project included Judith Andrea McLaughlin, *An Evaluation of Sport's Contribution to Community Relations in Northern Ireland*, unpublished PhD thesis, University of Ulster, 1995, which offered suggestive evidence on positive outcomes of cross-sectarian contact between the Belfast United boys.
6 For an overview of the historical context of arts-based interventions emerging in the 1990s, sharing many of the challenges of sport-based interventions, see Matt Jennings, "Building the dream in a theatre of peace: Community Arts management and the position of the practitioner in Northern Ireland", *Journal of Arts and Communities*, 4/3, 2012: 161–180 (first published 2009). See too Note 9 below.
7 The published contribution arising from the conference and feeding into the policy mix comprised the arguments in John Sugden, "As presently constituted, sport at an international level does more harm than good", *Peace and Understanding Through Sport: Journal of the Institute for International Sport*, ed. G. Cohen, 2/1, 1989: 63–68.
8 John Sugden and Alan Bairner, *Sport, Sectarianism and Society in a Divided Ireland* (Leicester: Leicester University Press, 1993).
9 The Centre for the Study of Conflict, under the direction of Seamus Dunn at the University of Ulster, contributed numerous reports in the 1990s on issues and interventions concerning the promotion and encouragement of research on community conflict across cultural and institutional spheres such as education, parades and policing.
10 John Sugden and Scott Harvie, *Sport and Community Relations in Northern Ireland* (Northern Ireland: Centre for the Study of Conflict, University of Ulster, 1995). Whilst the survey that provided the base of this report focused on 16 sports, we considered the findings representative of the wider culture of the sporting life of Northern Ireland. Also, the views expressed in the survey were very much those of the governing bodies of sport, and grass-roots experiences and opinion may well have been very different. Nevertheless, we could conclude with confidence that: "Most governing bodies do not see that a formal Community Relations agenda is relevant for their sports, believing that the formal introduction of Community Relations work could introduce issues which are best kept outside sport" (p. 92). This was a clear sign that the sport administrators were defendants of division for whom cross-sectarian interventions were anathema to their visions and beliefs. This survey and other complementary works contributed to a synthesis of research, *Sectarianism and Sport in Northern Ireland* published by the Northern Ireland Assembly in October 2001 (Research Paper 26/01); "compiled for the benefits of Members of the Assembly and their personal staff". This research paper confirmed the deep-rootedness of sectarianism in Northern Ireland's sporting culture, and presented a "selection of sporting initiatives aimed at reducing the impact of sectarianism in sport" (p. 1).
11 For a lucid and enlightening overview of the concepts of policy network and policy community as applied to sport settings, see Barrie Houlihan, *Sport, Policy*

and Politics: A Comparative Analysis (London and New York: Routledge, 1997): especially pp. 14–21.
12 Professor Brennan completed her PhD at the University of Ulster in 2000. Her thesis, on *The Role of Physical Activity in the Development of Female Agency and Empowerment*, indicates the expertise and awareness on gender equity that her involvement has brought to the F4P Ireland work. She authored the "eHoops" programme targeting the NEEET youth category (those not in education, employment or training) with sporting and educational opportunities designed "to give our young people a brighter future and enable them to become" active citizens in society. See sportchangeslife.com.

Chapter 3

SDP in the promised land – sport and peace-building in Israel

Introduction

I moved from Northern Ireland in 1996 when something resembling a peace process was beginning to take shape. At that time I had no intentions of taking the Belfast United model with me to the South East of England where I was taking up my new post at the University of Brighton, where I anticipated a rather more peaceful working environment than Ulster. Seeking out other peoples' conflicts elsewhere to meddle in was not on the agenda. There was enough to do, immersed in a large-scale study of maladministration, misrule and corruption taking place within the precincts of association football's world governing body, FIFA.[1] Indeed, the prospect of working more closely with my co-researcher on this subject, Alan Tomlinson, was one of the main reasons for accepting a Readership at the University of Brighton. But after the appearance of our first book on FIFA in 1998 it was through Tomlinson that, having escaped the metaphorical frying pan of Northern Ireland's murderous sectarian strife, I was to be drawn into the even more fiery and contested terrain of the Middle East.

A retired Baptist minister and former University of Sussex Chaplain, Geoffrey Whitfield, who had long-standing ties in Israel and Palestine, was trying to put together a planning group tasked with the challenge of developing a sport project that used sport with the specific objective of building positive relationships between Jewish and Arab youth in Israel. Aware of the social science-based research taking place at the University of Brighton, he approached Tomlinson and asked whether the University would be interested in working with his network, providing volunteers as well as research expertise that could monitor, evaluate and report on the project's initiatives and impact. Tomlinson explained to Whitfield that whilst the conflict-resolution area was not a particular specialism of his own, the Brighton group had a well-established profile in the critical, comparative and historical study of the place of sport in society. In May 1997 we had staged a symposium at the Sussex Arts Club in Brighton, spawning the edited volume *Sport in Divided Societies*.[2] In this we showed the role that sport played in culturally diverse and culturally divided societies; cases considered were India, Spain, Quebec, South Africa, Belgium, Switzerland, Germany, the USSR/Georgia, Northern Ireland and Yemen. So the cross-cultural expertise existed in Brighton, and Tomlinson told Whitfield that one of these experts who had recently joined the university had researched and written on conflict issues and sport in Northern Ireland: that academic was me, and Whitfield got in touch and invited me to attend one of his group's early planning meetings in an 'advisory capacity'.

Whitfield and his partners were at the time operating under the rather grand (and perhaps suggestively over-ambitious) name of the 'World Sports Peace Project' (WSPP), conceived in 2000; the meeting to which the University was invited took place in the offices of the London Marathon close to London's Waterloo Station and chaired by the then Race Director and former 10,000-metre world record holder, David Bedford. After not more than 15 minutes listening in on the discussion, several things became clear: firstly, those gathered were all very well-intentioned people driven by a real desire to make a positive contribution to peace-building in Israel; secondly, the existing members of WSPP's board had neither the knowledge nor the resources to effectively mobilise this desire by turning this goodwill into action on the ground in the Middle East. There was a straightforward choice: either continue to listen politely before walking away from the meeting without making any commitment to help; or roll up my sleeves, throw myself wholeheartedly into the project, and commit colleagues, resources and students from the University to the initiative. This book is testimony to the choice that was made!

The University's involvement could help in two important ways: firstly, from previous research and project-building – as outlined in the previous chapter – we could help the WSPP's Board glean the necessary contextual understanding that is essential to planning and implementing credible and sustainable conflict-resolution and peace-building programmes, whether they be at home or overseas; secondly, the kind of project that the WSPP's Board was imagining would need suitably qualified volunteers, and our University of Brighton department (the then Chelsea School of Sport that educated and trained large numbers of sport and physical education specialists), could provide access to a pool of suitably trained student volunteers, supported by a network of academic practitioners. The latter included, at this formative point, Gary Stidder, Andy Theodoloudes, James Wallis and John Lambert, who were to bring invaluable experience to the evolution of a model of implementation. A decade and more later, in a case study on the impact of the work among non-academic users, we would show how far in geo-political reach and policy impact the F4P model that was evolved out of the WSPP had travelled, its programmes having involved more than 8,000 children, 600 or so coaches and many community leaders. Its values were embodied in the project from the start, and fully articulated in 2004 as

Football 4 Peace's (F4P) Five Principles of Fair Play: neutrality; equity and inclusion; respect; trust; and responsibility; and subsequently it contributed to changing the policies of sporting organisations in Israel, Jordan, Palestine, Ireland, South Africa and South Korea.[3] How did the work, begun on such a modest level, develop so far? We will return to this later in the chapter, after providing an overview of the all-important context.

Israel and Palestine: the 'perfect conflict'

As already stated, when developing and designing programmes for strategic intervention in deeply divided societies, it is essential to nurture a deep understanding of the particular transcending social and political context. In this regard the significance of history must not be minimised. The problem lies in putting realistic boundaries around what is and what isn't relevant from the past to an understanding of the chemistry and architecture of contemporary conflicts. We have already seen that in order to comprehend the complicated patterns of institutionalised ethno-religious nationalism that framed the Troubles in Northern Ireland, it is necessary to take account of events and processes bound up with the legacies of historical conflicts. It is even harder to put sharp boundaries around a conflict that has its roots in the earliest recorded religious histories of the Western world, particularly when such biblical accounts continue to feed into and sustain narratives of the conflict between Israelis and Palestinians.

When preparing student volunteers for their participation in the F4P programme, in attempting to summarise this historical context in a way that helps them understand the political and cultural location and perspectives of the different groups they are likely to encounter, a broad brush approach is adopted, starting with a selective smattering of ancient, medieval and early modern history before moving on to a more detailed consideration of events immediately preceding and following World War II. 'History with hobnailed boots on' this may be, but it provides essential explanation of the origins of the narrative of exile and return that continues to exert a powerful influence on Jewish identity and nationhood. In this narrative, Jewish origins lie in the lands of what were Judea and Samaria in biblical times, a region to which the Jewish people believes it is destined to return. In various historic episodes since, under various conquering and colonising regimes, the most significant of which were the Egyptian and the Roman, large swathes of that population were exiled from these lands, a case of widespread examples of 'ethnic cleansing' characterising conquest and counter-conquest in the ancient world. What sets the Jewish experience apart is the strongly held belief, articulated and enshrined in Hebrew Scriptures, that they are a 'chosen people' destined to return from exile to the Promised Land – irrespective of who has occupied that land since and for how long.

In the period following the decline of the Roman Empire and in the wake of massive Jewish exile and migration, the region underwent a gradual process of Arabisation, accelerated in the sixth and seventh centuries by the emergence and spread of a Muslim Empire in the Middle and Near East and parts of Southern Europe. This in turn sparked the Crusades: a religiously fuelled series of conquests and counter-conquests between European Christian powers and the defenders of Islam for the control of the Holy Land and with it the Holy City itself, Jerusalem, where some of the most revered shrines and holy places of the world's three monotheistic religions – Judaism, Christianity and Islam – were located.

In the eleventh century, the Crusader presence in the region was all but eradicated by the victorious armies of Egyptian-based Muslim leader, Saladin, whose achievements on the battlefield and as ruler in peace-time helped to cement Arab dominance in the Levant. This period of Arab control prevailed for more than five hundred years when the greater Middle East, including Palestine, became part of an expanded Ottoman-Turkish Empire which, while not Arab at its heart, endorsed Islam as its official religion. The Ottoman Sultanate was nevertheless tolerant of other religions and this tolerance would be tested to the utmost in Palestine in the nineteenth century as it witnessed an ever-growing tide of Jewish immigrants fleeing persecution across Europe and returning to a Promised Land which by then was well and truly settled by multiple generations of Palestinian Arabs.

Zionism is the label given to the distinctive Jewish nationalist ideology that underpins the creation and preservation of an exclusive Jewish State in the Middle East. Hundreds of years of anti-Jewish discrimination throughout Eastern and Western Europe led to the emergence of Zionism, a philosophy and social and political platform that rejects notions of assimilation, instead arguing for the creation and preservation of a dedicated homeland for the wider Jewish diaspora – the globally scattered Jewish peoples who recognise their ancestral roots as belonging to the Jews who were originally exiled from the Roman colony of Judea in the early years of the last millennium. This history of exile and persecution is key to any understanding of the forces that come together to give powerful and enduring momentum to Israel's struggle for the right to exist.

The origins of Zionism are most closely associated with the teachings of Austro-Hungarian Theodor Herzl and were the product of debates among the Jewish middle and intellectual classes concerning how best to resist the alarming escalation of anti-Jewish sentiment and discriminatory legislation that spread across Europe from the mid-nineteenth century onwards.[4] The conclusion of these debates was that in the era of nations and nationalism, attempts to integrate Jewish minorities in the national projects of countries such as France, Italy, Russia and Germany had been abject failures. Instead it was argued that the only solution lay in the creation of a separate Jewish homeland wherein Jews could gather and control their own destiny.

Drawing upon a mixture of historical evidence and theological dogma, it was further argued that this homeland should be in what was then Ottoman Palestine.

Aided and abetted by a coalition of Palestinian Arabs and other fiefdoms across the Arabian Gulf, by the time the British wrestled control of the region form the Turks in 1918, the inward migration of Jews from across Europe had grown significantly. Set against the backcloth of the First World War it was in this period that the two mutually contradictory aspects of British rule in Palestine and Trans Jordan were established. Firstly, in order to garner support from regional Arab powers in their struggle to overcome the Ottoman Turks, the British promised that once this was achieved they would endorse the creation of an independent Palestinian nation.[5] Secondly, to foster material support for the war effort in western Europe from Britain's wealthy Jewish community, in direct contradiction of the promise of and commitment to an independent Palestine, the Balfour Declaration of 1917 pledged the British Government's support for the principle of an independent Jewish State in Palestine, stating in an official communiqué:

> His Majesty's Government view with favour the establishment in Palestine of a national home for the Jewish people, and will use their best endeavours to facilitate the achievement of this object, it being clearly understood that nothing shall be done which may prejudice the civil and religious rights of existing non-Jewish communities in Palestine, or the rights and political status enjoyed by Jews in any other country.[6]

This was received with great joy among Zionists, but, despite the caveats in the Balfour statement vowing to protect Palestinian rights, equal dismay by those local Arabs who had been allowed to believe in a vision of their own Promised Land; Balfour's Declaration wholly undermined this vision.

The peace that followed the 'War to End All Wars' in 1918 proved to be short-lived. Also complicating the situation, the terms of the Sykes-Picot agreement, known too as the Asia Minor Agreement, had in 1916 carved up the remnants of the Turkish Ottoman Empire among the victorious Allied powers. In this the British were given control of areas known as Palestine and Trans Jordan, all of which under British rule would be known as Palestine. As T. E. Lawrence's epic account of the British government's collusion with the Gulf Arab chieftans shows, in return for their co-operation in helping rid the region of Turkish rule, the Arab chiefs would be rewarded with control over Palestine; but this would become, of course, the preferred site for those supported in the Balfour Declaration in their aspiration to return to the 'promised land' of Israel. Anyone working in the field of conflict-resolution would have to understand and work with this historical knowledge and sensitivity – as we would emphatically demonstrate in the training programmes for volunteers working in the region.

The emergence of new and more virulent forms of ethnically driven ideological nationalism – some taking Fascist forms – swept across Europe in the 1920s and 1930s. Once more Jews were in the firing line leading to a dramatic increase in outward migration of those who sought sanctity through a return to their 'promised land'. With this influx the British found it increasingly difficult to govern in Palestine as Arab opposition to expanding Jewish settlements in the region developed a paramilitary dimension that was countered with the emergence of organised and armed Jewish resistance movements that not only sought to protect Jewish communities from Arab onslaught, but also agitated for an independent Jewish state.

The Holocaust, the regime of systematic slaughter during World War II when approximately six million Jews were exterminated across Europe under Nazi supervision, was the apogee of the millennia-long story of Jewish exile and persecution. It prompted a further flood-tide of Jewish migration into Palestine which the British struggled to resist and it further strengthened the moral position of those campaigning for an independent Jewish State. Finding themselves caught in the middle of what amounted to an unwinnable civil war between Jewish and Palestinian nationalists, in 1948 the British bowed to the pressure being exerted by the newly constituted United Nations and its powerful Security Council and agreed to the establishment of an independent Jewish state in Palestine.

While on the one hand the creation of the Jewish state is celebrated by Jews worldwide as a major achievement for the hitherto nation-less and Jewish Diaspora, in equal measure it is viewed by others as a catastrophe – or in Arabic *Nakba* – for the Palestinians on whose land the new state took shape. Moreover, the fact that the fledgling Jewish state prevailed in the first of the numerous ensuing Israeli-PanArab wars, the victor also occupying more land than was agreed in the original UN-brokered arrangement, deepened Palestinian wounds and the accompanying sense of injustice.

For neutral observers – and it is so hard to be neutral in the Palestinian/Israeli conflict – both the Jews and the Palestinians are heavily burdened with the weight of historical injustice. This is why Alan Dowty has described the situation in the region as "the perfect conflict": a conflict at the core of which is a series of zero-sum, counter-balancing claims of land-rights, injustice and victimisation:

> This sense of victimhood on both sides, on top of a strong belief that one is in the right, is what has made this into a 'perfect conflict', in the same sense as a 'perfect storm'. It would be difficult to design a conflict with more self-generating power for continued devastation and destruction.[7]

Anyone seeking to intervene in such a 'perfect' conflict must be alert and sensitive to the myriad of political, religious and cultural forces that have shaped the landscapes of 'devastation and destruction'. Such forces have determined the contemporary character of the countries and cultures, to which we now turn.[8] The demographic features of the contemporary Israel/Palestine conflict confirm the sedimented nature of such formative forces and determining influences. After its foundation in 1948 only 160,000 Arabs stayed in Israel.[9] The rest, approximately 640,000, fled, mainly to neighbouring Jordan, Syria and Lebanon. The Palestinian Diaspora has reached around 3.5 million, of which approximately 2.5 million Palestinians live in the Occupied Territories (West Bank and Gaza), some of the most densely populated places on earth. Perhaps rightly so, the situation of the Palestinians within the Occupied Territories, the plight of the Palestinian Diaspora and the Israeli state's engagement with these external factors attract most global attention. Often forgotten by the international community is the status of relations between the various constituencies which remained within the state of Israel after 1948.

In 2010 the total population of Israel stood at nearly 8 million; by 2016 it was estimated at 8,174,527. Of these approximately 6 million are Jewish Israelis, made up of a mixture of migrant first- and second-generation settlers from Europe and American, a small minority of *Falash Mura* from Ethiopia and a 'second wave' of European migrants from former Eastern Bloc countries who flocked to Israel when the Soviet Union began to disintegrate in the late 1980s and early 1990s. While in terms of religious persuasion the majority of the Jewish population considers itself to be secular, a significant minority is made up of devoted adherents to the Hebrew faith. This religious orthodoxy is a key dimension of Israel's fractured political make-up.

The number of 'Palestinian-Arab-Israeli' citizens is approximately 1.6 million, roughly 20% of the population. The order of its wording – Palestinian, Arab, Israeli – changes depending upon the political consciousness of the individual concerned. This too is an exceedingly complex identity, gathering together those Arabs whose roots are found in the families who remained in the state of Israel when it was created in 1948. It is further complicated via the religious and ethnic suffixes that can be added such as Moslem (Sunni and Shiite); Christian (varieties of Orthodox, Protestants, and Catholics); not to mention different tribal/ethno-religious affiliations, such as the Bedouin, Druze and Circassian which also contribute to the mapping of the country's complex sectarian geography. Much of this is a consequence of Britain's post-imperial policies and legacy.

Sport and football in Israel

Like everything else in Israel, sport is highly politicised. It is an important sphere of civil society, and it is terrain contested between Jews and Arabs and the various factions within each community. The politically contested dimension of Israeli sport has increased in proportion to the increasing numbers of

Israeli-Arabs who choose to participate.[10] Until relatively recently, for Arabs in Israel football was another contested aspect of mainstream civil society where they were losing ground. Traditionally, professional football in Israel has been linked to mainly Jewish political parties and political associations, including trades unions. In addition, as Ben-Porat has argued, along with other state-sponsored sports and sporting organisations, after 1948 football was an integral part of the process through which the cultural façade of the (Jewish) state of Israel was constructed.[11] This made it difficult for Israeli Arabs to participate at the highest levels. It also helped to exacerbate problems for Israel's participation in international football competitions, leading the Fédération International de Football Association (FIFA) to take the radical step of removing Israel from the Asian Football Confederation (AFC) to avoid confrontation with regional Arab states, and placing them first within the Oceania (Australasia and the South Pacific) Football Confederation (OFC), and later within Europe (UEFA) for future World Cup qualification purposes.[12] As noted below, the decision made by FIFA in 1998 to readmit Palestine into the 'FIFA family' – even though Palestine is not recognised internationally as a nation-state – led to problems for some talented Israeli-Arab-Palestinians who now have to decide to which football 'nation' they owe allegiance.[13]

However, after 1967, with the modernisation of Israeli society and the advance of post-1980s globalisation, the situation began to change with evidence of a professional/commercial performance pragmatic at work; professional football became more open to the participation of Arab players and Arab-owned teams:

> The globalization and liberalization of Israeli society since the 1980s, and the waning power of the political parties (the former patrons of soccer), have facilitated the commercialization of the game, introducing a profit motive and economic rationality of both players and owners.[14]

In other words, it is good business to recruit the best players, regardless of their race or ethnic/national identity because this produces better teams and more success. The net result is that, perhaps impelled by relative impoverishment and the perceived riches available in professional sport, more and more Arab-Israelis are taking up opportunities to play and watch football in settings that were formerly the almost exclusive preserve of Jewish-Israelis. This tendency has been encouraged by breakthroughs made by both Jewish and Arab players from Israel who play in the most prestigious European professional leagues. It is for these reasons, Sorek has further argued, that football, more than any other sporting sphere, has the potential to be an "integrative enclave" in Israel. However, this advance created other problems. Precisely because more Arab players, teams and their fans are now taking part, football also offers more opportunities for racial and ethno-national confrontation. For example, "death to the Arabs" and other more profane and racially vicious chants are sometimes heard coming from the exclusively Jewish terraces of Beitar Jerusalem, the team which is consistently at the top of the New Israel Fund's (NIF) weekly racism incitement index. This initiative to confront and document prejudice was introduced into the Israeli football league in 2004 in recognition of the increase in sectarian-related incidents in and around the country's football stadiums.[15] As well as working with the NIF, the Israeli Football Association (IFA) consulted with representatives from the English Football Association (FA) which, with its long experience of dealing with racism in English football, has helped to devise anti-racist strategies that are most suitable for the local context.[16]

Some of these contradictions are clearly revealed in the case of one Arab-Israeli team, Bnei Sakhnin. Based in a radicalised Arab-Israeli town in Galilee, Sakhnin won the national cup in 2004 and qualified for the UEFA Cup. Sakhnin won through the pre-qualifying stages of this prestigious tournament before being eliminated in a high-profile game against the English Premier League team, Newcastle United. Bnei Sakhnin is Arab-owned, has a Jewish coach and a mixed squad of players, including some who are not Israeli. Sakhnin's European involvement captured the imagination of the British media who portrayed them as an example of co-existence in Israel.[17] In Israel, the team's success attracted support from across the political spectrum and also some pan-Arab acclaim. The Israeli Prime Minister at the time, Ariel Sharon, and the then Chairman of the PLO, the late Yasser Arafat, made it a point to wish Sakhnin well. At the same time Sakhnin attracted criticism, particularly from some Arab groups in the region and elsewhere because they were flying the flag for Israel in Europe.

Furthermore, sport is an area where controversial issues of national identity and affiliation are easily evoked/provoked. Since 1998, talented Israeli-Arab footballers have been able to opt to play for either Israel or Palestine. In almost every case, because currently the Israeli national team plays at a significantly higher standard than its Palestinian neighbour – which faces infrastructural and military-political restrictions in its bid to develop a competitive 'national' team[18] – the best Arab-Israeli players choose to play for Israel. For this they are condemned in some Arab circles while, at the same time, they are not welcomed in the Israeli national team by all sections of Jewish society. For example, Sahknin player Abas Suan was lionised in the Israeli media for his heroic, goal-scoring performance against Ireland in a crucial World Cup qualifying game in 2005. However, when he returned to Israel for Sakhnin's game against Beitar Jerusalem, he was jeered by sections of the crowd who sang songs in praise of Baruch Goldstein, the Jewish nationalist who murdered 11 worshippers in a mosque in 1994. One fan was quoted as saying "we would rather have lost to Ireland than have Arabs score goals for Israel. You see, to us, when we say 'death to the Arabs!' we're not just trying to get a reaction. We mean it".[19] As these examples show, the integrative potential of football in Israel is heavily contingent, and the cleavages and divisions have shown little sign of diminishing or receding within the higher levels of the game in the region.

The findings of a study of football fandom in Israel and its relationship to national identity have suggested, its authors claim, that the sphere of football and fans' responses may contribute to "an ongoing process of diminishing Israeli hegemonic national identity".[20] But Jon Dart warns, in his review of the 'Boycott Israel' debate, and alongside developments that have seen FIFA, in 2013, invest US$4.5million into establishing an infrastructure for Palestine football, that the overall political debate may be hardening: "a crude characterisation used by the Israeli government, and its supporters, is seeking to neutralise any criticism of the State of Israel by labelling it as anti-Semitic".[21] At FIFA's 67th Congress in Bahrain in May 2017, the Israeli-Palestine issue was a major item. A FIFA Monitoring Committee, chaired by South African anti-apartheid activist Tokyo Sexwale, had recommended that Israeli football teams be given six months to stop playing in the occupied territories. The Palestinian case was that teams playing in the settlements of Kiryat Arba, Givat Ze'ev, Ma'aleh Adumim, Ariel, Oranit and Tomer were, by playing in territory widely recognised as part of a future Palestine state, breaching FIFA statutes concerning political interference in football. The Israeli riposte from IFA president Ofer Eini was scathing: "I do not intend to give a hate speech in return", he said, also proposing that a "match of peace" should be played between the two countries, with proceeds going towards a football school for the region. Israel's prime minister Benjamin Netanyahu had phoned FIFA president Gianni Infantino urging that the recommendation of Sexwale's committee be taken off the Congress agenda. Infantino duly put back the item, for further consideration by the FIFA Council later in the year, also adding, bizarrely: "I have been hearing in the press that President Trump is looking into this and hopefully he can find a solution. If he has an idea, I am happy to take it".[22] That the seriousness of the issue could be diluted in such a way is further and persisting evidence of the need for sensitive and informed interventions, such as the Football 4 Peace (F4P) project to which we now turn in detail.

Football 4 peace

It was against this backdrop that the F4P programme took shape. Since its beginning it has been the objective of F4P to make pragmatic and incremental grass-roots interventions in the sport culture of Israel, helping to build bridges between otherwise divided communities and, at the same time, contribute to political/policy debates around sport in the region. Specifically its aims are to: provide opportunities for social contact across community boundaries; promote mutual understanding; engender in participants a desire for and commitment to peaceful co-existence; and enhance soccer skills and technical knowledge.

The first formal phase of the project was in 2001 when, operating under the label of WSPP (World Sport Peace Project), six student-volunteer coaches from the University of Brighton, a staff leader (Gary Stidder), a research assistant (Pat Johnson) and the then Project Director (Geoffrey Whitfield) conducted a week-long coaching camp in the Arab town of Ibilin. The timing was a problem since the camp began during the second Intafada (uprising). The first Intafada had engulfed the West Bank and Gaza in the late 1980s and early 1990s. It appeared as a spontaneous and popular uprising of young Palestinians, protesting against the oppressive policies of the Israeli state and its security forces and, by implication, the failure of established Palestinian political groups, most notably the PLO, to protect them from such oppression.[23] Against a background of the failure of the Oslo Accord to deliver peace based on a graduated separate-state solution, the then Israeli opposition leader, Ariel Sharon, sparked a second Intafada in September 2000 when he led a demonstration into the sacred al-Aqsa mosque in the centre of Jerusalem. One of the key differences between this and its predecessor was that it spread from the West Bank and Gaza to include Palestinian Arabs living as citizens within the state of Israel. They took to the streets to protest against the brutal means being used by the Israeli authorities to quell unrest in the West Bank and Gaza and to draw attention to a perceived lack of civil rights within Israel itself. In Israeli-Arab towns such as Nazareth and Sakhnin (both partners in the F4P project), the security forces responded to the protest very aggressively, resulting in the arrests of many Arab-Israeli citizens and the deaths and serious injury of others.[24] This grievously damaged already fragile cross-community relations between Arabs and Jews within Israel in general, and in the region of Galilee in particular. The increasing use of suicide bombers as a strategy for resistance by several Palestinian extremist groups exacerbated a growing cross-community mistrust and polarisation.

For the first F4P intervention project, the original plan had been to partner Ibilin with a nearby Jewish municipality, Misgav. While the Project Director had made great efforts to secure the co-operation of community leaders in Ibilin, less attention had been paid to cultivating relationships within the neighbouring Jewish community. Given the broader political context, this proved to be a big mistake. A bus bombing in the neighbourhood also did not help matters and in the end Misgav chose not to send any of its children to the inaugural event. The 2001 project went ahead nonetheless in Ibilin, involving 100 Muslim Arab and Christian Arab children (10–14 years old). This reflected the sectarian geography of Iblin where Moslems and Christians lived in separate neighbourhoods. As noted earlier, community divisions in the region are more complex than simply between monolithic blocs of Arabs and Jews, and rifts and tensions within the Arab community in Galilee generated a problem that most of the UK team had not previously appreciated or accounted for.

Related to this was a realisation that for the project to have a future it could not afford to be associated with one particular faction. Most of the local key people who were involved with the Iblin pilot were Christian Arabs and this had alienated certain sections of the Muslim population. Coupled with the unproductive diplomatic efforts which contributed to the neighbouring Jewish community not sending its children, there was a danger that rather than contributing positively to inter-community relations, the football project could make matters worse. These were all very important lessons that would serve well the project's future development. This said, in the face of all the odds, the fact that the project took place at all was a considerable achievement demonstrating that, from a logistical point of view (fund-raising, volunteer recruitment, planning, travel, provision of equipment, programme implementation and so on) such programmes could be successfully organised.

Building on this qualified success a second project took place in 2002 with eight coaches and two staff leaders. This time, in addition to Iblin, the cooperation of the Jewish communities of Misgav and Tivon was secured allowing 150 Arab and Jewish children, including 20 girls, to share the coaching and playing experience. The inclusion of girls would later, for culturally sensitive reasons, prove problematic.[25] Local volunteer coaches and community sport leaders were more involved in planning the 2002 event and participated fully in the coaching project. The involvement of local people, and their increasing sense of partnership/ownership, was perceived to be a very important development and a key area in terms of the project's longer-term sustainability. The need to engage in more work year-round with volunteer coaches and community sports leaders from the participating towns and villages was also recognised. The impact that a week-long coaching project can have on longer term cross-community relations is important, but necessarily limited. The pre-project training day in 2003 was extremely useful, and the UK team was concerned to keep developing links and networks among the people who were not only key in terms of planning for the 2004 event, but also significant in the development of community sport policies in the region. In September 2003 Geoffrey Whitfield and David Bedford "entrusted" – Whitfield's word – the project he and Bedford had begun in 2000 to "The Chelsea School at the University of Brighton and the British Council in Israel".[26] The autonomous F4P was at that point confirmed as a "secular organisation . . . underpinned by a principle of neutrality", in the Brighton team's words, and unconnected to any religious or political group.[27]

Later in 2003 discussions and debates within the F4P leadership team led to the practical development of the F4P values-based training curriculum in 2004. By then the F4P project had been running and growing for three years. During our in-house evaluations of the 2003 intervention two significant observations were made. Firstly, while sport was an important 'hook' to encourage children to sign up to the programme, in and of itself getting a bunch of kids to play football together did not necessarily guarantee a softening of attitudes and the beginning of a journey to peaceful coexistence; on the contrary, left alone it was just as likely that the competitive element within sport would lead to further hostilities between groups of children who were already cultural enemies. The second observation was that alongside the on-pitch activities we had organised a series of seminar-based activities and discussions which required the children to consider a variety of issues germane to the conflict situation of their everyday lives, but these had proved difficult to put into action with any sense of engagement on the part of the children.

The team set out to rethink both the content of the F4P programme and the ways through which it delivered the F4P coaching experience, in terms of both the on-pitch programme and the off-pitch activities. Several of the F4P team were experienced Physical Education specialists, one of whom, Andy Theodoulides, was completing a PhD on the subject of personal and moral development though sport and had a keen interest in understanding the role played by sport in promoting positive social values.[28] While it was recognised that in the context of the level of inter-community hostility that existed between Jewish and Arab neighbours in Israel, just getting rival communities to allow their children to come together on the football field was without doubt an achievement in itself, this alone was not enough; rather than just let things happen in the hope that the children would make friends across the ethno-sectarian divide, we believed that we may be able to adapt the coaching curriculum in ways that might make this much more likely to happen. We would also reconsider and revise the programme of off-pitch activities. At the key meeting, following a period of brain-storming we were able to articulate a set of simple operational values that we believed would, firstly, if acted out on the sports field, be the embodiment of the principles of fair play as outlined in the introductory section of this chapter; and secondly, if embraced by the participants and taken with them beyond the boundary of the playing field, could contribute to building more harmonious relationships between otherwise antagonistic communities and thus aid the peace process.

Those original values have remained as the spine of the F4P approach, and taking them as foundation stones, the team, with John Lambert taking the initial lead, developed, designed and fleshed out an innovative values-based curriculum and coaching manual for F4P.[29] This included a wide range of imaginative practices through which these values could manifest themselves and be used to teach and reinforce the principles behind them. This cemented the distinctive F4P on-pitch approach. Coterminously, Gary Stidder, working with colleagues, led the thinking and discussions that generated the off-pitch strategy and manual. In the cycles of implementation, as more and new members of the F4P team became involved, these manuals have been amended, further developed and applied in different socio-cultural and, indeed, sporting contexts beyond football.[30]

'Teachable Moments' emerged as a particularly effective way of identifying instances of the core principles and values. In the F4P Coaching Manual they are defined as:

> those incidents and events that happen during the flow of the practices that the coach can seize upon to illustrate the main underpinning values that he or she is trying to get over to the children. This is especially important in helping to translate some of the five F4P principles which are concepts and abstractions into practical examples.

Teachable moments can be both positive and negative. For example, take the principle/value of Responsibility; if at the end of a given practice phase the children start to walk away without helping the coach gather in the equipment they have used, during the break this can be pointed out to them as an example of not taking responsibility. In another scenario the same value can be illustrated by highlighting how somebody, at their own volition, can take responsibility to help one of their teammates learn a particular skill. As is stated in the manual:

> For instance, during a session dedicated to turning, while trying to get the group to execute a particularly difficult turn, the coach sees one child who has mastered the skill help to teach one of the others that has not. At the appropriate time the coach can stop the practice and have the youngster demonstrate how he has helped his colleague. This not only helps teaching the required skill, but also gives the coach the opportunity to talk briefly to the group about how this illustrates one child taking responsibility for another.

Designing and delivering the F4P coaching curriculum in this way ensures that children can be encouraged to be more critically reflexive, not just about how well they perform technically, but more importantly, about how they behave towards one another both on the field of play and outside of the arena.

In parallel with our efforts to revolutionise what we did with the children when involved in the on-pitch programme, we turned our attention to the second problem that we had identified: the off-pitch activities. This was first raised as a logistical problem, caused by having two age groups of children using the same facilities at different times but sharing transport, meaning that while one cohort was engaged on the pitch the other would have two hours waiting time. Initially we saw this as a positive opportunity to introduce a programme of supporting reconciliation activities facilitated by local 'experts' who would engage the children in a variety of largely classroom-based encounters wherein they could explore their cultural differences. However, our evaluations of these often emotive encounters yielded considerable negative feedback leading us to conclude that by introducing mechanisms to encourage relatively young children to engage intellectually and verbally with problematic and controversial issues outside of the playing field was itself fraught with danger. If not handled with skill and sensitivity, then rather than enhance mutual understanding it could produce the opposite results, undermining whatever good was being achieved on the football field.

We decided that we needed to replace these classroom-based sessions with a programme of practical activities through which the goals of mutual understanding and reconciliation could be encouraged to mature in less obvious ways, whilst seeking to reduce any potential confrontation. Even if more playing fields had been available (which they generally were not), we agreed that we did not simply want more football. Instead we decided to engineer a parallel curriculum through which progressive social learning could be achieved through engagement with a range of less formal physical interactions. This development was led by, as noted above, Gary Stidder, who at the time, amongst other things, led the University of Brighton's Outdoor and Adventurous Activities (OAA) programmes. Stidder was assisted in this by a young visiting scholar from the German Sports University (Cologne), Adrian Hassner, who was at the time researching the pioneering work of Kurt Hahn, the German educationalist and former Headmaster of Gordonstoun School in Scotland. Hahn is widely believed to have been the founder of modern approaches that use OAA (Outdoor and Adventurous Activities) to promote a range of 'character building' attributes in young people.

Stidder and Haasner set about constructing a portfolio of basic OAA-type activities which, like the on-pitch curriculum, in neutral settings presented practical opportunities for the embodied experimentation with and demonstration of the values of trust, respect, equality and responsibility (four of the core principles of F4P).[31] The intention was to produce complementary on- and off-pitch programmes with quite different core activities but each underpinned by a common set of values making them mutually reinforcing.

Having designed the values-based curriculum the next step was to introduce a training programme through which international and local volunteer coaches could become familiar with the principles underpinning the values-based coaching methodology, and adept at the practical delivery of these values. This led to an influential initiative by the new autonomous body; the organisation, in March 2004, of a week-long training event in the UK at the University of Brighton, to which 30 Jewish and Arab community leaders were invited. All attended and, in addition, we invited the 28 student-volunteer coaches and seven leaders from the UK who would be involved in the 2004 project. After an introductory day of trust games and outdoor adventure activities (such as raft-building and orienteering), the remainder of the week was dedicated to working through the draft F4P Coaching Manual, incorporating the five core principles, and culminated in an escorted visit to the Premier League football club, Arsenal, in London. The Israeli visitors left the UK well prepared for the summer project and committed to building a network through which the work of F4P could continue. Questionnaire-based evaluations carried out by the British Council indicated that this training event was an unqualified success, and the Israelis left with a strengthened commitment to the values and principles that drive the F4P intervention. There can be no doubt that this training initiative enhanced the delivery of the project itself in July 2004, and it is a dimension that was then built into future projects. The Brighton training event served as a template for training initiatives run annually in either the UK or Germany to be attended by all new international volunteers and by delegations of sport coaches and community leaders from the regions where the F4P programme was running in any given year: such events have since been replicated in South Africa, South Korea, Gambia and Northern Ireland, followed by smaller, localised 'cascade' training events, staged by those who had experienced the international event, for other local volunteer coaches in the target country.

In taking part in the international training camp delegates from otherwise incompatible communities not only became versed in the F4P methodology, but also shared an intensive and intimate 'out-of-structure' experience in an alien and 'exotic' culture. Along with the task-orientated cooperation required of them throughout the training curriculum, this experience of 'otherness' undoubtedly helped to bring them closer together, in so doing helping them to act as role models for the children with whom they would be working back home. Genuine cross-community friendships that were born and flourished in this atmosphere, were carried back to the domestic environment to become pivotal to the strengthening of inter-community bonds upon which the F4P programme was sustained and grown in Israel for a decade and a half and more.

The 2004 project was much larger than in previous years, involving 700 children from 16 communities spread throughout northern Israel. The UK team worked alongside 60 local, Jewish- and Arab-Israeli volunteers at seven different project sites, including a girls-only project in Tiberias. The project began with a further training day for all of the local and UK coaches, held at the Israeli national sports university, the Wingate Institute. After four days of coaching at the separate sites, all 700 children were brought together in mixed teams to enjoy a grand finals day at the stadium of Nazareth FC. After the awards ceremony, when the winning teams were handed their trophies and every child was given a medal, as the anthem-like song 'all together now (in no-mans-land)' by UK pop band, The Farm, blasted out from the stadium's loudspeaker system, all 700 children, and their relatives and friends spontaneously flooded onto the field to dance and sing in celebration with the coaching teams. After witnessing such an emotional moment it would have been easy to conclude that the project had been a great success. However, the project team members were not prepared to trust their emotions; they had initiated a more structured and objective series of research and evaluation initiatives involving surveys of all the Israeli children and coaches, interviews and more in-depth, ethnographic studies. In subsequent years this holistic research-informed and evidence-based F4P framework continued to expand, initially in Israel through community partnerships beyond our Galilee heartland, and then in Jordan and the Palestinian Authority. This expansion also included metropolitan areas of Tel Aviv, Beersheba and eventually the most challenging place of all: Jerusalem.

Jerusalem: complexities and challenges in implementing the F4P model

The story of Jerusalem cuts to the heart of the Israel/Palestine conflict. There are no obvious geographical reasons for the city to be there in the first place. Rather than being planned, it has evolved on an arid cluster of hills and valleys at the crest of the Judean Mountains between the Judean Desert in the East and overlooking the Judean Plane, stretching west for 60 kilometres towards the Mediterranean coast. The patchwork conurbation which is today's city has taken shape after – estimates vary – around four thousand years of continuous if traumatic habitation that has been marked by invasion, conquest, slaughter, colonisation, ethnic-cleansing, exile, destruction and reconstruction. Since its earliest recorded history Jerusalem has been a divided and fought-over city and one of the key factors that has underpinned such conflict has been divergent religious and ethnic claims over the 'ownership' of the city in general and particularly the Old City within the walls of which, as noted earlier in this chapter, are to be found some of the holiest sites and relics of the three monotheistic faith groups, namely, Judaism, Christianity and Islam. While at times such conflicts have led to the destruction of the city at other times Jerusalem has learned to manage its differences and the various religious and ethnic groups that have laid claim to the rights of domicile there have lived relatively peacefully alongside one another in a shared urban space.[32]

In this context the situation in Jerusalem today is neither anomalous nor particularly extraordinary, but is rather typical. What then is the situation? The inauguration of the state of Israel in 1948 precipitated the first Arab-Israeli war when the fledgling state fought off an attempt by the Palestinians backed by the armies of five neighbouring Arab states to destroy Israel at birth. This was to be the first of several significant victories by the newly constituted IDF (Israeli Defense Forces) over its Arab neighbours and resulted in the eastern boundary of the UN-sanctioned Israeli frontier being pushed further into Palestinian and Jordanian territory which effectively saw Jerusalem divided into two sections with East Jerusalem being in Arab hands while most of the west of the city was ceded to the Jews. The armistice that followed led to the redrawing of the Eastern boundary (known as the Green Line) in Israel's favour and was the status quo until 1967 when after the 'Six Day War' the IDF conquered more Arab territory and occupied the whole of Jerusalem including the Old City and the 'Holiest of Holies', the Temple Mount and the Dome of the Rock. In the face of stern objections from the United Nations in the wake of this victory Israel proclaimed its right to governance of the whole of the city and declared Jerusalem as the nation's capital and proceeded to encourage the extension of Jewish settlement activity east of the Green Line. While this is the situation that prevails today, Israel's annexation of the Old City and East Jerusalem continues to be condemned by the United Nations as an illegal occupation and is viewed as one of the major stumbling blocks to achieving a peaceful resolution to the wider conflict.[33]

Clearly this is only the briefest of descriptions of what is an exceedingly complex situation. However, it does provide some important background information that helps to clarify why the prospect of taking F4P to Jerusalem was a considerable challenge and a trial for a critically sociological approach. On top of the transcending social and political context outlined above there were some more immediate concerns that needed to be considered. The opportunity to take the project to Jerusalem arose in 2009 when F4P was contacted by an organisation called the Jerusalem Foundation (JF), which itself had been given the opportunity to deliver inter-community football programmes in and around Jerusalem through funding offered by the German Football Association (DFB – *DeutscherFutball Bund*). The President of the DFB, Dr. Theo Zwanziger, who was a member of the Jerusalem Foundation's German branch, had been approached by the JF in an attempt to secure significant funding for the physical development of community sport facilities in the Jerusalem vicinity. Instead the DFB offered relatively modest support for project development involving children and football. The JF was willing to accept this funding but did not have the capacity to deliver a cross-community football programme. In order to overcome this lack of knowledge and expertise the JF turned to F4P which had a successful record of delivering such programmes in the North of Israel.

Before agreeing to such an undertaking it was important for F4P representatives to get more information about who they would be working and it soon became apparent that connecting with the JF could be problematic. Consultation with representatives of the Arab-Palestinian community in Israel and respected and knowledgeable sources from within the Palestinian Authority revealed that in these circles the JF had a reputation of being a Zionist organisation. A superficial examination of the JF's website suggests that this criticism is overstated as there are many references to promoting peaceful co-existence such as the declaration that "Jerusalem should be a city that unites all people, regardless of background, and serves as a bridge to create goodwill and tolerance for people of all faiths".[34] However a deeper reading suggests otherwise as the Foundation's *modus operandus* is underpinned by a philosophy that is suggestive of the broader Zionist mission. This is taken from its mission statement:

> With universal and Jewish values as the source of its inspiration, the Jerusalem Foundation seeks to create a just society for all citizens of Jerusalem. The Jerusalem Foundation works toward creating an open, equitable and modern society by responding to the needs of residents and trying to improve their quality of life. The Jerusalem Foundation will continue to pioneer change while at the same supporting efforts to preserve the history of the city.[35]

Regardless of any UN mandate, inspired by its founding father, former Jerusalem Mayor Teddy Kollek, the Foundation aspires to the establishment of a passive and reunited Jerusalem that sits at the centre of an extended Israeli state. In the eyes of its critics the JF is accused of pursuing strategies of 'normalisation' – that is, creating the conditions within and between Jerusalem's different communities that suggest local acquiesence to Israel's *de facto* illegal occupation. This criticism is not helped by the fact that out of a total of 14 people on the Board of Directors there was not, as documented in 2011 on the Foundation's website, a single Arab member.

In the course of matters it soon emerged that the DBF had not been aware of these complex political nuances. While F4P was happy to work with the DBF it was very guarded about getting too close to the JF. It cannot be overstated that establishing strong partnerships and building robust networks have been goals of critical importance to the sustainable success of F4P. However, while broadly supportive of F4P's aims, when it comes to making specific strategic decisions, each partner will bring divergent positions to the negotiating table depending upon their distinctive institutional vantage points. Then, on top of this there are the interpersonal standpoints to be considered – personal perspectives based on life experiences, values and belief systems.[36] This makes achieving a consensus quite difficult. In this case around the table sat representatives of the University of Brighton, the German Sports University, the British Council Israel (BCI) and the Israeli Sports Authority (ISA). From an institutional point of view the ISA as a government institution would not have great difficulty in taking a holistic view of Jerusalem's community structure. Whereas the BCI, in keeping with UK and UN foreign policy would not be favourably disposed to including areas of Jerusalem on the eastern side of the Green Line in any F4P project. The German Sports University had brokered the deal with the JF and DFB and, while without doubt sensitive to the issues outlined herein, had a vested interest in finding ways through which the project could be edged forward without opening up F4P to the charge of normalisation. As the founder organisation, likewise the University of Brighton wanted to make progress in Jerusalem without tarnishing F4P's reputation in the Arab communities in Israel and in the West Bank where, as we shall see, plans were being drawn up to run a programme in Bethlehem.

To further complicate the issue, these discussions took place in 2009 in the shadow of the IDF's assault on and temporary re-occupation of the Gaza strip which left hundreds of Palestinians killed and many more wounded. This led to some heated discussions among the F4P management team about whether or not going ahead with any F4P projects could be justified at a time when events on political and military fronts seemed to be moving in the opposite direction. It was our community partners who stressed that under such circumstances, in the face of accelerating conflict, it was more important than ever to keep the momentum of progressive civil society interventions like F4P. This, they stressed, is one of the few things that can give them hope for the future by providing a structure for active engagement through which they can feel that they are making a positive contribution to progressive social change, despite what politicians and war-mongers may say or do – in a C. Wright Millsian sense, a classic illustration of the dynamic relationship between 'personal troubles' and 'public issues'.

Taking all of these things into account and following the principles of critical pragmatism (further discussed below, and in detail in Chapter 6) it was decided to go ahead with the Jerusalem project with the following four provisos. Firstly, funding from the DFB to finance the training, transport and subsistence of the F4P volunteer coaching would be paid directly to the German Sports University; funding to support the delivery of the project in the communities would come via the JF into the Sports Department of Jerusalem Municipal Authority; the site at which the programme was to be delivered would be on the western side of the Green Line; and finally, children would not be recruited from parts of communities that were to the east of the UN-sanctioned border.

These conditions were met and in July 2010 F4P ran a successful project on the grounds of the Hebrew University in the west of the city with Jewish children from Jerusalem and Pet mixing with Arab children from Beit Safaffa, and the neighbouring town of Abu Gosh. Building upon this success and learning from some of the problems encountered in the 2010 enterprise a second project in Jerusalem was planned for 2011 with the added prospect of running two Jerusalem-based cross-community sports partnerships (CCSPs) in 2012 on the table. It was hoped that the DFB would remain involved, but the JF would no longer have a presence in the programme; instead, like all the other F4P CCSPs, the JF's involvement would fall within the embrace of the ISA's emerging cross-community sport strategy.

Whilst idealistic objectives drove the interventions, pragmatic compromises became recurringly important in realising the projects and initiatives. What this illustrates is that despite the many political and logistical problems that had to be overcome to mount such a project, through adopting a critical yet pragmatic approach, with grounded understanding, mutual sensitivity and lots of good will, it could still be achieved in ways that reflected and reinforced F4P's principles and goals. The genesis of these general principles of a critically pragmatic framework is described in Chapter 6.

Bethlehem: a bridge too far?

Were it not for the fact that Jesus Christ is widely believed to have been born in a stable there, Bethlehem would be seen alongside towns such as Nablus, Hebron and Ramallah as one of the main hillside Arab population-centres in the besieged West Bank. While this is the case, it is also widely regarded by tens of millions of Christians around the world as the sacred centre of their universal church. Because of this Bethlehem, like Nazareth in the North of Israel, has long-since had a significant Christian Arab population as well as a prominent presence of overseas Christian clerics and pilgrims. However, while the clerics and pilgrims remain in force the proportion of Arab Christians living in the town has been in sharp decline in the last three decades.[37]

Attempts to set up an F4P-style project in the West Bank can be traced back to 2002 when three staff travelled to Bethlehem and Beit Sahour to carry out a feasibility study. As already explained, these were extremely tense times in the wake of the second intifada with suicide bombings in Israel's major towns and cities and nightly gun-battles between Palestinian militia and armed Jewish settlers in the West Bank.[38] As we inspected some possible sites for the proposed project it became clear that the security situation was deteriorating rapidly. Through the US Ambassador the Israelis warned that if the attacks on the settlements did not cease and if there were any more suicide bombings the IDF would move in and reoccupy the areas of the West Bank that had been given a level of autonomous control following the Oslo Accords in 1993 and 1995. That night the shooting went on as usual and there was another suicide bombing in Jerusalem. We were warned by our hosts to leave the West Bank which we did the next day only moments before the IDF's tanks rolled in.[39] Clearly under the prevailing circumstances to try to go ahead with a F4P project was neither feasible nor justifiable. Nonetheless as we left we determined that when the conditions improved we would endeavour to return and fulfill our commitment to community development in this very needy area.

While the IDF eventually withdrew its invading forces, this was followed by the enforced isolation of the West Bank when in 2003 the first segment of a separation barrier between it and Israel was moved into place. Eventually, either as a barbed wire fence or concrete wall, the barrier would snake around the Samarian and Judean Mountains for more than 700km. The UN declared the barrier to be illegal, but the Israelis justified it in terms of security, particularly as a means of keeping out Palestinian suicide bombers. Palestinians and other opponents of the wall see more sinister motives, especially since the barrier did not follow exactly the route of the Green Line, but ate further into Palestinian territory, sometimes slicing villages in two and cutting off farmers from their grazing pastures and olive groves.

The Israeli strategy was more than a disguised land grab and, as Tanya Reinhart argues, it represents the fulfilment of former Israeli president Ariel Sharon's desire to turn the Arab-populated areas of the West Bank and Gaza Strip into a quarantined series of giant prisons, overlooked by an ever-increasing scatter-gram of Israeli settlements.[40] The movement of Palestinians to and from Israel was severely restricted with access to and from the patchwork of Palestinian towns and villages closely controlled by IDF check-points, and activities within these 'townships' placed under maximum surveillance. Thus, while the IDF no longer had so many 'boots on the ground' in the autonomous areas of the Palestinian Authority, for all intents and purposes Palestine remained under military occupation.

It was not until 2009 that F4P personnel began to reconsider the prospects for returning to the West Bank. Once more it was prompted by a potential funding partnership brokered by colleagues at the German Sports University, this time with the City Council of Cologne which has a civic twinning arrangement with the town of Bethlehem. After gathering information and taking soundings from credible sources, especially those in the Palestinian authority, it became obvious that the standard F4P model of bringing together children from Jewish and Arab communities would be both untenable and undesirable. Untenable because, despite the rhetorical claims made by some other organisations, under the current conditions of the time, while it might be possible for Arab children to come into Israel to engage with their Jewish counterparts, there was no possibility of Jewish children moving in the opposite direction. It was undesirable because such an asymmetrical arrangement only serves to reinforce the oppressive power relations between Israel and Palestine. In addition to which it would go against the principles of 'passive resistance' to the occupation which is the main plank of Arab protest against the wall and all that it stands for. Within the scope of 'passive resistance' any form of co-operation with Israel and its institutions is frowned upon and should be boycotted.

Thus, if we were to do anything progressive in the Palestinian Authority it would have to be self-contained within the West Bank and not have any formal associations with anything Israeli. We also needed a credible local partner that was not associated with any particular political faction. We found this in the University of Bethlehem and it was in cooperation with staff from the University's Sport and Recreation Department we were able to plan and eventually execute a project that brought together Palestinian Muslims and

Christians, girls and boys, and children from the refugee camps. In addition to this we were able to invite and host four local Palestinian volunteers to participate in the annual F4P training camp held in 2010 in Cologne. As with the pilot programme in Jerusalem, from a logistical point of view the project in the West Bank was a great success. Which is why it came as a surprise and disappointment when, during a post-project visit with our local partners, we were told that the project could not be repeated in 2011.

The reasons for this were far from clear at the time. While there may have been some difficulties concerning the use of facilities (sports venues are extremely scarce in this region) and the management and flow of funding, it is also possible that the prevailing unfavourable political climate, the continuation of settlement development and the intensifying of the occupation have led to the boycott being intensified. Even though F4P ran the programme in the West Bank in isolation from any of the programmes in Israel – including the printing of separate t-shirts that did not have any of the partner logos on (including that of the Israeli Sports Authority) – it was impossible to disguise the fact that the umbrella organisation did operate over the other side of the wall, particularly when all the details were published on the F4P website. There is evidence that this, coupled with the fact that Palestinians had participated in the training camp alongside Israelis, invited pressure on the local organisers from various political factions to desist from cooperating or further co-operating with F4P. Bloggers on Palestinian-based websites had picked up on the fact that some key Palestinian sport personalities, including the then captain of the Palestinian women's football team, had participated in a F4P training event in Cologne prior to running the Bethlehem project. Photographs were published online, showing Palestinians and Israelis cooperating together with German and English student-volunteers to learn the F4P methodology. This provoked online responses that the F4P scheme itself was a form of 'normalisation' and went against the underpinning principles of passive resistance to the occupation.

The key figures in F4P fully understood the position of their local partners in Bethlehem and were respectful of this local decision. Given the prevailing politics, no plans were made to run any programmes in the West Bank. Changes in local circumstances could, we observed, reactivate the Bethlehem project(s), and in January 2011 in a historic deal brokered by the President of the IOC, Jacques Rogge, the President of the Israeli Olympic Committee, Zivi Varshaviak, met his Palestinian counterpart, Major General Jibril Rajoub, and agreed to ease the travel restrictions placed on Palestinian athletes in the build up to the 2012 Olympics in London. In addition Varshaviak offered to give such athletes access to elite training facilities on Israeli soil. If such deals can be struck at an elite level, we reflected, it may signal hope that cooperative sport-development programmes, including that of F4P, could be resumed in the needy communities of the West Bank. But five years on from that agreement, no such programmes, to our knowledge, exist in the West Bank. So despite such positive overtures as the 2011 agreement emerging in the world of sport, a word of caution is always required. If progressive reconciliatory moves made by senior sports administrators are not matched by similarly progressive attitudes and policies in political society nothing much changes. It is deemed to be counter to the principle of social justice if the basic human right of freedom of movement is given to elite athletes while the overwhelming majority of the Palestinian population continues to be imprisoned in its own lands.

A note on normalisation

So, in the Bethlehem initiative, were we, F4P, 'guilty' on the charge of 'normalisation'? Normalisation is a charge levelled at civil society interventions which, in the views of their critics, do no more than reinforce the status quo in deeply divided societies with prevailing and significant socio-political imbalances between dominant and subordinate ethno-religious groups.[41] In the context of sport, anti-normalisation became the conceptual driver for the anti-apartheid and sport boycott movement in South Africa in the 1970s and 1980s and found expression through the campaign slogan: "no normal sport in an abnormal society".[42] In recent years there have been calls to adopt a similar position with regard to sporting initiatives in Israel, in the context of which F4P and other civil society peace-building organisations that operate in this sphere have been accused of aiding and abetting normalisation. There are undeniable similarities between South Africa and Israel with regard to the significant advantages in status, economic opportunity, political power and general life-circumstances enjoyed by Israel's Jewish citizens in comparison with their Arab counterparts. Indeed this is the very ground upon which F4P operates with the promotion of equality being central to its operational philosophy. With regard to our work in Israel the F4P position on 'normalisation' has been prominently addressed, as unequivocally stated on the front page of the F4P website:

> The philosophy underpinning the Football 4 Peace programmes in Israel and neighbouring countries is one that emphasizes social justice and human rights as the moral principles that underpin and guide the search for equality and peaceful co-existence among different ethno-religious communities and political factions. We are not doing this in support of the status quo and neither are we involved in the business of normalisation. Instead, we see our bridge-building work between Arab and Jewish communities inside Israel as part of a broader challenge to influence progressive social and political change in the wider region, including, when possible, making a contribution to the preconditions beyond which a mutually acceptable and balanced peace agreement

between separate and independent Israeli and Palestinian states can be achieved.

What makes the South African case distinctive is the fact that until the end of apartheid in the 1990s racial inequality was structured into the social order and legally enshrined as part of the constitution, so rendering incremental and progressive social change through civil society intervention impossible to achieve. This is yet to be the case in Israel, but if it were to become so, as some extreme right-wing Jewish nationalist interests have been campaigning for, F4P would cease to operate there.

Presenting on this subject it has often been effective to invoke words attributed to the eighteenth-century political philosopher Edmund Burke: "the only thing necessary for the triumph of evil is that good men do nothing". Burke has been adopted – however informally – as the unofficial patron of F4P, and this quote has been acknowledged as "the most popular quotation of modern times", in a poll of specialists in the field.[43] Yet although the saying has provided a useful shorthand to raise moral issues and justify interventions, there is no actual evidence that Burke said or wrote these words. He pronounced on the consequences of inaction though in his *Thoughts on the Cause of the Present Discontents*, a volume running to its third edition in 1770: "When bad men combine, the good must associate; else they will fall, one by one, an unpitied sacrifice in a contemptible struggle".[44] Working in Israel and Palestine it would be presumptuous and foolish to stake out any single position claiming the moral high ground, but forms of co-existence are an essential foundation for a mode of resistance to the combinations of the bad; association and co-operation in the name of co-existence are also strategies for survival, ways of avoiding being picked off "one by one" and sacrificed to the cause of extremist ideologues. Working in SDP contexts such as F4P it has been inevitable that we have had to make choices, choose sides. Value neutrality, a feature of particular models of objectivity in the formative phase of sociology, has never been allowed to over-determine the F4P work; the coaching manual itself, professing principles of neutrality, is in essence an articulation of alternative values that might challenge the cultural realities of a people, place or time.[45] It is to be hoped though that the adoption of a critically pragmatic approach to sport in the service of conflict-resolution and peace can provide activists – including sociologists – with both reason and method for doing something positive. However, as the cases and contexts discussed in this chapter illustrate, such a critical approach does have its limitations and there will be times when, after a full and balanced assessment of the transcending social and political context, the local needs, the levels and calibre of resources available, the security situation, and combinations thereof, the reluctant but sensible decision might be to stand back. Thankfully our judgement was that as things stood, this was not for the most part the case in the work accomplished in Israel, Jordan and Palestine in the first decade of the F4P story.

Concluding comment

We have in this chapter told the story of an SDP initiative seeking to challenge stereotypes and prejudices, taking sport as an arena where positive cultural changes might be encouraged, imagined and realised. It might appear at times to be a peripheral sphere of activity in the midst of conflict and devastation. But it is just one sphere among many in which actions can be taken to bring divided constituencies and communities together. At a general level such change has been urged by theorists and influential activists. The late and highly respected Palestinian academic and activist, Edward Said believed that co-existence, not separation, is the way forward if a lasting peace is to be achieved in Israel. He points out, "we cannot coexist as two communities of detached and uncommunicatingly separate suffering . . . the only way of rising beyond the endless back-and-forth violence and dehumanisation is to admit the universality and integrity of the other's experience and to begin to plan a common life together".[46] Likewise, Naim Ateek, a senior Christian-Arab cleric, argues that any lasting peace in the region must be based upon reconciliation which itself is dependent upon mutual recognition of and respect for different cultural traditions and the history of oppression and suffering that underpins those traditions. "Before the process of peacemaking can begin, a change in attitude of Israeli Jews and Palestinians towards one another is necessary. They need to face each other with candour, to create the new attitudes that will be the foundation for peace and stability in the region".[47] These arguments are fundamental in providing a rationale for civil society interventions like F4P.

At an ICSSPE international conference on *Sport as a mediator between cultures*, hosted at the Wingate Institute a little outside Tel Aviv in 2011, F4P played a central role alongside the British Council and the Israeli Ministry of Culture and Sport (IMCS) in debates on initiatives and interventions.[48] By the time of the conference F4P had trained in excess of 50 individuals, numerous of whom had undertaken the programme multiple times to further their expertise. So much so that, supported by the IMCS, it was felt that the Israeli trainers had enough experience to now run their own programmes without direct input from F4P. With this legacy in place, the F4P team considered its mission to be accomplished; we felt that we had fulfilled what we had promised, and that this was the appropriate time to withdraw from direct involvement in delivery and implementation, so leaving the door open for future collaboration. The achievement in the partnership was by now well-established, and the British Council's Jane Shurrush observed, in 2013 (see Appendix D) that "engagement with the University of Brighton research team and the development of F4P" had positive influences on the Council and its partner institutions in Israel", leaving behind "a sustainable model for continued cross-community sports activities in over 30 communities". [49]

F4P's contribution at the Wingate conference included a demonstration, led by student and community volunteers working with local children, of the values-based approach to delivering sport-based peace-building interventions. It was also argued in the conference that, based on our F4P work, social change through sport is incremental; adopting our framework of critical pragmatism, we can make interventionist splashes that turn into ripples, and ripples may become waves (to use the metaphor of our fully developed model presented in detail in Chapter 7).[50] These contributions received very positive feedback from the international delegates, among whom was Professor Cora Burnett of the University of Johannesburg, South Africa. Professor Burnett saw potential for developing similar programmes in South Africa, and in order to facilitate this she recruited one of F4P's most experienced student volunteers to undertake a three-month visiting fellowship at the University. The visiting fellow would work with Professor Burnett and her colleagues to develop a life-skills coaching manual based on the F4P model.[51] In the following chapter we resume contact with Professor Burnett in a consideration of the contribution of sport to the culture and polity of post-apartheid South Africa, including tracking the inputs of F4P to the genesis of a national PE curriculum in the 'Rainbow Nation'.

Notes

1 This resulted in three jointly authored books. See John Sugden and Alan Tomlinson, *FIFA and the Contest for World Football: Who Rules the Peoples' Game?* (Cambridge: Polity Press, 1998); *Great Balls of Fire: How Big Money Is Hijacking World Football* (Edinburgh and London: Mainstream Publishing, 1999); and *Badfellas: FIFA Family at War* (London and Edinburgh: Mainstream Publishing, 2003).
2 John Sugden and Alan Bairner eds., *Sport in Divided Societies* (Oxford: Meyer & Meyer Sport, 1999).
3 See *Football4Peace*, Impact Case Study, REF2014 (Research Excellence Framework), Higher Education Funding Council England (HEFCE), F4P CS 39771, impact.ref.ac.uk/casestudies2/refservice.svc/GetCaseStudyPDF/39771, 2013, accessed 12 May 2017.
  On the core principles of the values-based model see John Lambert, "A values-based approach to coaching sport in divided societies. The Football 4 Peace coaching manual", in *Anyone for Football for Peace? The Challenges of Using Sport for Co-Existence in Israel*, eds. John Sugden and James Wallis (Oxford: Meyer & Meyer Sport, 2007): 19–20.
4 Theodor Herzl's Zionist manifesto *The Jewish State* was published in 1896, and the following year he initiated the first Zionist Congress focusing upon strategies that could support the goal to establish the Jewish state. See herzlinstitute.org.
5 This whole saga was chronicled in great detail in T.E. Lawrence, *Seven Pillars of Wisdom: A Triumph* (London: Jonathan Cape, New Edition, 1940), brought to wider popular attention in David Lean's cinematographic, epic retelling of the

tale in *Lawrence of Arabia* (1962). The production of *Seven Pillars* was in itself an epic. Around Christmas 1919, Lawrence wrote, he "lost all but the Introduction and drafts of Books 9 and 10 at Reading Station" (p. 15). Rewriting from memory he produced a privately printed version of the book in 1926, not published for general circulation until 1935, the year of his death. In his Introduction to the book he refers to the British Cabinet's "definite promises of self-government" to the Arabs in exchange for their support in fighting the Turks. But he knew all along, throughout his time as a British army officer liaising with and supporting the Arabs, that "if we won the war these promises would be dead paper", and that "a fair settlement" of the Arab claims was an unlikely outcome. "Arabs believe in persons, not in institutions", he also astutely observed, conceding that he was unlikely to "defeat not merely the Turks on the battlefield, but my own country and its allies in the council-chamber"; and as such was himself a victim of institutions, of the "essential insincerity" of the British establishment. Direct quotes are from pp. 23 and 24. More generally on Lawrence's life, see Lawrence James, "Lawrence, Thomas Edward [Lawrence of Arabia] (1888–1935)", in *Oxford Dictionary of National Biography* (Oxford: Oxford University Press, 2004); online edn, Jan 2011, www.oxforddnb.com/view/article/34440, accessed 13 May 2017.

6 Letter from the United Kingdom's Foreign Secretary, Arthur James Balfour, dated 2 November 1917, to Lord Rothschild, a leading figure in Britain's wealthy Jewish community and prominent Zionist. Writing from the Foreign Office, Balfour stated that the "declaration of sympathy with Jewish Zionist aspirations has been submitted to, and approved by, the Cabinet". The letter concluded with the request that Rothschild "bring this declaration to the knowledge of the Zionist Federation". On Balfour himself, see Ruddock Mackay, H.C.G. Matthew, "Balfour, Arthur James, first earl of Balfour (1848–1930)", in *Oxford Dictionary of National Biography* (Oxford: Oxford University Press, 2004); online edn, Jan 2011, www.oxforddnb.com/view/article/30553, accessed 13 May 2017. For the text of Balfour's letter/statement, see a reproduction of the original in Leonard Stein, *The Balfour Declaration* (New York: Simon and Schuster, 1961): frontispiece.

7 Alan Dowty, *Israel/Palestine* (Cambridge: Polity Press, 2008): 222.

8 H.A. Harris has pointed out that "easy generalisations about Jews" should be avoided and that Jewish peoples should not be treated "as if they formed a homogeneous unit in the ancient world". He cites the hippodrome at Tarichaeae and the stadium at Tiberias as "massive pieces of evidence" of how Hellenised the Jews of Galilee and Judaea may have been, of what everyday life might have been like "around the Sea of Galilee at the beginning of the Christian era". Harris's meticulous researches remind us that generalities can distort contemporary understanding of historical influences, and we have sought to remain sensitive to such nuances despite our, historically speaking, hob-nailed boots overview. See H.A. Harris, *Greek Athletics and the Jews* (Cardiff: The University of Wales Press, 1976): 101.

9 For overall demographic data on Israel, see the regularly updated *The World Factbook* (Central Intelligence Agency),www.cia.gov/library/publications/the-world-factbook/geos/is.html, accessed 14 May 2017.

10 Tamir Sorek, "Arab football in Israel as an 'integrative enclave'", *Ethnic and Racial Studies*, 26/3, 2003: 422–450; and *Arab Soccer in a Jewish State: The Integrative Enclave* (Cambridge: Cambridge University Press, 2007).

11 Amir Ben-Porat, "The commodification of football in Israel", *International Review for the Sociology of Sport*, 33/3, 1998: 269–276; and "From community

to commodity: The commodification of football in Israel", *Soccer & Society*, 13/3, 2012: 443–445.
12 John Sugden and Alan Tomlinson, *FIFA and the Contest for World Football*: 39–40.
13 E. Taylor, "For occupied Palestine, just turning up is a struggle", *The Guardian*, 8 September 2004: 33.
14 Guy Ben-Porat and Amir Ben-Porat, "(Un)bounded Soccer: Globalization and localization of the game in Israel", *International Review for the Sociology of Sport*, 39/4, 2004: 421–436.
15 See New Israel Fund, www.nif.org/tag/israel-religion-and-state-index/. The NIF professes a commitment to "the best values of Judaism, humanism and liberal democracy" adding that its "ideals are equality, tolerance and social justice". See nif.org.
16 The FA, "United they stand on both sides of the line", *Communiqué* (The Football Association's International Newsletter), Issue 12, 2005: 2.
17 S. Adar, "Middle East United", *The Sunday Times*, 12 September 2004: 11; and Donald Macintyre, "A sporting chance for peace", *The Independent Review*, 6 July 2004: 4.
18 Taylor, "For occupied Palestine".
19 Gabriele Marcotti, "Peacemakers edge closer to their goal", (The Game), *The Times*, 11 April 2005: 20.
20 Ilan Tamir and Yair Galily, "When the private sphere hides from the public sphere: The power struggle between Israeli national identity and football fandom", *International Review for the Sociology of Sport*, 52/2, 2017: 189–208, p. 204.
21 Jon Dart, "Israel and a sports boycott: Antisemitc? Anti-Zionist?", *International Review for the Sociology of Sport*, 52/2, 2017: 164–188, pp. 171 and 179.
22 Liam Morgan, "Infantino decides FIFA Council should rule on Israel-Palestine issue", *Inside the Games*, Thursday 11 May 2017, www.insidethegames.biz/writers/24079/liam-morgan, accessed 11 May 2017.
23 Amos Elon, *A Blood-Dimmed Tide: Dispatches From the Middle East* (New York: Columbia University Press, 1997).
24 Edward Said, *The End of the Peace Process: Oslo and After* (London: Granta, 2002).
25 Jayne Caudwell, "On shifting sands: The complexities of women's and girls' involvement in Football for Peace", in Sugden and Wallis, *Football for Peace*.
26 Geoffrey Whitfield, "The down to earth miracle 2000–2003, and thereafter" (Foreword), in Sugden and Wallis, *Football for Peace*: x. See too Geoffrey Whitfield, *Amity in the Middle East: How The World Sports Peace Project and the Passion for Football Brought Together Arab and Jewish Youngsters*. (Eastbourne: Sussex Academic Press/The Alpha Press, 2006). Geoffrey Whitfield took an MA in conflict studies at the University of Sussex in 2011, at the age of 77. He died in 2017, and we would like to reaffirm his invaluable contribution to the peace-building initiatives of F4P in the Middle East.
27 'Foreword', *Football for Peace*: x.
28 Andy Theodoulides and Kathy M. Armour, "Personal, social and moral development through team games: Some critical questions", *European Physical Education Review*, 7/1, 2001: 5–23.
29 This section of the chapter draws heavily on the work of John Lambert, a colleague at the University of Brighton, and senior member of the F4P Management Group with particular responsibility for football-related matters. Lambert led the development of the F4P training materials a record of which can be found in

his unpublished MPhil thesis, *A Values Approach to Coaching Sport in a Divided Society*, University of Brighton, 2011. See too, for general context in relation to values-based coaching, Jean Whitehead, Hamish Telfer, and John Lambert eds., *Values in Youth Sport and Physical Education* (London and New York: Routledge, 2013). This includes John Lambert, "How can we teach values through sport? Teaching values through sport in divided societies", pp. 152–165; and "How does coach behaviour change the motivational climate? The creation of a learning environment conducive to the transmission of prosocial values", pp. 166–177.
30 A list of contributors to the evolution of these materials is included in the Appendix to this book. We are particularly grateful to Graham Spacey for his committed and assiduous work in documenting the progress of F4P over the last decade and a half.
31 Gary Stidder and Adrian Hassner, "Developing outdoor and adventurous activities for co-existence and reconciliation in Israel: An Anglo-German approach", *Journal of Adventure Education and Outdoor Learning*, 7/2, 2007: 131–140.
32 Simon Sebag Montefiore, *Jerusalem: The Biography* (London: Weidenfeld and Nicholson, 2011).
33 Elisha Efrat, *The West Bank and Gaza Strip: A Geography of Occupation and Disengagement* (London and New York: Routledge, 2006). See too B. Wasserstein, *Divided Jerusalem: The Struggle for the Holy City* (London: Profile Books, 2002).
34 The Jerusalem Foundation, www.jerusalemfoundation.org/board.aspx?MID=546&CID=555&SID=705, accessed 11 April 2011.
35 Ibid.
36 For reasons of confidentiality and personal privacy it would be inappropriate to comment any further on specific cases, but the general point holds.
37 Efrat, *The West Bank*.
38 A vivid memory persists of lying awake in a cell-like room in the Franciscan White Sisters hostel next to the Church of the Nativity listening to the rattle of automatic rifles as gunmen of the Al-Asqa Martyrs Brigade exchanged fire across a nearby valley with Jewish settler communities.
39 Subsequently we learned that in the early days of the occupation one of the locals who had shown us around possible facilities in Beit Sahour had been shot dead by Israeli troops.
40 Tanya Reinhart, *The Road Map to Nowhere: Israel/Palestine Since 2003* (London: Verso, 2006).
41 Munther Danjani and Gershon Baskin, "Israeli-Palestinian joint activities: Problematic endeavour but necessary challenge", in *Bridging the Divide: Peace Building in the Israeli-Palestinian Conflict*, eds. Edy Kaufman, Walid Salem, and Juliette Verhoeven (Boulder, CO: Lynne Rienner Publishers, 2006).
42 This was the rallying cry of South African activists, including the veteran anti-apartheid campaigner and sport administrator Sam Ramsamy, member of the IOC Executive Board from 2006. Ramsamy relates the story of the rising opposition across the international sporting world to apartheid, in "Apartheid, boycotts and the Games", in *Five-Ring Circus: Money, Power and Politics at the Olympic Games*, eds. Alan Tomlinson and Garry Whannel (London: Pluto Press, 1984). In this story, the Gleneagles Declaration of June 1977 did not mince its words, urging governments to "combat the evils of apartheid" by cutting contacts and competition with "organisations, teams or sportsmen from South Africa" (p. 51). We have noted the distinction between the South African and the Israel/Palestine situations, but it is worth reminding ourselves of the

range of strategies that could be mobilised in informed and principled opposition to deeply embedded and persisting conflicts fuelled by prejudice, ethnocentrism and racism.
43 "Quote Investigator: Exploring the origins of quotations", quoteinvestigator.com.
44 *The Oxford Dictionary of Quotations, Second Edition* (London: Oxford University Press, 1953): 101.
45 Max Weber, in his "'Objectivity' in Social Science and Social Policy", in *The Methodology of the Social Sciences*, trans. and eds. Edward A. Shils and Henry A. Finch (New York: The Free Press, 1949), insisted on an important distinction. This was between an analysis of reality through concept construction such as in the production of ideal-types, and – less sociologically credible – "the *value-judgement* of reality *on the basis of ideals*". Without such a sharp and precise distinction, he argued, "serious and foolish blunders" (p. 98) would occur. We hope to have avoided such blunders in our analyses, observations and interventions.
46 Said, *The End of the Peace Process*: 208.
47 Naim Stifan Ateek, *Justice, and Only Justice: A Palestinian Theology of Liberation* (Maryknoll, NY: Orbis Books, 1990): 168.
48 Joint hosts for the conference were Germany's Federal Ministry of the Interior and Israel's Ministry of Culture & Sport (and its Ministry of Regional Cooperation), which saw the event as the first joint measure of the two countries' ministries having in November 2010 signed a Protocol on Cooperation in the field of sports; UNESCO also served as a patron of the event. See "Greetings" by Dr. Hans-Peter Friedrich, member of the German Bundestag and Federal Minister of the Interior, in *Proceedings: Sport as a Mediator Between Cultures*, eds. Ronnie Lidor, Karl-Heinz Schneider, and Katrin Koenen (Berlin: International Council of Sport Science and Physical Education, 2012): 9.
49 To facilitate the implementation plans, the Israeli Ministry inaugurated an F4P-based model entitled 'Sport for Life' (S4L), which recruited local volunteers of whom the vast majority had been trained by F4P. The model continues to attract attention and research, a recent example of which is Jim Buttery, "Conflict Transformation and Values-Based Approaches Through Sport: The Experience of 'Football for Peace' in Israel", unpublished Master's dissertation (MSc in Development Management), Open University, UK, April 2017. Buttery, UK Attaché for Education and Culture and Director of British Council Kazakhstan, wisely notes the continuing need for fuller longitudinal studies of the effects of the model on children and on their views of the future in a potentially less conflictual world. He also recognizes the appropriateness and possibility of co-operating with F4P globally, for instance in Central Asia.
50 John Sugden, "Turning drops into ripples and ripples into waves. Critical Pragmatism and social change through sport in deeply divided societies", in Lidor et al., eds. *Proceedings*: 51–64.
51 The South African model is included in the Appendix as Appendix E.

Chapter 4

SDP over the rainbow – sport and peace-building in South Africa

Introduction

The title of this chapter is inspired by the words of Nelson Mandela in his presidential address in 1994, when he talked of the newly democratised South Africa as the Rainbow Nation. As already referred to in Chapter 1, when learning our trade among a handful of people who called themselves 'sport sociologists' in the 1970s and 1980s, South Africa was the outstanding example that made a nonsense of the then popular view that 'sport and politics don't mix'. Sport had always been hugely significant in South Africa, particularly in the white community whose members viewed it not only as a highly visible theatre within which to act out the principles of racial segregation, but equally importantly as a global arena for the display of white racial supremacy. From the early 1960s onwards, anti-apartheid activists began to understand that alongside political and economic sanctions, if the rest of the world wanted to damage South Africa's self-belief and international standing, attacking the country's revered sporting institutions would chronically weaken the apartheid regime. Volumes have been written about this volatile period in South Africa's sporting history.[1] Suffice it to say here that if sport played a major role in the undermining and dismantling of apartheid, its social significance did not stop there; in the transition to democracy it would be expected to play an equally significant role in the shaping of the new South African nation. In this chapter we assess the progress that has been made in the democratisation of South African sport since the restoration of political democracy in 1994 and ask what contribution, if any, has sport made to peace and reconciliation there.

In Ashwin Desai's book, roving across the country's most prominent sports – rugby union, cricket, athletics, soccer and swimming – a collection of journalists, sports administrators, academics and hybrids thereof, reflect critically on the reformist achievements of South Africa's sports order in the two decades since the dismantling of apartheid's political apparatus. The broad conclusion drawn is that long after the Rainbow Nation's after-glow of the near-miraculous victory of the Springboks in the Rugby World Cup on South African soil in 1995 had faded, while intentions might have been honourable, little or nothing had changed, and if anything, in the world of sport at least, South Africa was more divided than it had ever been. Desai states: "What is clear is that the divide between the two halves of sport in South Africa (*white and non-white*), like that between Mbeki's (*Tarbo Mbeki, then South African President*) two nations is increasing".[2] Fieldwork visits in June 2010 and May 2012 gave us the opportunity to return to South Africa to delve beneath Desai's rather depressing conclusion.[3]

South Africa in context: the state of the sporting South African nation

Arriving at Johannesburg's Oliver Tambo International Airport – so named after the prominent anti-apartheid activist, former President of the African National Congress (ANC) and life-long associate and friend of Nelson Mandela – on our respective field trips, we recalled our similar journeys back in January 1996 when researching the politics of African football for the book *FIFA and the Contest for World Football*. We were there to experience and observe one of South Africa's post-apartheid 'magical sporting moments' as the national football team *bafana bafana* (boys boys) lifted the African Nations' Cup in early February in Soweto's packed FNB stadium, defeating Tunisia 1–0 in the CAF final. This was just 18 months after the recently elected ANC President of the Republic, former Robben Island inmate, number 46664, Nelson Mandela, handed over the Web Ellis Cup to François Pienaar, the white captain of the South African rugby team the Springboks, after his side's emotional victory over New Zealand in the final of the 1995 Rugby (Union) World Cup. South Africa's freshly rehabilitated national cricket team was at the same time whitewashing the touring English in a series of Test Matches: it really did feel like the Gods had blessed the role of sport in the Rainbow Nation's nation-building project. The image of Mandela wearing a Springbok shirt became truly iconic; "when the final whistle blew, this country changed forever", Pienaar recalled on Mandela's death in December 2013.[4] Mandela would also attend Pienaar's wedding, and act as godfather to his children. But had South Africa, and South African sport, really changed?

The usual indicators of the sport mega-event that South Africa had so desperately sought were visible. The brand new high-speed *Gautrain* was launched in the days preceding the 2010 World Cup, and had attracted proud locals with their digital cameras and phones to be among the first to sample the new and novel facility. This was a welcome and comfortable legacy project and on our rides into the city we both mused over how sport's capacity for nation-rebuilding had fared over the intervening years. Was it possible that sport, something so emblematic of this country's divisive and racially segmented social fabric under apartheid, yet so instrumental in the resistance and revolution through which the white supremacist regime was undermined and brought down, could be further reformed in the service of peace-making, reconciliation, and democratic nation-building?

This is a multi-dimensional puzzle that requires consideration of the condition of top-class, high-performance, 'spectacular' sport in contemporary South Africa; the health and status of the underpinning 'farm systems' that feed that high performance sport; the government-sponsored institutional order that sustains sport and physical education nationally and has the lead responsibility for the nature and quality of sport in the community; and, finally, the parallel role of the ubiquitous NGO sector.

Elite and professional sport in South Africa

The school report card of top-level sport in South Africa would read something like this: 'showing signs of progress in some areas but not fulfilling its potential in others: definite room for improvement'. Albeit tainted by the injustices of apartheid, South Africa has a rich sporting heritage and, other than during the boycott years – the mid-1960s to early 1990s – sat at the top table of world sport for both Olympic and non-Olympic events and settings for much of the last century. In the immediate years after democratisation and the reintegration of South Africa into the fold of international sport, it did not take long for the activities most favoured by white South Africans, Rugby Union and cricket, to reassert their prowess on the world stage. In 2012 South African cricket was ranked second in the world behind England by the International Cricket Council (ICC) and second behind India in 2017 and rugby was ranked third behind New Zealand and Australia by the IRB (International Rugby Board) though behind England and Ireland too in its fifth position in 2017. This was made possible largely because the elitist talent-development structures and processes that underpinned white South Africa's sporting success during the apartheid era remain largely intact. Famously, under the leadership of Nelson Mandela, once it came to power in the immediate post-apartheid period, contrary to the fears of the white community, the ANC opted not to dismantle the sporting system that had served white South Africans so well, often to the detriment of the majority non-white population. Given what sport had stood for during apartheid, Mandela and his ANC colleagues could have been forgiven for destroying the whole edifice. Instead he endeavoured to harness it to the cause of his new nation-building project. That the Springboks would win the Webb Ellis trophy in Johannesburg during the first term of his presidency was nothing short of miraculous. He was a key player in the behind-the-scenes struggles that saw the unlikely transformation of the Springbok emblem from a symbol of white sporting supremacy to one of multi-racial, national unity. This event served as the inspiration for film director Clint Eastwood's *Invictus*, in which Morgan Freeman's Mandela uses the nineteenth-century

Victorian-era poem of the same name by William Ernest Henley to inspire the Springbok captain, Matt Damon's François Pienaar, in much the same way as Mandela had used it to shore up the morale of his fellow inmates when incarcerated for many years on Robben Island. Mandela's biographer noted in 1999 that the man who became "master of his own prison" on Robben Island still liked to quote a particular line from the poem: "I am the master of my fate, I am the captain of my soul".[5]

While there can be little doubt that the Springboks' triumph in 1995 was a hugely significant moment in the awakening and bonding of the Rainbow Nation, it should not disguise the fact that this victory was delivered only by harnessing a talent-development system that remains heavily dependent on the legacy of elite and exclusive clubs and a network of private schools only accessible to the relatively well-off. When the Springboks pulled off that unlikely victory in 1995 only one non-white player, Chester Williams, pulled on the famous green and gold jersey. Williams was classified as mixed-race or coloured, a sub-group making up approximately 9% of the South African population. The 80% black African segment of the population had no representatives, hardly surprising given that rugby had only recently re-emerged from the shadow of apartheid and opportunities for non-white players to develop the skill levels required at international level remained severely limited.

What is both surprising and disappointing is that 12 years later, when the Springboks took to the field in Paris in the 2007 World Cup Final against the English, there were more black faces on the English team than in the ranks of their South African opponents even though less than 15% of the English population are non-white compared to South Africa's 80%. In fact only two of the victorious Springboks in Paris that day were non-white. A further five years on, despite promises to make elite sport in South Africa, including rugby, more representative, the racial complexion of the 2012 Springboks was much the same with black Africans being notable mainly by their absence. For the 2015 World Cup, South Africa was struggling to find the required quota of non-white players, seven for a 23-man squad.

A similar story can be told for cricket which at a national level continues to be dominated by white players. Nevertheless in the case of cricket, because the game has a strong traditional base for both spectatorship and participation in the country's Indian-Asian population (2.5% of the total), the South African test side boasts more players of colour than does its rugby counterpart, but once more black South Africans, with the exception of standouts such as pace bowler Makhaya Ntini, who became the first black African to play test cricket for South Africa against England in 1995, are very thin on the ground. These high-profile examples of the continuing legacy of apartheid do little to encourage the view that South African society is becoming more egalitarian. Moreover, by continuing to overlook those swimming in the non-white talent pool, top-level sport in the country is not getting the most out of the human resources potentially at its disposal while at the same time continuing to alienate large sections of the fan-base in ways reminiscent of the apartheid era.

Yogo Coopoo, an Indian-Asian academic, recalls supporting "anybody but South Africa, the English, the All Blacks, the Australians, whoever came to this country . . . and at that stage, anybody who played South Africa, we obviously supported them". He had good reason to adopt such an attitude and vividly recalls as a young boy playing cricket with his brother against white boys in the back streets at a time when it was illegal to do so, and "we whopped these guys almost every weekend", white boys who went on to play at representative levels for the province, when the Indian-Asian boys were ineligible and had no opportunity to pursue their sporting ambitions.[6]

In recognition of such glaring inequalities, as part of a general trend towards positive discrimination in favour of black South Africans, early in its administration the ANC introduced a quota system for sport whereby elite sport teams and organisations had to ensure that a prescribed number of non-white athletes were selected to play and perform at the top levels of senior and junior sport, irrespective of relative ability. While this did lead to a slight increase in non-white athletes taking part, by violating the meritocratic principle upon which all sport is based, it damaged, albeit unintentionally, the competitive subculture of South African sport. In different ways the quota system impacted negatively on both white and non-white athletes. According to Denver Hendricks, former Director General of the National Department for Sport and Recreation (NDSR), the quota system has been a mixed blessing; it has created an openness in previously inaccessible sports, but has also placed some black sports people in teams at levels beyond their talent or capacity, so puncturing confidence and at times making a scapegoat out of them if teams performed poorly. Hendricks adds that lack of achievement by black athletes at higher levels has also been framed by structural factors: "It's about where they come from. It's about what opportunities are available, what facilities, what coaching, all those kind of things that are available to them"; or not.[7]

Not surprisingly, despite benefiting from advantaged upbringings, talented white athletes feel resentful when less able non-white athletes are selected ahead of them. This has led to many white athletes leaving sport altogether or electing to play their sports outside of the country of their birth. Perhaps the most high-profile case is South African-born cricketer Kevin Pietersen, who, citing quota-related injustices experienced in his junior domestic cricketing career in South Africa, elected in 1997 to exploit his British-born mother's national affiliation and play for England for whom he went on to enjoy an exceptional international career.[8]

According to Cora Burnett, the Pietersen case is but the tip of a pernicious iceberg that is doing much damage to the talent pyramid of South African sport. White players feel cheated and non-white players feel uncomfortable about being selected when they know better players are sitting on the bench.

And it is not just individuals who are suffering. After interviewing a representative range of elite junior rugby players Burnett concludes that it "is clear that the legacy of apartheid and the implementation of racial quotas as a strategy to redress the racial representation in the branding of nation-building have devastating unintended consequences. In-outsider affiliations are strengthened, the racial divide deepened and 'no normal society created in the abnormal (world) of South African Rugby'".[9]

A related issue is that in some cases, in order to fill their quotas, rather than using resources to develop their own non-white talent pool by engaging with and developing potential in local disadvantaged communities, instead some clubs raid the established farm systems of those few non-white clubs and associations that are producing good players; this undermines the capacity of non-white teams to compete at the highest levels. According to Ashwin Desai and Zayan Nabi the most glaring victim of this trend is the Jaguars Rugby Club which for several seasons was the only non-white team playing in the Kwa-Zulu Natal Premier league. Because of their success with an established and renowned production line of talented black ruby players, each game was well attended by rugby talent scouts from rival top clubs throughout the country. They were there for conventional reasons, to identify potential recruits, but also a part of their mission was to short-cut the quota system by bringing in non-white talent that had been developed elsewhere.[10] Denver Hendricks agrees with Desai's and Nabi's analysis:

> That's exactly what is happening at the moment. I mean Blue Bulls Rugby – you know the Blue Bulls Rugby team, one of the top rugby teams in the country. They don't develop their players here. They go to the Eastern Cape where rugby is a sport for black players. They don't identify the talented youngsters over there they just buy them![11]

In March 2012, after a thorough review of impact of the 1994 quota policy, the ANC finally took the decision to do away with quotas for top-level sport in favour of a new scorecard system for monitoring 'transformation targets' for grassroots sporting federations and organisations. In so doing the intention was to put more emphasis on the provision of adequate facilities and coaching resources as well as talent-identification programmes. Nevertheless, new government-led guidelines or quotas were reintroduced in 2016, which would be unlikely to tackle the central issue of the equalisation of provision, participation and opportunity at the school level. In September 2016 *The Economist* reported that "only 20% of all primary schools in South Africa play cricket", and in the country's poorest province, Limpopo, that plummets to 4%. As experienced cricket administrator Ali Bacher starkly observed: "For a black player to make it in South African cricket they have to go to one of the traditional cricketing schools in the country. It's as simple as that".[12] Goolam Vahed placed this everyday reality in its broader context as early as 2001, noting that some degree of post-apartheid reform and transformation has "loosened race identity" in sports, but "cricket has failed to create an imagined South African community", continuing to reproduce class privileges and the status quo: "the elite-centred nature of transformation . . . is validating the established capitalist status quo by providing opportunities for select Blacks".[13] Our observations and investigations over the last 16 years have offered us little evidence to dispute this picture of the reproduction of entrenched privilege in the world of South African cricket.

Soccer, 'the people's game', is far and away the most popular sport for black South Africans. Its professional sides – such as the Kaizer Chiefs – garnered huge support during the apartheid era, and were coached at one stage by the former English professional Eddie Lewis. Lewis had played for Manchester United in the early 1950s, one of the Busby Babes, moving on to enjoy a solid career with Preston North End, West Ham United and Leyton Orient. His playing days behind him, in the 1970s he emigrated to South Africa and built a long career in coaching and managing at the country's top levels. As a coach at Wits University (University of the Witwatersrand, Johannesburg), he was instrumental in giving access to the University's resources to the Chiefs, after befriending Kaizer Motaung, chairman and managing director of the club. Motaung recalled that Lewis was "the first *mlungu* (white) to find comfort in an otherwise discredited community of impoverished blacks".[14] Lewis himself recalls the first multi-spectator football match between two black teams, the Kaizer Chiefs and the Orlando Pirates, in 1975 as an historic occasion: "The wonderful scene made a mockery of apartheid in sport, and I thought to myself the next thing to happen must be multi-racial teams playing in one professional league".[15]

Indeed, one might be forgiven for expecting that during a period of liberation, transformation and reform the game of the people, building on foundations such as were achieved despite the odds during the apartheid period itself, would have flourished and become more integrated. But prejudices and resentment can remain deeply embedded, as the South African football world was reminded soon after the country's victory in the Africa Cup of Nations, when white footballer Sean Dundee accepted German citizenship, claiming that he had been discriminated against, as a white, within South African football. In early 1997, too, the Springboks' rugby coach André Markgraaff was dismissed after calling black South African sports and rugby administrator Mululeki George a "'fucking kaffer'", a "massively derogatory term used by some whites to describe blacks . . . during the segregation and apartheid eras".[16]

After an initial glorious opening spell of the new era, in the two decades and more after the democratisation of the country, when measured in terms of success on the field soccer's fortunes have declined. There is little or no evidence that it is being taken up in significant numbers by South Africa's white population – at least not in terms of local interest. On the surface this seems counter-intuitive. During 1996, when South Africa won the African Cup of Nations, *bafana bafana* were ranked number 19 in the world by FIFA and number 1 in Africa. In 2012 South Africa had slipped all the way down to number 67 in FIFA's list and languished in ninth place in Africa. Staging the 2013 African Cup of Nations did nothing for the decline; in all likelihood South Africa would not have qualified but for its hosting role, and it crashed out to Mali in the quarter-finals. In Equatorial Guinea in 2015, losing finalist Ghana knocked out the *bafana bafana*, and in Gabon in 2017 the 16 finalists did not include South Africa, still languishing in sixty-seventh position in FIFA's rankings.

When in 1996 *bafana bafana* took the field in Soweto's FNB stadium they were led out by white captain Neil Tovey. Two other white players, Mark Fish and Eric Tinkler were in the starting 11 with a further three white men on the bench. In 2010 when the national team took the field in the opening game of the World Cup Finals, all of the starting players were non-white. With stats like this, how are quotas working here, one might feel obliged to ask? Crowd attendances in the domestic professional leagues have been lamentably low and television audiences proportionately small.

Kirsten Nematandani, when President of SAFA (South African Football Association), bemoaned the situation in a postgraduate seminar at the University of Johannesburg, blaming corruption and the influence of powerful club owners who have little or no interest in the fortunes of the national game. He blamed poverty too, lamenting the lack of resources being deployed at the grass-roots level and a general state of disorganisation at the lower levels of the game. This he argued dissuades young people, particularly from white communities, from taking up the game in the first place. Instead they are choosing to channel their talents into better organised rugby or hockey clubs. Moreover, while the fortunes of the 'big two', the Kaiser Chiefs and the Orlando Pirates may be of some interest to the black community, there is a tendency for most fans and enthusiasts to reserve most of their interest and passion for the teams playing in the English Premier League and other Euro-based competitions, a predilection that is shared with significant numbers of white South Africans.[17]

Having said this, when it comes to displaying collectivist civic pride around the notion of South Africa as a member of the global football family, an evaluation of the country's response during the hosting of the 2010 FIFA World Cup suggests that all shades of South Africa's population got behind their nation. At squares and malls in the centre of Johannesburg, bordering in one case the exclusive suburb where the Mandela domestic residence was, mixed groups of varying ages, genders and races watched the opening matches, rooting in particular for South Africa's deficient but gritty national team. Sitting with one group of city bankers and their wives for *bafana bafana*'s final match, in which a dogged defeat of France could not save the team from elimination, the collective enthusiasm for the event was infectious, and unprecedented: "This is like nothing before it, perhaps only the Rugby or the African Cup. But it is bigger than the Rugby victory. We are all sitting here together. We can now speak truly of the new South Africa".[18] This is definitely a post-apartheid phenomenon. In tacit recognition of how white South Africans saw their God-given supremacy reflected through their sporting achievements, before the dismantling of this odious regime the attitude of the vast majority of black and coloured South Africans in anticipation of the outcomes of South Africa's various international rivalries was, as in Yogo Coopoo's boyhood experience of cricket, 'anybody but South Africa'. The post-1994 'magical period' changed all of that. As Mandela wove his charms and cast his spells, on the field at least, no matter what colour the skin of the players wearing the green and gold, the shirt no longer symbolised servitude and oppression for the masses. It represented instead a new and reunified republic; a thrusting Rainbow Nation. Despite some poor performances on the field since then, and a lack of proportionate representation of non-white athletes at the elite level, as a spectacular celebration of South African solidarity, it seems that sport has retained some capacity to unite.

The hosting of the Football World Cup Finals in 2010 is an illuminating illustration of this. One of the most important reasons behind FIFA's decision to bring the tournament to the African continent for the first time was to contribute to Mandela's great project; the rebuilding of the Rainbow Nation, politically, economically and culturally. Notwithstanding some pre-tournament and in the event groundless fears, about organisation and security, both inside and outside the country, it is generally accepted that as spectacular mega-events go, South Africa was an exemplary World Cup host.[19] The impressive stadia were ready on time, hotel rooms were plentiful, pristine and welcoming, the overhaul of the country's transport system was more or less completed before kick-off and the predicted crime-wave never came. When the home team played, multi-racial crowds in replica kits turned out in large numbers to noisily cheer and trumpet for *bafana bafana* and only once they had failed to get beyond the qualifying group stages were allegiances switched to other African and world teams which were then supported with the same enthusiasm that had been afforded to *bafana bafana*. Regardless of the failure of the national team to make much headway in the competition, the very hosting of the event allowed large swathes of ordinary South Africans to feel good about themselves and their place at the top table of global sport. In May 2004 Mandela had held the World Cup aloft in Zurich when South Africa secured the decisive vote, greeting the outcome with zestful commitment, claiming: "I feel like a young man of 50".[20]

But beyond the dazzle of the spectacle, early evaluations suggested that this 'feel good' factor was at best an ephemeral moment and the much-lauded 'legacy' effect of South Africa's World Cup 2010 has turned out to be less than positive for the vast majority of ordinary citizens.[21] After surveying the immediate impact of the tournament, Eddie Cottle commented on the transient nature of the collective euphoria of the event, the "cohesive effects . . . almost immediately disappeared with the spectre of xenophobic attacks on foreign nationals raising its ugly head and well over a million public sector workers were preparing for strike action across South African cities". And the economic promises evaporated swiftly.[22] South Africa would be no different to previous World Cup Final tournaments on this financial front. Whatever the promises or the rhetoric, FIFA would take the *largesse* of its sponsors and its media partners, leaving the host nation with the burden of debt and unwanted facilities, as observed by Glynn Davies: "although the tournament may be highly successful and profitable for FIFA, it says nothing of the potentially debilitating effect the need for massive host country investments can have on the local economy".[23]

The splendid high-speed *Gautrain* that is now the choice of affluent travellers and well-off locals, carrying tourists, consumers and commuters into the corporate heart of Johannesburg and beyond to the seat of government in Pretoria, is a post-World Cup bonus for the domestic, metropolitan elite and the international visitor, but it is a futuristic and unattainable luxury for the urban poor in townships such as Soweto and Alexandra. Fears over security and distance meant that numbers of overseas fans attending the tournament were far below than expected, leaving thousands of hotel rooms, bars and restaurants empty. It was even reported that there were far fewer punters than anticipated for local sex workers. Generally, South Africa's informal economy – an important source of income for the country's most disadvantaged groups – was depressed as this kind of trading in and around the competition venues and in the city centres was shut down by the South African authorities at the behest of FIFA and its marketing partners. But funded largely through the public purse, blue-chip construction companies saw their profits soar on the back of new stadia and related World Cup building programmes, with no responsibility for the upkeep of numerous facilities which had little or no utility once the tournament finished.

When it hosted the African Cup of Nations in 1996, with the exception of Soweto's FNB national soccer stadium, the South African Football Association (SAFA) had sensibly used existing Rugby stadia in which to play most of the matches. For political reasons this was never going to be good enough for the FIFA Football World Cup, an event through which black South Africa hoped to showcase its coming-of-age in the lavish facilitation of its own national sport. Even so some compromises might have been made, and much more thought given to the size and location of facilities that were not only extremely expensive to build, but equally expensive to maintain once built. A classic example of this is Cape Town's iconic Green Point Stadium. Eric Dalton, Commercial Manager of Durbanville Football Club in Cape Town, a function he used to perform for the city's leading professional club

Ajax, worked at Green Point for several years. Dalton has been involved in local football for more than 40 years and while he believes that hosting the World Cup was good for South African morale and national pride, he remains damning on the topic of the post-event legacy.[24] According to Dalton, FIFA had too much say over everything that was done and not done in the name of the World Cup, including the location of the stadiums. If they had to build a new stadium in Cape Town – a decision he disputes – why couldn't they build it on the other side of the city, closer to the Townships, making it easier for those who actually support soccer to go and watch their own teams play once the World Cup was over? For Dalton the villain of the piece is the FIFA President himself, Sepp Blatter, whose arrival one day by helicopter in 2007 prompted the commitment to the new build. Blatter liked the look of Green Point and "after that SAFA said if you don't build that stadium there Cape Town will get no World Cup games and eventually they decided to build it".

To make matters worse, because of a dispute between city officials and SAFA, the renamed Green Point, now Cape City Stadium, was not used as a venue for the 2013 African Cup of Nations. Dalton argues that the stadium, like its counterpart in Durban, remains a classic White Elephant: "It's a most beautiful, magnificent stadium, but today, if they play five games of football there a year, it's a lot! They might have two big concerts. The Eagles were there a month ago but otherwise it stands there and it costs them over a million rand a month in maintenance! They'd be better off tearing it down". Which is precisely what the municipality of Cape Town was seriously thinking about doing at the end of 2012, only two years after the last ball was kicked in the 2010 World Cup. Nevertheless, in 2016 a newly formed football club Cape Town City took up occupancy at the site, and perhaps Dalton's concern and pessimism have since receded. For FIFA and its corporate commercial partners, both within South Africa and elsewhere 'off shore', World Cup 2010 produced a high-profit windfall, leading Cottle to conclude that a commitment to "minimal tangible costs" combined with "significant" direct benefits was the predictable rhetoric of the civic boosters and the corporate and entrepreneurial classes. FIFA would adjudge the 2010 World Cup "a major success from both an organisational and a financial perspective", reporting "a positive four-year result of USD 631 million", allowing the world body to survive relatively unscathed the 2008 global financial crisis.[25] But at the grass-roots and community rather than elite levels World Cup 2010 had little significant medium- or long-term impact. In locations such as Nelspruit, close to the border with Mozambique, the newly constructed Mbombela Stadium hosted games with little sign of any planned future. The town had no high-level sporting team, construction was reported to be mired in administrative corruption, there was no local belief that a use could be found for the facility in the future, and even on a match day, it was sad to see the punters head straight out of town to the calm and comfort of a hunting lodge or boarding house in the high veldt. Few Chile or Honduran fans looked to be swelling the coffers of the local merchants: "The neutrals among us trailed away sadly, wondering how Mandela's dreams and aspirations might have worked out better for this small, essentially rural town".[26]

Of course, given the scale of the challenge, the reform of South Africa's sport nexus was never going to depend on whether or not the quota system was successful or *bafana bafana* had an extended run in the World Cup finals. In fact, given the highly politicised role that sport had played in the destruction of the apartheid regime, other than the reform of political institutions themselves, the transformation of sport was one of the fledgling 'rainbow' nation's biggest challenges in the decades after democratisation. How could sport operate as a realm in which the goals of equality, social cohesion and nation building could be advanced, whilst at the same time looking to regain and retain South Africa's place at that top table of global sporting excellence: how was this circle to be squared? Ashwin Desai, speaking in the Wanderers Hotel adjacent to the famous test cricket ground of the same name in the outskirts of Johannesburg, responded to this question. He was there to attend a meeting of a committee of Cricket South Africa looking into the problematic relationship between the game's commercial partners and the governing body. Desai is a 'coloured' (Indian-Asian) academic and freelance journalist whose first passion is cricket but has been a tireless campaigner for the holistic reform of South African sport both during and after the apartheid years. His promptly delivered answer to the question was the obvious one: "with great difficulty".

After 1994 when Nelson Mandela's ANC became the ruling party, the South African Government faced colossal challenges to ensure that the country's quest to reform a deeply divided society didn't degenerate into a violent social and political revolution. Desai argues that the ANC had to choose one of two pathways: to opt for a fast-track, broadly socialistic and redistributive transformation strategy; or to reform South Africa more gradually by embracing the globally dominant neo-liberal capitalist agenda and open up South Africa for free-market commerce and investment in the hope that generated wealth would 'trickle down' to improve the lot of the impoverished masses. The first was believed to carry the highest risk of sparking a violent revolution so it was the neo-liberal reformist course that was set.

Of course, within South Africa itself it was those who already had access to wealth and resources – i.e. white South Africans – who stood to benefit most from the embrace of the neo-liberal doctrine. Also, as the country declared itself open for business it developed as Africa's leading business nation and attracted entrepreneurs and fortune seekers from all over the continent and further afield. Wealth was indeed generated on a vast scale but little if any of it trickled down to those historically disadvantaged groups most in need. Desai's arguments are based on more than speculation: in 2013 South Africa had a GINI coefficient of 63.1%, the second highest in world. This index is a measure of income inequality, or the scale of the average difference in wealth between the poorest and the richest in a given country. Since 1994 – the formal end of apartheid – South Africa's GINI coefficient has risen. In other words the gap between rich and poor is rising, rather than falling as one might have expected.[27]

With elitist economic structures left largely in place, while the already well-off white community prospered along with a small minority of rising black African middle classes, the so called 'black diamonds' – many of whom were from outside South Africa – the vast majority of the 80% non-white population was not pulled along and up by this neo-liberal surge. This dislocation is a feature of South African society at large and is replicated in the world of sports. Desai explains this by using a metaphor borrowed from rugby, that of the 'truck and trailer'. This is a move whereby the strongest and heaviest forwards, 'the pack' or 'truck', use their might to power through the opposition defence while lighter forwards and backs, 'the trailer', attach themselves to this rolling maul with the ball in hand to make progress up the field. Of course this move breaks down when the trailer becomes detached from the truck, which, according to Ashwin is precisely the case with the reformist approach to South African sport. At the elite level South African sport is more or less holding its own, but it has little or nothing in the trailer. In other words there is a disconnect between high- performance sport, talent-identification, and mass participation. In the two decades and more of democratisation there have been multiple policy statements, white papers and national plans issued by the South African Government and directed to the wholesale reform of grass roots sports in South Africa. According to Desai almost all of these statements are high on reformist rhetoric but low on strategies for implementation and the resources to carry through serious reform. In the next section we look at the governmental domain focusing particularly upon this issue of implementation, or, more precisely, the chronic lack of policy implementation.

State interests and governmental and educational issues

From the areas around the *Gautrain* the lived reality of neo-liberal South Africa is visible. Johannesburg is an urban sprawl with no obvious centre. Located in the North of the City, Sandton City is Johannesburg's, South Africa's and Africa's commercial financial hub, with sky-scraping corporate headquarters vying for space with four- and five-star hotels and opulent shopping malls. In the Summer of the 2010 World Cup its smartest hotels were monopolised by the FIFA elite – past and present – and the business dealmakers of the global football industry. Deals were still being struck, or sought, with the decision-makers who, as members of the FIFA Executive Committee (ExCo), had the votes that would at the end of the year hand the men's World Cup Finals to the Russian Federation (2018) and Qatar (2022). Not all members of the ExCo would make it through from Johannesburg or Durban (the favoured bases for the FIFArati) to Zurich in December; several would by then have been suspended for breaches of the FIFA ethics code, for making it known, for instance, what level or kind of offer they might listen to in exchange for a (secretly) declared commitment to vote for one of the candidates.

In Sandton City in June 2010 though it was business as usual for much of the football world, luxuriating in a first-world city in a third-world country, the urban centre of which looks and feels like many US city centres with suited businessmen scurrying between offices along heavily secured walkways and squares while the daily influx of township workers and street traders mills about in a parallel universe in the streets below. There was obviously no shortage of money here, an impression reinforced by a stroll through the opulent gated residential neighbourhoods surrounding Sandton. This remains a world away from Johannesburg's sprawling townships where the vast majority of the city's black population people lives, eking out a living, cheek by jowl in ramshackle, makeshift homes. While sold as generic improvement in the city's otherwise inefficient/non-existent public transport system in the build-up to the 2010 FIFA World Cup, it was plain to see that a primary purpose of the *Gautrain* is to facilitate the speedy passage of international travellers, corporate executives and civil servants to South Africa's capital and centre of government 30 kilometres north in Pretoria.

In Pretoria, Bernardus Van Der Spuy, then Chief Director, Strategic and Executive Support in the National Department of Sport and Recreation (NDSR) provided a government perspective on sport in the Rainbow Nation. A former Olympic weightlifter, he occupies a distinctive vantage point from which to comment upon the topic at hand. Unable for many years to compete on the world stage, he felt the impact of South Africa's sporting isolation during the anti-apartheid era and has been a senior government sports administrator for more than two decades. He has been involved in the disestablishment of apartheid-style sport and its democratic reform from the earliest days of the new South Africa and is one of the few senior white administrators to hold and keep a position in government. Van Der Spuy admits that he never believed he would be kept on once the ANC took over, but the Minister of the time Steve Tshwete told him: "Bernardus the time of fighting is over. It's now time to work and I believe that you have a role to play". A "very emotional" Van Der Spuy has been involved in the development of almost all of the NDSR's (or its equivalent previous incarnation's) sport policy documents produced over the last 23 years. He recollects that one of the first challenges that had to be overcome was the reunification of South African sport's otherwise splintered administrative order, and he recalled the "passion of sport" that fired both white and non-white groups that "led to the compromises and led to the willingness to get together". He is adamant too that the vision and charismatic intervention of Nelson Mandela in the build-up and triumph in the '95 Rugby World Cup was absolutely vital in ensuring that sport would play a positive role in the rebuilding of the South African nation: "Doing it at the rugby stadium. If you have to pick one day in the history where I think peaceful co-existence really became a reality it was then!" After that momentous occasion people began to believe that sport could be a force for unity throughout South African society. But for that to turn into a reality, a clear strategy had to be developed, backed by the resources necessary for implementation, the lack of which explains in large part the failure of the transformational project of South African sport.

Scarlett Cornelissen is a Professor of Political Science at Stellenbosch University in the Western Cape and her views on this matter, echoing those of Ashwin Desai's and Denver Hendricks, she sees as "fairly typical. We've got a track record of having the most wonderfully conceived and conceptualised plans and policies, really good policies, really good plans" but implementation has been wholly lacking, and "sport and development has had a belated entry into the South African policy environment".[28] An analysis of sport development policy in the South African case has stated explicitly that government "should ease up on developing a perfect, all-encompassing policy and create mechanisms that take into account the results of greater monitoring, evaluation, reflective observation and active experimentation".[29] It added too that an over-prescriptive, what one might call a pseudo-comprehensive, approach can "devalue opportunities" for greater creativity, from other spheres of government as well as sport, but also from civil society. A third challenge noted is to give ideas and policies time to "cascade to the lower levels of participation" and to allow "ordinary conversations" to influence the process. And a fourth issue points to the consequences of streamlining state-based sport institutions, in that multiple voices are marginalised, the "broader range of community-based civil society influences" having less and less influence on the policy-making process. Taken together, these issues or challenges show that a well-intentioned but cumbersome system could turn out to be a process of ossification and procrastination rather than progressive intervention.

Van Der Spuy, one of the authors of many government policy documents on the reform of sport, certainly does not dispute the pertinence and power of such arguments, recognising that the implementation question certainly "is the challenge", with policies and policy documents reiterated and revised but rarely if ever implemented. And the participatory process could be very elongated, in seeking a consensus to underpin the policy vision. For the key ingredients of one new white paper – the National Sport and Recreation Plan 2012–2020 – the Government organised a national sports *Indaba*, held in the outskirts of Johannesburg in November 2011. This two-day event was preceded by a series of Provincial Sport *Indaba*s, the conclusions of which were fed into the national level by representatives of all of the country's major stakeholders including the governing bodies, charitable NGOs, academics, journalists and athletes themselves.

The National Sport Plan has since been produced, prefaced by a 'Transformation Charter for South African Sport' hammered out at the sports *Indaba*. It is a weighty document,[30] with the central objective to broaden the opportunities for participation across all sections of South African society, particularly for the underrepresented black majority, as a means of not only improving the nation's health and wellbeing but also of widening and deepening the pool wherein talent can be identified and elite sporting excellence developed. Once more, Van Der Spuy was involved in the production of this text. The plan's Mission Statement states the primary, and ambitious, goal: "to transform the delivery of sport and recreation by ensuring equitable access, development and excellence at all levels of participation and to harness the socio-economic contributions that can create a better life for all South Africans". Similar rhetorical flourishes can be found in almost all national sport policy reviews/reports/plans/white papers published since 1994. Kobus van der Walt, Director of Sport and Recreation at the University of Pretoria, has seen a plethora of National Plans and policies come and go and saw this latest *Indaba* and the ensuing Government White Paper as yet another exercise in empty rhetoric calling it, "a talk show, it's just another talk show".[31] To paraphrase Van Der Walt, in his view the tractor still floats free of its trailer. What, Bernardus was asked, will be different this time? He believes that unlike previous grand declarations, the National Plan has teeth. The key issue, he maintains, is a coherent funding strategy and the resources to back it up: "I think – and there was also at the *Indaba* last year a principal decision that no funding will be approved at the national – at the Government level – or even at your private sector level, if it's not in support of the Sports Plan".

The decision was also taken at the *Indaba* to restore Physical Education to the state-sector school curriculum, but this would inevitably encounter huge problems in implementation in a neglected and run-down public education system. For Denver Hendricks the picture is bleak, a combination of scarce resources and existential priorities:

> People living in absolute squalor, not having access to clean water, to electricity, in some senses it is worse than what it was during the apartheid here. The schools in the townships are dysfunctional. Education has gone to the dogs completely for black people who can't afford to send their kids to these nice schools across the road.

But Hendricks understands why this situation has evolved, not through malicious intent, but a simple case of opportunity cost: resources were scarce and the scale of the problems facing the ANC when it came to power was overwhelming: "it was an issue of resources. You had to focus on what you thought were the important things that had to be focused on and physical education wasn't a part of that". Budgets could not be increased, merely reallocated "so obviously everything's going to take a dip". Van Dur Spuy from Sport South Africa agrees with the drift of Hendricks's argument, pointing out from his perspective that when it comes to dealing with local government it is hard to persuade them to prioritise sport and recreation,

> especially at the lower principality level, where we urge the municipalities to build sport and recreational facilities where the people can play – because there is nothing! But then they tell you, 'Listen how can we build the sports facilities if there's no running water, if there's no electricity?' and then you don't have a foot to stand on.

The future of sport for the majority of South Africans depends, argues Hendricks, on the vitality of the state education system. "The primary area that we have to focus on, which we are not doing, is in education . . . black sports people tended to come through the school system . . . education provides the basis". But the vast majority of township-based black South Africans children are denied a decent basic education in general, and physical education is virtually non-existent. Only the relative handful of upwardly mobile middle class of non-white South Africans – again, the so-called 'black diamonds'- can afford to buy access for a decent education for their children. Those who aspire to give their offspring the chance to excel at sports must, if they can afford it, send them to a private school. Thokozil Mkhonto, or Kelly as she is known to her friends, is one such case.

'Kelly' Mkhonto, when interviewed, was Chief Director of Mass Participation in Sport and Recreation South Africa (SRSA). She is a middle-class black South African parent who has the financial resources that make an actual choice of schooling for her child a possibility; one of only a few such parents in the overall population of the country. Professionally her role at SRSA was to develop strategies to help bring sport and physical education to the masses and she is a passionate believer in the principles of non-elitist equity and inclusion. She has a young son who is an able sportsman and rather than send him to the nearest state school she elected to spend a considerable part of her income sending him to a private school in Johannesburg:

> I had to take him to a private school. Why couldn't I take him to a public school? Because public schools – you know we have a school very close to my house – it's Sandown High. That school is a public school but it's so neglected! The Principal of the school is white and most of the teachers are white. The kids are black. They have no interest. There's no sport programme.[32]

Mkhonto made significant moral and financial sacrifices to send her son into private education:

> It would have been a lot easier for me to take my son to that state school. He could actually even walk to the school but I can't let him because the system is very weak, results poor, year in year out ... Now he's going to Michael House and his fees are about 80,000 Rand per annum. Had I taken him to Sandown High, I would have paid something like 10,000 Rand. So now this 70,000 I could be using it you know, for other things. Every time I get my bonus I can't enjoy it, I have to throw it into the fees, but now he is in the 'A' Team and I just feel really that my hard work is paying off, you know?

Mkhonto articulates a dilemma common to many more affluent and financially secure families in post-apartheid South Africa, but for a black person in the Rainbow Nation her dilemma and decision are testimony to the divisions and cleavages that still characterise South Africa's social, educational and sporting landscape. Cora Burnett, Professor in the Department of Sport and Movement Studies at the University of Johannesburg, points out that the restoration of Physical Education in schools is likely to be a slow process as all the courses/departments that used to train Physical Education specialists have been closed for a number of years. With no capacity for the training of PE teachers, she asks, who will be able to impart physical literacy to future generations of South African children?

Filling the void: NGO initiatives in the SDP mould

Much of the slack in community-based physical activity and school-based physical education is being taken up by a plethora of interventions from the NGO (Non-Governmental Organisation) and INGO (International Non-Governmental Organisation) sectors. Sub-Saharan Africa in general has been at the cutting edge of the burgeoning SDP movement. With long histories of civil and military conflict, economic failure, poverty, unstable political structures, weak civil-society institutions and the social and health-related problems that accompany such levels of under-development, the countries in this region have long since been prime targets for traditional international aid programmes. Unsurprisingly they are also at the forefront of some of the more innovative SDP interventions as the field has flourished.

Post-apartheid South Africa has been a particularly fertile ground for SDP NGOs and INGOs. It is a microcosm of the wider region in that within its own borders, to paraphrase former ANC President Thabo Mbeki's speech made in 1998 at the dawn of the new South Africa,[33] it contains two nations: one a relatively prosperous nation supported by a 'first world' economy that benefits a minority of largely urban-based South Africans; the other an abjectly poor and desperately needy 'third world' country to be found in the townships and rural areas where the vast majority of South Africans abide. With HIV at epidemic levels, youth crime and gang warfare rampant, and violence against women on the increase, not to mention the lingering and socially divisive wounds left behind by the apartheid system, the SDP movement has found plenty of work to do in South Africa.

The NGO/INGO sector in the Western Cape provided illuminating accounts of targeted interventions fuelled by sport and development ideals. Khayelitsha is a sprawling township of ramshackle tin huts and cabins stretching as far as the eye can see in the westerly outskirts of Cape Town, with an estimated residential population of a million, many the diaspora of the non-white families that were cleansed from the inner city after the imposition of the 1966 version – or 'Consolidation' – of the Group Areas Act (1950).[34] This population has since been supplemented by a significant influx of people from South Africa's impoverished rural areas, and immigrants from neighbouring countries.

Lunga Sidzumo lives in Khayelitsha and works as a Supervisor for an Organisation called Grassroots Soccer which uses football programmes in the townships to raise awareness about HIV and help to combat other social problems. It is one of many such programmes that have been adopted under the umbrella of Streetfootballworld, and a partner of football's world governing body, FIFA, in its Football For Hope initiative, launched in 2005. Former UN Secretary-General Ban Ki-Moon has praised FIFA in this action, for releasing football's capacity to "instill confidence, hope and pride in the underdog and promote teamwork and support".[35] Working with locally based organisations like Grassroots Soccer, in the build up to the 2010 Football World Cup FIFA got together with Streetfootballworld to try to establish 20 community soccer hubs across the African continent. Lunga's centre in Khayelitsha is one of them. Meanwhile, in the buildup to the 2010 World Cup, FIFA's Finance Committee chair, as was revealed in 2016, was signing off his approval for Sepp Blatter's 11 million Swiss Francs bonus from the proceeds of the 2010 World Cup financial cycle.[36]

Lunga explains that there was a two-fold strategy to developing the centre at this particular site. Firstly, there was a complete lack of any facilities in the neighbourhood where young people could come, not just to take part in organised sport, but also to engage with related youth and adult education programmes. Secondly, as a criminologist might put it, Khayelitsha is a 'criminogenic environment' and, as described by Lunga, the site on which the centre has been developed used to be a notorious space for criminal activity. "Before this place was built there was a lot of water with trees around and it was the most dangerous place. It was a tapping (*mugging*) place whereby people who are going to the railway station, thugs were robbing them".[37] By clearing and illuminating the site and populating it with supervised SDP activities, not only is the centre helping to occupy and educate deprived local youth, but also, by its very physical presence, it is helping to eradicate (at least in the public space that the initiative has transformed) crime.

Deep in the heart of Khayelitsha, hemmed in on all sides by shantytown homes and shops, can be found the 'Chris Campbell Memorial Field' – a facility developed with the support of the US family of a young soccer player of the same name who died suddenly on the pitch – where another, German-based NGO, AMANDLA (the Zulu word for 'power'), runs a range of sport-plus programmes. They are overseen by Karl Voysey who explains that AMANDLA takes an holistic approach to their work. The bedrock of the project is a Fair Play League for approximately 500 of the Township's children. The League has a scorecard that is used to assess behaviour and performance on several categories such as team work, respect, dealing with setbacks and failure throughout all of the football activity, in all of the games that are played. Secondly, there is the Life Skills Programme where participants in the League also go through an educational programme that is designed to help them to lead safe, healthy and sensible lives in the community. Additionally, a tutoring programme takes a smaller group of children through more intensive training and this feeds into the Leadership programme. Voysey explained how this works:

> There are roughly 40 trainee Leaders at the moment and they have three main components to that programme. There's a practical experience component, an employability training component and a personal development component, and their practical work experience is based on them implementing the football and the life skills and the tutoring.[38]

There are also mentoring and employability programmes associated with the Fair Play League and on top of all this the Crime Prevention League which happens on Friday evenings and is designed to attract young people away from the streets and alleyways during the times when crime is most prevalent. Overall, this constituted a comprehensive SDP intervention strategy with accompanying joined-up structures for implementation.

Twice a week during term time, once school's out in mid-afternoon in Kayelitsha small groups of chattering boys and girls make their way excitedly out of the township, snaking over the sand dunes towards the nearby Monwabasi Beach at the North end of False Bay. Overlooked by Fish Hoek Mountain and Cape Point in the far distance, with its startlingly white sandy esplanade contrasted against a deep blue ocean, the contrast with this scene and the teeming streets of the Township they have left behind could not be starker. They are heading for ISIQUALO's Waves for Change Centre. ISIQUALO is another community-focused NGO that has sought to use sport to combat some of South Africa's most pressing social problems, namely, HIV, substance abuse and violence against women. It was operating two 'Waves for Change' programmes that eschew conventional sports – like soccer – and use the offer of training in the lifestyle sport of surfing to attract township youth into a range of social education programmes.

Once at the Centre each child is given a wet suit and a surfboard before being escorted onto the beach to participate in a number of creative warm-up exercises, all designed in ways that would enhance their appreciation of the dangers of HIV-Aids. In role-play the menacing image of the avaricious, man-eating shark is evocatively invoked to amplify the threat posed by those sexual predators who seek multiple partners.[39] The Director of Waves for Change was a young Englishman, Tim Conibear, who explained that, like the AMANDLA programme, ISIQUALO seeks to use the hook of a physical activity or sport to introduce in innovative fashion a wide range of life skills, including teamwork, mentorship, leadership, self-esteem, employability and personal health and hygiene. After 20 minutes of such exercises the members of the team pick up their surf boards and march off bravely into the foaming and ice-cold South Atlantic to work on their surfing technique under the studied eyes of qualified coaches, some of whom themselves came out of the shanties of Khayelitsha.

This kind of work of the NGO sector in Khayelitsha is repeated in townships throughout the land. There can be no doubting the well-meaning nature of programmes like these and in most cases their intention is matched by positive action. In a drought any drops of moisture are welcome, but it is better to have a steady and reliable water supply. If the NGOs and INGOs provide what would otherwise not be on offer in communities such as Khayelitsha, can they ever, though, make up for the serious lack of comprehensive and systematic government-led support for sport and recreation in the community? Lucy Mills, Cape Town-based Manager for Streetfootballworld's Southern Africa Programmes offered a very qualified 'yes' to this question. She believes that the sector does make an important contribution, but her own research has suggested that the main beneficiaries might be the "Sport for Development NGOs that have a connection with Global North", rather than the communities that they target: "In Cape Town you've got the very struggling, poor community structures, government structures, school structures – you've just heard that school sports are basically non-existent and then you've got these thriving NGOs that are now the service deliverers of sport".[40]

Norman Brook is the Southern Africa Regional Manager of Coaching for Hope, an INGO that comes under the wing of another umbrella organisation, Skillshare International. Responsible for the organisation of activities throughout sub-Saharan Africa, most of his work takes place within South Africa itself. He runs a classic sport-plus organisation and explained that this is not "the business of sport for sport's sake". Rather, "we're an International Development Agency and we're about addressing social issues, so it's either HIV prevention or gangsterism . . . drug abuse or the environment, whatever the issue is"; and in such contexts his organisation's primary goal is that of "engaging young people to teach life skills". Brook believes that the dearth of provision, particularly in the black communities, provides the space and justification for organisations like his to operate, to fill the gap where there is "nobody on the ground organising sport", a problem exacerbated by the lack of a volunteering tradition among both black and white communities. This and the absence of government support for sport and recreation creates the pretext upon which NGOs and INGOs can justify their presence in the Townships and pursue funding opportunities. Like others before him, Brook singled out the absence of Physical Education in Township schools as another important reason why the NGOs are needed there. Hitherto the government has proven reluctant to admit to a mistake in getting rid of PE, and is not always comfortable with NGOs moving into schools, "filling that vacuum"; government has begun in some cases to oppose such inputs, but continues to offer no alternative provision.

In the idealism of democratisation and fuelled by the reconciling optimism of Nelson Mandela, post-apartheid South Africa's first government made great efforts to galvanize the positive side of sports around the perceived "need to entrench" the country's "new democratic ethos in sport as part of the transformation process for the upliftment of the quality of life of all South Africans", as the national Department of Sport and Recreation put it in 1995. Nothing was to be overlooked in the mobilisation of sport as:

> a unifier, healer of wounds, creator of work opportunities, booster of the national image, promoter of national health, consolidator of international ties, restorer of the culture of learning and teaching, redeemer of the so-called marginalized youth, etc.[41]

With such a wish list, it is scarcely surprising that in the political realm of South African government the vision of sport as a positive progressive force has achieved so much less than anticipated; in such a political and bureaucratic, unrealistically comprehensive, climate, "the dreams that you dare to dream" rarely do come true.

Concluding thoughts

The end of apartheid in South Africa and the ANC's accession to power coincided with the end of the Cold War and the triumph of neo-liberalism as the paradigm for global government and national and transnational business practice. This was the model adopted by Nelson Mandela as he sought to rebuild and rebrand his 'Rainbow Nation'; in his inaugural speech as president, on 10 May 1994 he proclaimed:

> each one of us is as intimately attached to the soil of this beautiful country as are the famous jacaranda trees of Pretoria and the mimosa trees of the bushveld.

We have triumphed in the effort to implant hope in the breasts of the millions of our people. We enter into a covenant that we shall build the society in which all South Africans, both black and white, will be able to walk tall, without any fear in their hearts, assured of their inalienable right to human dignity – a rainbow nation at peace with itself and the world.[42]

This powerful blend of the poetic and the political embodied the hope that South African society would emerge from the shadow of apartheid, "out of the valley of darkness" as Mandela added in the inaugural speech; the aspiration and hope that for the first time previously excluded population groups would enjoy unbridled opportunities and equal access to possibilities and futures. For this to happen, though, free-market mechanisms and the generation of wealth would need to have cascaded downwards to benefit the whole society, not just the white elite as had been the case previously. Instead, as part of the pragmatic compromise through which white South Africa traded political power for guarantees of continued socio-economic privilege, benefiting from a generous injection of overseas investment as the South African economy expanded, existing business elites got even wealthier. A new black African bourgeoisie hitched a ride on this commercial rollercoaster, but the vast majority of their countrymen and women remained as impoverished as ever. In fact they got even poorer and in 2012/13 South Africa with a score of 63.1 was second only to Lesotho on the GINI index of inequality.[43]

This dynamic has impacted all sections of the new South Africa and sport has been no exception. In South Africa in the second decade of the new century we expected to find many examples of programmes and projects the prime concern of which would be to improve community relations between the racial categories established under apartheid – particularly between white and non-white populations. But a widespread absence of such programmes greeted us. Despite the country's racialised political history, there seemed to be a consensus that 'racism' – in a conventional Western sense, open discrimination and prejudice against an individual or group because of their skin complexion and ethnic categorisation – was no longer a big problem in South Africa. Instead, people across the spectrum were in agreement that it is socio-economic differentials – in the old money, social class – that keeps the population divided in the new South Africa. Norman Brook agrees that poverty and inequality remain rife: "It's driven by poverty and it's driven more by the social economic status of people than it is by the colour of their skin". This is a moot point. There is no doubt that based on economic success a democratic South Africa is more open to meritocratic social mobility than it was under apartheid. But, as already discussed, at the dawn of the neo-liberal state, those who already possessed economic advantages were best placed to capitalise most on their position, to the disadvantage of late-comers to the race, and the back markers in the field are almost exclusively indigenous black Africans.

In Cape Town, Coaching for Hope was hosting a party of 20 or more budding young stars from the English Premier League's elite academies. As they prepared for careers in the richest soccer league in the world, the rationale for the trip was to keep them grounded by exposing them to some of the harsher conditions experienced in other cultures. Sight-seeing included trips to Robben Island where Mandela had been incarcerated and visits to the city's Townships where the prodigies took part in community coaching sessions on some of the few threadbare open spaces that can be found in these shanty towns. To help them to understand more of the 'two nations' thesis and the lived consequences of the country's GINI coefficient, Brook had taken them on a tour of Masiphumelele, one of the city's Townships where they "just sat with the kids and they ate with their hands and stuff like that". He then took the incipient superstars to a restaurant in an affluent suburb where people from the Township could not dream of visiting, telling them "that's inequality – that's what it is". The delegation was also granted a reception at the British High Commissioner's residence in Cape Town. Surrounded by neo-colonial splendour – all that was missing was pith helmets and ostrich feathers – Harry, an intelligent young player from Norwich City, confessed to being "blown away" and "humbled" by what he had experienced in Masiphumelele, which he confessed seemed a world away from where we now stood.

Whilst peaceful co-existence among the racial categories of the South African population has been in part achieved, this cannot be allowed to mask the deep socio-economic divisions that continue to define the life chances of the majority of the population. Education is a key sphere whereby people's opportunities can be broadened. We have seen in this chapter how the education system in South Africa since the end of apartheid has not delivered such opportunities, not least in the remnants of a sport or physical education-based educational provision in state-run schools. In this regard, the University of Johannesburg in partnership with the University of Brighton is seeking to revive a national physical education curriculum. While not a proverbial pot of gold, this new initiative provides hope for still marginalised and culturally disenfranchised communities. The F4P model is a major component of the proposed revitalisation, and Professor Burnett and her colleague Professor Kobus Roux confirmed, in October 2013, the influence of F4P upon training and policy for physical education in the country, noting that collaboration with F4P has resulted in "developing two 'Life Skill Manuals' – one for primary school and one for secondary school . . . based on the F4P methodology with the utilization of indigenous games from South Africa (primary school) and sports (secondary school) as the activity bases. Not only is this very novel, but these manuals will serve to educate students (during recreation camps) and in formal coursework of

Life Orientation/Physical Education training (about 200 students) to implement in schools and recreation centres" (see Appendix E for their statement). We hope that this emphasis on values of mutual tolerance and inter-cultural co-operation may deliver, on however modest a level, serious possibilities for transformation in the lives and life chances of the younger generation for whom the Rainbow Nation metaphor remains little more than an illusory mix of poetry and myth.

Notes

1 There is an extensive literature on sport and the South African context. Here we refer to just a few sources of particular relevance to the narrative of this book, and the core themes of this chapter. An early, ground-breaking study by Robert Archer and Antoine Bouillon, *The South African Game: Sport and Racism* (London: Zed Press, 1982) provided invaluable starting points for the early phase of scholarship on the politics and sociology of sport in the country, providing what one reviewer, André Odendaal (*Africa: The Journal of the International African Institute*, 54/2, 1984: 106 and 107) called "the most rounded and authoritative picture so far of the whole South African sports issue" and "in a unique way" placing the issue in its historical and social context, also demonstrating "the necessity and profitability of social and academic analysis of sport as an important aspect of South African social life and history. More such studies should follow". And they most certainly have followed. Grant Jarvie, acknowledging the importance of prior studies on race and the apartheid issue, and with a striking dependance upon the historical narrative and policy documents provided by Archer and Bouillon, emphasises "the concepts of class conflict, ideology and cultural struggle as axial principles for analysing the nature, meaning and political significance of South African sports policy"; see *Class, Race and Sport in South Africa's Political Economy* (London: Routledge and Kegan Paul, 1985): 1. Jarvie also expresses his gratitude for the support of scholars at Queen's University, Kingston, Ontario, in particular Rick Gruneau, his Master's supervisor. We can see Jarvie's pioneering study as another example of the confluence of critical work in the sociology of sport emerging in the early 1980s, as discussed in Chapter 1 of this book. John Nauright, *Sport, Cultures and Identities in South Africa* (London and Washington: Leicester University Press, 1997), has provided an insightful contribution to the understanding of the complex dynamics of identity and sport in the South African setting, presented with the sensitivity of an historian's craft also honed at Queen's University, Kingston. Important contributions have been published in journals such as *Sociology of Sport Journal* and the *International Review for the Sociology of Sport*. For an early example, see March L. Krotee, "Apartheid and Sport: South Africa Revisited", *Sociology of Sport Journal*, 5/2, 1988: 125–135. See too Adrian Guelke, "Sport and the end of apartheid", in *The Changing Politics of Sport*, ed. Lincoln Allison (Manchester and New York: Manchester University Press, 1993); and, for a fluent and sophisticated analysis of sport's symbolic significance and place in the politics of communication and identity in the 'new nation' of South Africa, see Douglas Booth, *The Race Game: Sport and Politics in South Africa* (London: Frank Cass, 1998).
2 Ashwin Desai ed., *The Race to Transform: Sport in Post-apartheid South Africa* (Cape Town: Human Sciences Research Council/HSRC Press, 2010): 11.
3 We are grateful to the University of Brighton for awards of sabbatical leave and associated funding that made our trips possible and that allowed us to update

our knowledge of the South African situation both during and after the country's staging of the 2010 men's football World Cup.
4 David Smith, "Francois Pienaar: 'When the whistle blew, South Africa changed forever'", *The Guardian* (online), Sunday 8 December 2013.
5 Anthony Sampson, *Mandela: The Authorised Biography* (London: QPD/Harper Collins, 1999): xxvi.
6 Yogo Coopoo was interviewed in his office on campus at the University of Johannesburg, 14 May 2012.
7 Denver Hendricks, Professor and Director of University Relations at the University of Pretoria, was interviewed on 12 May 2012.
8 On Pietersen's South African background see Marcus Stead, *KP: The Biography of a Rebel* (London: John Blake Publishing Ltd., 2009).
9 Cora Burnett, "An open letter from Rugby Boys in No-Voice-Land. Reflections on Rugby and Race by South Africa's 2007 schoolboy players", unpublished paper, University of Johannesburg: 13.
10 Ashwin Desai and Zayn Nabbi, "Inside 'The House of Pain': A case study of the Jaguars Rugby Club", in Desai ed. *The Race to Transform*.
11 Denver Hendricks interview.
12 T.A.W., "A new racial selection policy for South African cricket", *The Economist*, 19 September 2016, economist.com.
13 Goolam Vahed, "What do they know of cricket who only cricket know? Transformation in South African cricket", *International Review for the Sociology of Sport*, 36/3, 2001: 319–336, quotes from 319 and 333.
14 Neilson N. Kaufman and Eddie Lewis, *The Eddie Lewis Story: From Manchester to Soweto* (Derbyshire, UK: Derwent Press, 2008): 35–36.
15 Ibid., 190. These occasions were also recounted in an interview in Johannesburg, 28 May 2010.
16 David R. Black and John Nauright, *Rugby and the South African Nation: Sport, Cultures, Politics and Power in the Old and New South Africas* (Manchester: Manchester University Press, 1998): 147.
17 Kirsten Nematandani was interviewed informally after a postgraduate seminar held at the University of Johannesburg, 11 May 2012. In August 2012 as part of the FIFA Fair Play and Social Responsibility initiative, he hosted a two-day Interpol "Integrity in Sport" workshop, attacking match fixing as "a cancer that robs the game of its innocence", and hailing the event as "a wonderful chance to learn more about this threat" (David Hills, "Said & Done 2016-2017 awards", *The Observer*, 28 May 2017: 7). Following a FIFA-led investigation into corruption in South African football, Nematandani was, later that year, required to take 'voluntary leave of absence' while the investigation into match-fixing continued. For more details see Paul Kelso, "Corruption shakes Africa to the core", *Daily Telegraph*, 19 December 2012: S8. In 2016, FIFA's Ethics Committee proposed that Nematandani be banned for a minimum of six years for alleged bribery and corruption violations. He had been replaced as SAFA president in September 2013 having received no nominations for re-election. See BBC Sport, "FIFA proposes six-year ban for Kirsten Nematandani", 24 August 2016, www.bbc.co.uk/sport/football/37107137, accessed 15 May 2017.
18 Fieldwork observations, Johannesburg, 22 June 2010.
19 As the back-slapping continued in the mutual appreciation society that was Sepp Blatter's FIFA Executive Committee, the fact is that if it wasn't for some very dubious horse-trading and unexplained absenteeism that took place during the crucial 2000 vote that gave the 2006 tournament to Germany, it is likely that South Africa would have hosted the tournament four years earlier. For further

details see John Sugden and Alan Tomlinson, *Badfellas: FIFA Family at War* (London and Edinburgh: Mainstream Publishing, 2003).
20 See Alan Tomlinson, *FIFA: The Men, the Myths and the Money* (London and New York: Routledge, 2014): 114–120, for a brief overview of the cultural, economic and political dimensions of the South Africa 2010 World Cup finals.
21 Careful sociological analysis also warned beforehand that much of the promised urban legacy of the World Cup would be unforthcoming, as is the case with almost any contemporary case of the mega-sport event. See Udesh Pillay, Richard Tomlinson, and Orli Bass eds., *Development and Dreams: The Urban Legacy of the 2010 Football World Cup* (Cape Town: HSRC Press, 2009).
22 Eddie Cottle ed., *South Africa's World Cup: A Legacy for Whom?* (South Africa: University of KwaZulu-Natal Press, 2011): 2.
23 Glynn Davies, "Managing the alchemy of the 2010 World Cup", in Pillay et al., eds. *Development and Dreams*: 49.
24 Eric Dalton was interviewed in his office at Durbanville F.C., 22 May 2012.
25 Tomlinson, *FIFA*: 119.
26 Ibid., 118. See too Richard Jones, *Rainbows for Goalposts: A Journey to the Heart of the World Cup* (Brighton: Pitch Publishing, 2010): 77–83. On the 2010 event as a political project, as a process in the making and not just a staged event, see Scarlett Cornelisson and Kamilla Swart, "The 2010 football World Cup as a political construct: The challenge of making good an African promise", in *Sports Mega-Events: Social Scientific Analyses of a Global Phenomenon*, eds. John Horne and Wolfram Manzenreiter (Oxford: Blackwell, 2006). On the marginality and exclusion of local populations at the event itself see Chris Bolsmann, "Representation in the first African World Cup: 'World class', Pan-Africanism, and exclusion", *Soccer & Society*, 13/2, 2012: 156–172. Bolsmann concludes (p. 169) that though the event was being portrayed in a positive light in that its staging represented the arrival of South Africa on the world-stage, "the traditional football-supporting public in South Africa was, in many cases, absent from the stadiums of the tournament".
27 Two years earlier, in 2011, South Africa had been at the top of this inequality index. For more detail on the GINI index, see Note 44 below.
28 Scarlett Cornelissen was interviewed in her office at the University of Stellenbosch, 18 May 2012.
29 See the 'Country Report: South Africa' chapter in *Sport and Development Policy in South Africa: Results of a Collaborative Study of Collected Country Cases*, eds. Marion Keim and Christo de Coning (Cape Town: Interdisciplinary Centre of Excellence for Sport Science and Development/ICESSD, Sun Press and UWC/University of the Western Cape, 2014): 149. See too Marion Keim, *Nation Building at Play: Sport as a Tool for Social Integration in Post-apartheid South Africa* (Aachen: Meyer and Meyer, 2003) for arguments supporting the positive potential of sport to bring people together and achieve mutually beneficial and respectful outcomes; and on the reconciliation theme, Kristine Höglund and Ralph Sundberg, "Reconciliation through sports? The case of South Africa", *Third World Quarterly*, 29/4, 2008: 805–818.
30 South African Department of Sport and Recreation, *The National Sport and Recreation Plan 2012* (Pretoria: Government Publications, 2012).
31 Kobus van der Walt was interviewed in his office at the University of Pretoria on 13 May 2012.
32 Kelly Mkhonto was interviewed in the Balalaika Hotel in Sandton City, 12 May 2012.

33 Statement of Deputy President Thabo Mbeki at the Opening of the Debate in the National Assembly, on Reconciliation and Nation Building, National Assembly Cape Town, 29 May 1998.
34 See www.sahistory.org.za/article/group-areas-act-1950, accessed 15 May 2017.
35 Tomlinson, *FIFA*: 125.
36 John Sugden and Alan Tomlinson, *Football, Corruption and Lies: Revisiting "Badfellas", the Book FIFA Tried to Ban* (London and New York: Routledge, 2017): 236.
37 Lunga was interviewed at the Khayelitsha community football centre on 16 May 2012.
38 Karl Voysey was interviewed in his office in Cape Town on 18 May 2012.
39 Sharks are widely feared in South Africa's black community, which is one reason why, despite a proximity to the ocean, swimming in the sea is not widely practiced by Khayelitsha's residents.
40 Lucy Mills was interviewed at the Khayelitsha community football centre on 16 May 2012.
41 These quoted words from the 1995 *Sport and Recreation in South Africa* report are also quoted in Alan Tomlinson, "South Africa 1996: Scenes from Soccer City", in Chapter 2 of Alan Tomlinson, *Sport and Leisure Cultures* (Minneapolis: University of Minnesota Press, 2005): 46.
42 Nelson Mandela, *Inaugural Speech, Pretoria*, published online by The University of Pennsylvania, African Studies Centre, www.africa.upenn.edu/Articles_Gen/Election_Victory_15727.html, accessed 15 May 2017. The use of the phrase 'Rainbow Nation' in the South African context is widely attributed to veteran anti-apartheid campaigner Archbishop Desmond Tutu, in welcoming the outcome of the April 1994 election that confirmed post-apartheid South Africa as a constitutional democracy.
43 "To understand how many inhabitants of a country are poor, it is not enough to know a country's per capita income. The number of poor people in a country and the average quality of life depend on how equally or unequally income is distributed across the population. A Gini index value of 0 represents absolute equality, and a value of 100 indicates absolute inequality". From *Gap Between Rich and Poor: World Income Inequality* (Infoplease.com), www.infoplease.com/world/statistics/inequality-income-expenditure.html#ixzz1vCf7oRW5.

Chapter 5

Can sport save the world? – SDP in cloud cuckoo land

Introduction

"Sports Saves the World" screams the headline of a feature in *Sports Illustrated* (*SI*) by Senior Sports Writer, Alexander Wolf, for the September 25, 2011 edition of the world's most widely read sports magazine.[1] Wolf was examining the putative 'social movement', Sport for Development and Peace (SDP), which took root and blossomed in Western Europe in the 1980s and flourished globally in the first decades of the twenty-first century. He visited five continents to examine SDP programmes from the *favelas* of Rio de Janeiro to Palestine's West Bank, in the former killing fields of the Balkan civil wars and the shanty towns of sub-Saharan Africa, interviewing practitioners and experts, looking to shed light on this topical and controversial subject.

Wolf himself is not so sure about sport's healing qualities. Beneath the rhetorical headline he adopts a more measured tone asking, "can such (sport) projects make a lasting difference, or is the dream of salvation through sports too grandiose?" At an SDP conference hosted by North Eastern University in Boston in 2010, he tested the waters with the academics and researchers. He had visited Belfast in 1994 at the height of the 'Troubles', part of an *SI* team covering events surrounding Northern Ireland's toxic home World Cup qualifying match with the Republic of Ireland.[2] There, in Windsor Park, Northern Ireland's national football stadium, he had experienced one of the most vicious manifestations of sectarian hatred that could be generated by a sporting fixture. At the same time he had spent time investigating the *Belfast United* cross-community sports programme, the core focus of Chapter 2 of this book, and had been intrigued by the contrasting messages he was receiving from the same sport in these two very different contexts. Was sport a force for confrontation and violence or was it a force for social good? He recalled the Belfast assignment as a powerful memory that had stayed with him, and the Belfast United initiative as the inspiration, a decade and a half on, for his global quest to find new answers. In this chapter we will take a more in-depth look at the genesis of the question, weighing the generic arguments for and against sport's capacity to make the world a better and more peaceful place.

The debate

The efficacy of sport as a peacemaker was the subject of a debate that featured in a conference entitled *Peace and Understanding through Sport* held at the University of Rhode Island (URI), USA, in 1988,[3] the year before the first incarnation of the Belfast United initiative in Northern Ireland. Brian Gowdy,[4] a graduate of an early sport studies cohort at the University of Ulster, by now an intern at the new Institute for International Sport, was given the task to set up an international conference on sport and international diplomacy. Targeted delegates comprised an eclectic mixture of politicians, journalists, academics, former international athletes and graduate students. Gowdy was familiar with the conceptual territory and the lived realities of sectarian-generated conflict contexts.[5] He proposed his old University of Ulster tutor as a speaker.

At a pre-conference informal reception for speakers at an elegant eighteenth-century colonial manor house, perched on the bluffs outside Narragansett overlooking Long Island Sound, the young academic from the University of Ulster mixed with athlete activists, politicians and academics.[6] These included Mary Peters, Great Britain's 1972 Olympic Pentathlon champion and Northern Ireland's First Lady of Sport, and the iconic double gold medallist (400 and 800 metres) at the 1976 Montreal Olympics, the Cuban Alberto Juantorena. He had retired from competitive sport and was working for the Cuban Government's Sport's Ministry, INDER.[7] The Cold War was still in progress and it was quite unusual for Cubans of any political stature to be allowed either out of Cuba or into the United States. Juantorena duly arrived via Mexico and Canada.[8]

Serendipitously, the young academic became the former world-champion's running partner on early morning jogs around URI's leafy campus. In those sessions the world was 'set to rights' in conversations across the widest range of subjects. The Cold War was cooling, winds of change were beginning to blow strong and Juantorena was feeling them, anticipating challenges but with optimism. Talk focused on how the changing global political and economic climate might affect Cuba and its sports system in particular. Juantorena described his country's systematic approach to using sport as a development tool for less developed nations – albeit restricted then to allied countries within the communist bloc. We saw this first-hand the following year when his invitation to study Cuba's sports system led to a research visit. We saw how Cuba, having benefited from importing sport expertise and resources from other, longer-established and wealthier Communist nations, had developed its own distinctive approach to popular and elite sport (claiming an integration of the two into a system/principle of 'massivity') that it was now sharing with its allies, and with sympathetic non-aligned nations such as Spain and the Irish Republic. Much later, when Juantorena had been elevated to the position of Sports Minister, he oversaw a complex international sport policy nexus that combined elements of philanthropic development goals, political influence and diplomacy, and the economic necessity to earn 'hard currency' through Cuban sporting excellence.[9]

In the days before the conference formally began, the politician and the young academic, accompanied by Juantorena's 'minder' Angel Pino, from the Cuban Interest Section in Washington DC,[10] toured the area and shared lunches and evening drinks in a developing friendship. This seemed suddenly in jeopardy when the still awestruck young academic learned on the eve of the conference that he was to share his room with another conference speaker, David Kanin, listed on the programme as being from the 'Washington School of Law and Diplomacy'. Having to share the room with a man who had written about sport and international relations was of no real concern, but his institutional affiliation rang alarm bells and, given the developing closeness to the Cubans, raised suspicions that he might be a US government secret agent.

Up in the shared room a determination to wheedle the truth out of Kanin was sidelined, and little wheedling needed, when Kanin, who was sitting on his bed, simply responded to a greeting – "Hi, I'm John Sugden, University of Ulster . . . Pleased to meet you", with "Hi, I'm David Kanin, CIA". He went on to explain that he wasn't a spy but a backroom analyst and that his being in the shared room had nothing to do with the Cubans.[11] This was not particularly convincing, to either Kanin's room-mate or the Cubans, who had been alerted to the situation by 'their people'. A difficult and demanding conversation ensued to convince the Cubans that there was no plant in their midst in the form of a young Englishman working for the CIA or as an MI6 informer. So much for sport being a tool for international diplomacy, though it would not have been the first time that sport was used as a cover for activities related to espionage.[12]

On the conference podium it was John Sugden versus Senator Claiborne Pell, Chairman of the US State Foreign Relations Committee, debating the proposition that 'sport as a tool of international relations does more harm than good'. Here, it required a debater's rhetorical strategies combined with hard evidence to make the case in defence of the proposition. Drawing on the Northern Ireland case it was argued that there were more examples of international sport damaging community relations than of its positive contributions to peace and understanding. The audience was asked to consider the deep historical roots of modern sport, whether or not there was something in the essential make-up of sport – its DNA if you like – that made it totally unsuitable for peace-making. It is usual for those who champion the moral value of sport to dress it up in the vestments of Ancient Greece. In the present era, when distant wars are fought from hi-tech facilities in

Silicon Valley and remote desert outpost, using smart bombs, drones and other disembodied military hardware, it is easy to forget that for most of history the most important weapon of warfare has been the human body itself. Sport in the ancient world grew out of the close relationship between physical training and military prowess and performance. Indeed the competitions that featured in the ancient Olympics – boxing, wrestling, running, javelin, horse and chariot racing, discus, *pankration* (mixture of wrestling and boxing) – were derived in large part from military-training regimes. There are strong arguments to suggest that sport and warfare in the ancient world were one and the same thing. Sport became the theatre within which combatants honed and displayed skills also used in recurrent wars and conflicts of the times.[13] The sport curriculum may have evolved over time, but elements of its deep-structure, its confrontational and competitive chemistry, remain from that formative past. Eduardo Galeano even calls football "choreographed war", a "ritual sublimation of war, eleven men in shorts . . . the sword of the neighbourhood, the city or the nation".[14] So, if originally sport was the handmaiden of war and remains its direct by-product, can it ever be reincarnated as a vehicle for peace?

Those opposing this argument claimed that sport could be, first and foremost, a force for good. The fabled Olympic Truce, *Ekecheiria* – the period of time before, during and after the ancient Olympics when hostilities between city sates and kingdoms were said to have been suspended to ensure the unhindered staging of the Games and the safe passage of participants and spectators – was cited as a key example.[15] Indeed, as Wolff points out in his *SI* feature, set against the backcloth of a vicious civil war in the former Yugoslavia, it was the re-invocation of the spirit of the Olympic Truce at the Winter Games in Lillehammer, Norway in 1994 and the birth of Olympic Aid and its successor organisation, Right to Play, that is seen by many as a watershed moment for the emergence of the SDP movement in general. Another *SI* writer, Leigh Montville, caught in the optimistic web of that 1994 moment, saw Lillehammer as "the fairy-tale Games, drawn from the imagination . . . Reality cannot be this good".[16] Sitting in the icy cauldron of the Albertville stadium for the opening ceremony of the 1992 Winter Olympics, it was a genuinely moving moment to see a 'Unified Team' comprising five former republics of the Soviet Union, and a single, unified German team march into the stadium. But the mythical truce of the ancient Olympics was never more than a transient moment: once the Games were over the truce expired and conflicts and hostilities were resumed.

The impromptu Christmas Day armistice on the Western Front at the beginning of the Great War in 1914, involving 'friendly' football matches between British and German troops in the no-man's land between the trenches across 20 miles or so of the British lines, offered an equally flawed argument in support of sport's pacifist credential. There is powerful testimony to the desire of troops on both sides to sustain the informal armistice into Boxing Day and beyond, and one German soldier in the XIX Saxon Corps, Vize-Feldwebel Lange, recalled the reluctance of his comrades to obey the order of their officers to fire, to resume hostilities on Boxing Day: "the men *struck*. We can't – they are good fellows, and we can't". The response of the German officers was "Fire, or we do – and not at the *enemy!*"[17] What the Christmas Day events really signified was the strong wish of soldiers on either side to recognise their commonalities, in the belief too that the 'phoney war' would prove to be short-lived. And

> football was the *lingua franca* of the truce . . . one of the things that the British and German soldiers had in common along with their vulnerability, fear and their mutual enemies of cold, wet, rats, lice, hunger and the high command. For a brief period of time football offered an escape from their fear and anxiety.[18]

Even where there were no rubber balls, or footballs, or spherical objects of any adaptable kind available, soldiers still yearned for the release of play with the enemy. A young English soldier in the trenches, a Private Pickering from Burnley, Lancashire, recalled meeting with his German counterparts, exchanging Christmas box contents that they had received from home: "We shook hands with the Germans and they gave us cigarettes and cigars. They wanted to play us at football but we had no ball. It made us think the war was over".[19] And of course nothing could have been further from the truth than such wishful and tragic thinking. The fact that in some cases soldiers were forced back into the trenches – on both sides – at gunpoint by their commanding officers confirms the transience of the ceasefire and the poignancy of the young private's hopes.

Less well-known than the Christmas story, at Loos (1915) and the Somme (1916), soccer and rugby footballs were punted forward by British soldiers to encourage the troops to make bolder and more energetic attacks on enemy trenches.[20] It is not difficult to counter arguments favouring sport's positive side: another dramatic case of sport acting as a catalyst for conflict and the stimulation of wider conflict was the 'soccer war' between Honduras and El Salvador in 1969 when a series of hotly contested World Cup qualifying matches between two countries already in conflict over territorial and trade interests sparked a short but brutal war that left more than 30,000 killed or wounded. Although the veracity of the reportage of the author of *The Soccer War*, Kapuściński, has been challenged in relation to a number of his other works, some critics arguing that his war writings have bordered on the fictional, there is no doubting the part that a football match, contested between national sides, played in further igniting the sparks of tension between the rival nations.[21]

The metaphorical relationship between sport and war – one through which theatres of conflict are analysed and talked about in the language of sport – is almost as old as modern sport itself, further popularised in Britain in the uncorroborated utterance, attributed to the soldier and statesman Arthur Wellesley the Duke of Wellington, that the 1815 "Battle of Waterloo", the decisive victory over Napoleon Bonaparte, was "won on the playing-fields of Eton". Wellesley was no sportsman, though; even at preparatory school he was in his own (later) words "a dreamy, idle and shy lad", with, as a consequence of indifferent health, "a careless and lethargic manner"; at that early age he "would never take part in playground games but 'lounged' against a large walnut tree watching the players and picking out those who cheated".[22] For three unhappy, lonely and unsuccessful years in the early 1780s, Wellesley was a schoolboy at an Eton that had no playing fields, "no compulsory, organized games . . . and even the most casual cricket or boating did not attract Arthur".[23] The first written claim that he uttered the famous words was in the writings of a French political historian published in 1855, three years after Wellington's death; there is no trace of remotely corroborating evidence of the Duke of Wellington having said anything connecting games, Eton and military victory.[24] The thinness of the claim though has not diluted the potency of the myth;[25] in the popular imagination of the mid-nineteenth-century day, the qualities of discipline, leadership and sacrifice demonstrated on the battlefield were attributed to the values of an emerging games cult.

The sporting metaphor also featured in Britain's most popular late Victorian poem, Henry Newbolt's *Vitai Lampada* (*They Pass On The Torch of Life*), published in his collection of ballads, *Admirals All* (1897), with the cricket square framed as a great classroom for life, competition and combat: "Play up! play up! and play the game!" is the last-line refrain of each of three stanzas that takes the boy from the public school to the military encounters of the Sudanese desert, a journey through life sustained by the gritty spirit of the games ethic.[26] Rudyard Kipling's *The Islanders* (1902) offered a starkly opposing view of the sport culture, casting the cricketers as "flannelled fools at the wicket" and footballers as "muddied oafs at the goals", ill-equipped by their public school sporting prowess for the demands of the Boer War, and capable of misguided acts of heroism of little or no use in the harsh reality of 'modern' military conflict. What these poems share though is a preoccupation with sport's place in Britain's imperial journey. As we have already seen, given that many of the world's regions that are most in need of development assistance – including the three case studies covered in earlier chapters of this book – were at some point part of the British Empire, the re-introduction of sport into these regions as a transformative device to promote progressive social change might be seen by some as a retrograde if not reactionary step.

Back on the Rhode Island podium, the targeting of sporting events by terrorists also featured in the argument. The hostage-taking of Israeli athletes by the Palestinian militants, Black September, in Munich in 1972, ultimately resulted in the deaths of 11 Israeli Olympians. And it is undeniable that contemporary sport was becoming, and has continued to become, a more militarised space than ever before. The 'war on terror' declared in a speech by the US President George W. Bush, in September 2001, had dramatic effects on sport globally, particularly in the USA and the UK, two countries joined at the hip in theatres of combat from Iraq to Afghanistan. On both sides of the Atlantic shortly before a major game or sports event commences, to the accompaniment of the marching bands, the pre-match show features tributes to service men and women fighting and dying overseas. In this regard the attractiveness of Westernised sports events for terrorists is enhanced by the fact that not only do they generate large crowds, but they also venerate and valorise the very conflicts which the terrorists stand against and use to justify their actions.[27] Since Munich '72, while there have been no overtly geo-politically motivated attacks on the Olympic Games, there have been isolated incidents involving rogue individuals, the most serious of which was the pipe bomb blast in the Olympic Park during the Centennial Games in Atlanta 1996, attributed to Eric Robert Rudolf, who was found to have neo-Nazi leanings but no links with any global terror organisations. Despite the relative lack of terrorist involvement in the Olympic Games since Munich, international terrorism remains the number one concern for host cities of major sporting events. The destruction of New York's Twin Towers World Trade Centre by *Al Qaeda* on 11 September 2001 turned that concern into nothing short of a moral panic, providing successive Olympic host cities and their respective governments with the licence to do almost anything, no matter the cost to the tax payer or civil liberties, in the name of counter-terrorism and security. There have been further terrorist-related attacks on high profile individual athletes and teams, such as that on the Sri Lankan cricket team in Pakistan in 2009 and on Togo's men's soccer team during the African Cup of Nations in Angola in 2010. The increasing militarisation of the sporting spectacle since the Rhode Island debate has done little to enhance sport's credibility as a peace-making tool or strategy.[28]

A mid-twentieth-century contribution to these debates was made by George Orwell in his widely quoted sentiment that sport is "war minus the shooting". Orwell had a distinctly dystopian regard for sport, harbouring bitter memories of his experiences of sports and games at Eton where, as an athletic underachiever, he had been dominated, bullied and brutalised by muscle-bound sports captains and tyrannical games masters.[29] Years later he coined the phrase "war minus the shooting" in an essay about the Moscow Dynamo soccer team's post-war tour of Britain in 1945. Here are two key passages from Orwell's essay 'The sporting spirit', on "serious sport":

> It is bound up with hatred, jealousy, boastfulness, disregard of all rules and sadistic pleasure in witnessing violence: in other words it is war minus the shooting. . . . If you wanted to add to the vast fund of ill-will

existing in the world at this moment, you could hardly do it better than by a series of football matches between Jews and Arabs, Germans and Czechs, Indians and British, Russians and Poles, and Italians and Jugoslavs (sic.), each match to be watched by a mixed audience of 100,000 spectators.[30]

This statement must be understood in its historical context. Just before the Second World War, in 1936 Orwell had watched with alarm the 'Nazi Olympics' in Berlin and like others saw it as a thinly disguised prelude to the Third Reich's quest for world domination. After the war the recent fact of the dramatic and devastating hydrogen and atom bombs destroying the Japanese cities of Hiroshima and Nagasaki and the long shadow of the Holocaust were making Orwell's world a darker place. European empires were on the eve of fragmentation and the Cold War was looming. In his essay Orwell argued that far from helping to improve international relations between the West and the Soviet Union, which was the stated intention of the tour organisers, by providing opportunities for public and collective displays of aggressive sportive nationalism, contests such as this were likely to make the impending cold war even icier. Ten years later Orwell's words looked prophetic at the Olympic swimming pool at the 1956 Melbourne Games as Hungarian and Soviet water polo players fought a bloody, surrogate battle against the backcloth of the Soviet's brutal suppression of the Hungarian revolution back in Europe.[31]

Countering Orwell's own dystopian view of sport, there are those who have used the phrase to propose that sport can serve as a cathartic alternative to war, arguing that the playing of competitive sports provides distinctive communities (nations, regions, towns and so forth) with opportunities to express distinctiveness and rivalry without threatening the wider social order: sport *instead* of the shooting. Examples of this that are often cited are political overtures between nations in conflict such as 'ping-pong diplomacy' between the USA and China in the early 1970s, or 'cricket diplomacy' between India and Pakistan in the 1990s and 2000s – although the highly complex, contingent and extremely fragile nature of these processes are rarely stressed.[32]

Other supporters of this position, mainly sports administrators, allied Governing Body blazers, vote-hungry politicians and current and former successful athletes themselves go a stage further and are even more optimistic about sport's capacity to promote peace and understanding, believing that it offers more than a temporary haven for the suspension of conflict and can go beyond the reach of conventional politics to achieve results that government officials cannot. Most advocates of this position will have gone to the right schools and have been long-time sports participants and enthusiasts. If sport was good for them, it must be good for others and the intrinsic value of sport as a social good is rarely questioned. They believe in the fraternal and character-building qualities of sport and in its capacity to bring together diverse people and communities as demonstrated in global sport festivals, such as the modern Olympics or the World Cup Finals. The literature of the modern Olympic movement and other national and world sports governing bodies reflects this and is littered with the rhetoric of this Sports Evangelism. It was precisely this kind of rhetoric rather than reasoning that had formed the main thrust of Senator Pell's arguments at the Rhode Island event.

For Pell and others like him it was less about the logic of what had been said and more about the stature of those who had said it. But, even in relation to evidence-based arguments, such largely rhetorical claims could, backed by the testimony of several former Olympians, carry the day for Senator Pell. The lessons were clear as to how the Pell model of the SDP world worked: firstly, the veracity of what is said has been less important than how it is said and by whom; and secondly the belief that sport can change the world is an article of faith that easily withstands empirical challenge no matter the weight of evidence-based counter-arguments. The rhetoric of the SDP world is littered with the pseudo-wisdom of current and former athletes and the vacuous platitudes of vote-hungry politicians and global sports tsars who exploit their status and fame earned in a different sphere of life as a platform from which to proclaim their assumed expertise. Just because you can sing, play guitar or play football extraordinarily well, does not automatically make you an expert on all things musical and sporting, much less on affairs of state and international relations. Likewise, statesmen like Senator Pell can be guilty of trading on pedigrees earned in international political circles to pontificate as experts on other fields about which they are not really qualified to speak.

The power of sport? Evangelists and critics

These Sports Evangelists can even draw the greatest of figures into their hyperbolic world. Of all the world statesmen that have commented on sport's healing capacity, as we saw in Chapter 4 Nelson Mandela has the greatest credibility. But even he has made the mistake of taking sport out of its context and assigning to it intrinsic universal value and magical powers. Take this extract from his speech given at the Laureus Sport for Good Foundation's Inaugural Achievement Awards in Monte Carlo, 25 May 2000:

> Sport has the power to change the world. It has the power to inspire. It has the power to unite people in a way that little else does. It speaks to youth in a language they understand. Sport can create hope, where once there was only despair. It is more powerful than governments in breaking down racial barriers. It laughs in the face of all kinds of discrimination.[33]

The words "governments" and "discrimination" are not always included in the oft-quoted extract, and the Laureus Foundation sometimes chooses to cut the statement short in its replay of what it likes to call "the speech that changed the world".[34] Mandela's words are given almost biblical authority by the SDP faithful and since first uttered the address has become a standard part of any political speech writer's text on the subject. We draw upon personal experience to provide the final example of this kind of de-contextualised, over-sentimentalised thinking, from a 1997 interview with João Havelange, the outgoing President of FIFA, world football's governing body. We asked him whether before he stepped down he felt that he had anything left to do; his response spoke of his last great ambition in terms that run directly counter to Orwell's views, expressed 50 years earlier:

> One day during the World Cup (USA '94) I had a telephone call from Al Gore (vice-president of the United States). At that time Gore was involved in negotiating for a peaceful settlement in the Middle East. Mr Gore said he really had no experience of football before, but he was amazed that the World Cup (USA 1994) could be so perfectly organised and that so many people could become so passionately involved. He was greatly inspired by this and asked would it not be possible to have a match between Palestine and Israel, organised by FIFA? The project is now indeed to have such a match, Palestine versus Israel, ideally in New York – New York being the seat of the United Nations – just to show the politicians football can do things that they cannot!

Like Orwell before him, Havelange singled out 'Jews and Arabs' for special treatment, but as we saw in Chapter 3, the capacity to unravel and resolve conflicts the roots of which go back more than two thousand years is a bit too much to ask of a football match. Self-serving and simplistic sentiments are typical of the naiveté and haughty arrogance that we have come to expect from international sport's preening and posturing dictators.[35] Havelange's views provide a particularly stark example of the kind of idealistic thinking that is in danger of infecting the whole SDP universe. It had not escaped our attention that as he eulogised the peace-making capacities of sport, two heavily-armed guards caressing sub-machine guns posed alertly in the corridor outside the room where we conducted the interview.[36] Clearly the FIFA president was not taking any chances that one or other of the Middle East's warring factions might violently oppose his views on a FIFA-brokered peace deal between Israel and Palestine!

Hitherto, the views on the positive, curative role of sport from within the academic community have been ambivalent. According to Norbert Elias and Eric Dunning, for instance, the experience of sport has, over time, had a moderating effect on social behaviour beyond the playing field itself and as such makes a positive contribution to human social development; for them, affect control and incremental increases in constraints on behaviour and conduct have informed an overarching civilising process in which sport has played its part in modifying violent practices.[37] Sport, they argue, has offered opportunities for the socially approved arousal of moderate excitement, gradually leading people to exercise stricter control over their public behaviour. In short, codified sport became a *"civilising"* influence, not just at a local or national level, but also between nations;[38] outbursts of hooliganism or in-play violence can be absorbed in the overall theory as examples of a 'de-civilising spurt'. Others are more sceptical; believing that modern sport encourages aggression and violence, homophobia, racism, sexism, nationalism, political submissiveness and a host of other social ills.[39]

Undoubtedly sport is a very important element of collective identity, carrying meaning beyond anything intrinsic to the activity itself. Even in (relatively) stable societies, a high degree of social stratification and racial/ethnic heterogeneity means that expressions of shared identities through sport are complex, often ambiguous and can be generative of class distinctions and cross-community animosity and conflict. Sport concurrently includes and excludes, and can exaggerate difference. Where there is a lack of shared understanding about what precisely constitutes "the nation" and/or a legitimately sovereign state, the function of sport in the politics of community identification and celebration is even more problematic. As illustrated by the football match in Belfast in 1994 mentioned at the beginning of this chapter, under such circumstances, sport in its 'natural state' is much more likely to promote conflict than it is to foster mutual understanding. In this sense, the case for the generation of informed interventions offering alternative models of values-based sporting practice can be made even more strongly; without them, the sporting sphere could become an uncontrolled Darwinian arena.

Conclusion

Who is right, then, Orwell or Havelange, Senator Pell or the sceptical but informed critical academic? From the evidence of history and contemporary politics and sociology, Orwell is incontestably right in believing that sport in its 'natural state' is anything but a panacea. However, as is implicit through accounts of the SDP work presented in earlier chapters, it can also be argued that sport can be manipulated in such a way as to serve peace-building and broader development goals. The theoretical framework for this, and a potential model for implementation, are outlined in succeeding chapters.

For now, note should be taken of Bruce Kidd's view that, in and of itself, sport is of no intrinsic value: it is a socio-cultural, political construction, neither naturally good nor irrevocably bad. It is, like all collective human endeavours, a malleable practice shaped by the social forces that surround it. Kidd captures this position well when he says, "caution should be taken not to 'essentialise sport' and the role it plays in societies – in fact it would be preferable to think of 'sport' as a plurality of forms that have different results in different contexts".[40] This is why sport can be claimed and proclaimed in the name of both complementary and contradictory social goals and practices and in this regard context is everything. The truth of this position has been demonstrated in the preceding case studies, and we conclude this chapter with a brief review of the current state and status of the SDP movement, asking who and/or what is in the driving seat and in what direction SDP is, as currently constituted, heading.

Fred Coalter (2009) has provided a comprehensive critical review of the emergence of 'sport-in-development' as a policy-related social movement. In doing so he points out that, while there is a wide variety of traditions and typologies characteristic of this field, the dominant model is based on the *apriori* assumption that in and of itself sport is a social good. This blind faith in 'the power of sport' has driven an 'alphabet soup' expansion of government and non-government agencies, and sadly, academic organisations that have latched onto the SDP bandwagon. Helpfully, scholars and researchers – such as Simon Darnell, Richard Giulianotti and Roger Levermore among numerous others[41] – have provided detailed classifications and taxonomies that attempt to make sense of this evolving organisational flowchart. As stated in our introduction, it has not been the intention in this book to rehearse in detail what has already been well said elsewhere. The key point is that what these authors have attempted to describe is a process of institutionalisation that is threatening the vitality of the SDP sector, a process to which they and all of us working in the area are – wittingly or otherwise – contributing. Jacob Naish provides a Foucauldian framework to argue that a technology of governmentality has overdetermined the practices of SDP organisations, the "capillaries of power" and associated alignments of key players or actors coming together to distort and undermine the aspirations and the stated ideals of the SDP interventions.[42] SDP practitioners and theorists alike should dwell on their contributions to such unintended but very real outcomes.

As Darnell argues, in terms of its origins the SDP movement has been a largely grassroots-led phenomenon. That is, in its early phase it was characterised by a scattergram of very loosely-knit and disconnected small voluntary clubs and organisations, most of which have their roots in sport rather than the International Development sector per se. Several of these, like the aforementioned Olympic Aid, were the products of individual vision and initiative; they were in large part set up by those who had rich experience in playing, coaching and organising sport at a variety of levels, and through this had come to believe in sport's capacity to assist in the achievement of wider development goals beyond the boundaries of the playing field. To what extent this experience-based belief turns into blind faith in the 'power of sport' is a moot subject to which we must inevitably return.

In order to ensure a level of sustainability and longevity, and enhance opportunities for fundraising, many of these small, relatively informal groupings, sought and achieved NGO (Non-Governmental Organisation) status. This allowed them to consolidate and even expand their theatres of operation. Some of the more ambitious organisations used this platform to engage in more widespread regional and global initiatives. Then a series of umbrella organisations began to emerge; as instanced above, the evolution of Right to Play out of the chrysalis of Olympic Aid. Examples of other overarching SDP institutions would include Coaching for Hope and Streetfootball World, Beyond Sport World and the Laureus Foundation. These organisations fulfil a range of functions by both initiating new SDP programmes and clustering together existing projects, offering support with project management, programme development and evaluation, and, crucially, fundraising. Some offer awards at glitzy international ceremonies and all have sophisticated websites and may have permanent staff and office buildings.

As SDP came of age and its global profile grew, it began to attract the attention of global government and non-government organisations inside and outside of the world of sport. FIFA and the IOC have already been mentioned and in their quest to be seen to support and associate their names with SDP they were joined by global heavyweights such as the European Union and the United Nations, the latter with a dedicated office for SDP in its Geneva headquarters. At the same time, in the private sector, the growing resource needs of the SDP movement are seen to chime with the main tenets of the CSR (Corporate Social Responsibility) agenda; Naish argues that SDP services "have been configured to a rational and corporate understanding of how to administer the doing of good".[43] Essentially, CSR is a bit like volunteering to pay extra for carbon offsetting when you take an international flight; you know that the main business of the airline inevitably damages the environment, but you can assuage your conscience by making a contribution to help fund relatively minor, environmentally friendly initiatives elsewhere. This is especially pertinent for the blue-chip global corporations which already have strong links with the major global sport governing bodies and the mega-events that they have facilitated. The big beasts of the athletic apparel world, like Nike and Adidas, with questions never far away about what goes on in the far-flung factories and workshops where most of their running shoes and track suits are made, have shown themselves willing to support and embrace CSR-orientated SDP work. But this is a far from purely philanthropic gesture. Poor people covet training shoes too. Whether it be in the townships of South Africa or the *favelas* of Brazil, getting the Nike and Adidas logos into such neighbourhoods via the sponsorship of a local SDP programme opens up new market opportunities and is good for business as well as image and conscience. This raises obvious ethical questions for SDP organisations, but with limited funds available and competition for such funding fierce, when the likes of Nike come calling it is hard for threadbare voluntary organisations to turn them away.

Such observations do not play well in the SDP sector where securing the resources to engage in SDP work is the most pressing challenge. This has important implications for shaping what actually goes on at the level of the grass-roots and the community, and for how interventions and initiatives are represented. Whether it be from a corporate sponsor, an umbrella INGO, an IGO or a mixture of all three, ethical questions notwithstanding, in order to secure initial funding and keep such revenues flowing in, grass-roots SDP bodies have to convince potential funders that the activities they support are of value, or, to use the phrase of the moment, that they have impact.

For SDP practitioners this leads to two related problems when making the case for support. Firstly, in order to get potential funders to 'buy into' the concept of SDP, when making their presentations they have to wear the mantle of True Believers. If you want to come away with a cheque, the corporate boardroom is not the place to give a lecture on critical realism, rather it is the place to invoke the utopian idealism and platitudinous wisdom of the likes of Mohammed Ali, Nelson Mandela and other greats who have pronounced upon the 'power of sport to change the world'. If your sermon shows signs of swaying the congregation you will then need to back up your belief with evidence and this is the second problem.

The vast majority of recent and contemporary literature about SDP comments that there is not sufficient research and evaluation or adequate evidence. More accurately, it appears to us that there may even be too much research and evaluation, but most of it is of the wrong type. Government and non-government corporations alike understand numbers rather than people and when it comes to evaluation and 'measurement' they tend to operate at the hard, positivistic end of the research paradigm. This is why the vast majority of evaluation schemas that are associated with SDP work are pseudo-scientific and numbers-based. In the context of the F4P programme (covered in Chapter 3, and informing the discussions in the final chapters), when asked "how do you know that what you do is making a difference?", our standard response has been another question: "how do you measure a change of heart?" We have used pre- and post-pencil-and-paper attitudinal surveys, but know too that what is really going on in an Arab child's mind after s/he has encountered and played with a Jewish neighbour for the very first time cannot be captured in a standardised questionnaire format. Get that same child to recount a story about that encounter though and this might generate illuminating insights into how if at all this experience has had real and potentially enduring impact. But such story-telling won't play hard in the boardroom. There the pitch must include glossy reports, packed with pie-charts, histograms, ANOVAs and multiple regression analysis, put together by independent and 'objective' Research and Monitoring teams at considerable expense using precious funds that could have been used in delivering the project.

The problem with this approach to programme evaluation is exacerbated by the fact that it is usually in everybody's interest to put the maximum positive spin on the results. As a practitioner, you need the project to be supported and funding agencies want to show that they are not wasting their money, whether it is from the public or private purse. Despite the glossy, mediated façade, nobody is any the wiser as to what is in actuality happening in the field and what the impact of the intervention is. The net result of this institutionalisation is that the larger a SDP organisation becomes and the more overheads it has, then the pressure to produce positive if rather superficial reports increases to justify and sustain its growing number of specialised functions and supporting administrative offices and officers. Following a classical Weberian formulation, formal rationality pushes aside substantial rationality and in this scenario the survival and strengthening of the SDP bureaucracy becomes the superordinate organisational goal.[44]

The academic community is playing its part in the institutionalisation of and, arguably, mortification of SDP in much the same way as 'development' per se metamorphosed from being a vibrant area of praxis and activism in the 1960s and 1970s to becoming a respectable and relatively conservative sphere of multi-disciplinary academic discourse in the 1980s and 1990s.[45] In a parallel universe to the organisational delivery structures referred to earlier, SDP is in the process of being overwhelmed and colonised by the academic community for its own purposes. University courses and modules at undergraduate and postgraduate level that prominently feature SDP are springing up on both sides of the Atlantic and in Australasia. The 1988 Rhode Island symposium on *Peace and Understanding through Sport* was a very rare event, but three decades later SDP is a very common theme on the international academic conference circuit. Likewise it has become an important focus for research and academic scholarship and published research in the field has exploded with a proliferation of books, specialised journals and special issues of established journals covering all aspects of SDP. This expansion and wider dissemination of the body of knowledge and the training of increasing numbers of well-qualified SDP specialists should be viewed as a positive development. However, as so often happens with these kind of exercises, intellectual ambitions in the expansion of new fields, alongside rivalries for academic status and position, gradually moves the field away from its activist roots. As Wright Mills warned, the excesses of the sociological imagination can distort at the extremes: on the one hand, generating endless databases in forms of abstracted empiricism that tell us more and more about less and less; on the other, theorising from the library or the desk, with unanchored conceptualisation and obliquely articulated forms of grand theory pronounced in dense and inaccessible language.[46] We seek in this study to avoid either of these extremes in a critically and conceptually informed, empirically grounded assessment of the realistic potential of SDP principles and interventions based in disinterested analysis and feasible forms of social action; critical proactivism, as we argue for in the remaining chapters.

The calendar of global sports competitions is increasingly accompanied by the soundtrack of the SDP movement. As we saw in the previous chapter, nowhere was this more in evidence than when South Africa hosted the football World Cup 2010. Likewise, in this regard, because of its mythic heritage and obsession with legacies, every four years the modern (Summer) Olympic Games provides a high-profile forum for showcasing the work of the SDP sector, an element in what Toby Miller labels "growth evangelism".[47] In his comic play *The Birds* Greek dramatist Aristophanes gave the Chorus a playful task, to find the name for the new capital city of the Birds, distinct from any wording with overtones of Sparta.[48] The respondent Pisthetairos, eulogising the city for its clouds, proffered the splendid or grand, but utopian, option of a new city between earth and heaven, its name constructed from the word for a cloud and the word for a cuckoo: Cloud-cuckoo-town (or land, as we have come to call it). In the hands of disingenuous apologists, quixotic fantasists, idealistic do-gooders, abstracted empiricists, and grand and obscurantist theorists, the growth of SDP has led many into a maze of interconnected cul-de-sacs justifying SDP as something really rather grand. In our remaining chapters we seek to get SDP out of the maze, back on track, based upon the fusion of critical social science and cultural and political activism that has fuelled the work documented in this book.

Notes

1 Alexander Wolff, "Sports Saves the World", *Sports Illustrated, Vault*, 26 September 2011, www.si.com/vault/2011/09/26/106112004/sports-saves-the-world, accessed 17 May 2017.
2 As a sidebar to the main event, Wolff was still interested in the cross-community sport work involving the Belfast United initiative that he had encountered a decade and a half earlier on his visit to Belfast.
3 The proceedings of this event were published in Greta L. Cohen ed. *Peace and Understanding Through Sport: A Monograph* (Rhode Island, USA: Institute for International Sport, University of Rhode Island: 1989); the subtitle remains somewhat of a mystery.
4 Sadly Brian lost his battle with cancer and passed away prematurely in 2010.
5 In 1983 Brian was present in the lecture on Sport in South Africa when the IRA bomb detonated, killing several policemen attending a lecture in a nearby building. This incident is discussed in greater detail in Chapter 2.
6 This impressive building was owned by Dan Doyle, Director of the Institute for International Sport, who, it was widely believed, had had the whole edifice jacked up and moved about a hundred metres so that he would have better views out to sea. At the time of writing Dan Doyle was awaiting sentencing for fraud and corruption, having been found guilty on 18 counts – the jury announced "guilty" 216 times – of embezzlement and forgery, criminal misuse of state and university funds. See Tom Mooney and Katie Mulvaney, "Dan Doyle guilty of all charges, including embezzlement and forgery", *Providence Journal*, 5 December 2016, providencejournal.com, accessed 17 May 2017.

7 At the time of writing Alberto Juantorena was Minister of Sport for Cuba.
8 At that time there were no direct flights between Cuba and the USA. Almost three decades later, despite the end of the Cold War, there are only very limited direct connecting flights between the two countries and travel options across the Florida Straits remain severely limited.
9 For further details of the results of the study tour to Cuba see John Sugden, Alan Tomlinson, and Eamonn McCartan, "The making and remaking of white lightning in Cuba: Politics, sport and physical education 30 years after the revolution", *Arena Review*, 14/1, 1990: 101–109; reprinted in Andrew Yiannakis, Thomas D. McIntyre, and Merrill J. Melnick eds., *Sport Sociology: Contemporary Themes, Fourth Edition* (Dubuque, IA: Kendall/Hunt Publishing Company, 1993). For a more contemporary account of Cuba's approach to international sport development see Robert Huish, Thomas F. Carter, and Simon Darnell, "The (soft) power of sport: The comprehensive and contradictory strategies of Cuba's sport-based internationalism", *International Journal of Cuban Studies*, 5/1, 2013: 26–40.
10 Until July 2015 Cuba and the USA had no diplomatic relations and as such did not have embassies in the respective countries. Prior to that there was a range of inter-political functions that had to be carried out and for these purposes each nation had an Interest Section in Washington and Havana. With good reason, the Cuban Government was worried that once abroad their athletes and/or officials might be tempted to defect so they were rarely if ever allowed to travel alone. Interestingly Juantorena's minder's luggage had mysteriously vanished during his circuitous journey to New England. During an early summer heatwave the poor man had to wear the same suit and clothes for five days before his baggage was recovered.
11 David Kanin went on to work for the CIA for more than 30 years, finishing his career as a Senior Analyst. At the time of writing he was Adjunct Professor of European studies at Johns Hopkins University, Washington D.C. For a more detailed consideration of the Rhode Island incident see John Sugden, "Sport and spies. The dark side of sport and international relations", in *Image, Power and Space: Studies in Consumption and Identity*, eds. Alan Tomlinson and Jonathan Woodham (Oxford: Meyer and Meyer Sport, 2007).
12 Fortunately the Cubans believed the young academic from Britain and the friendship remained, and endured. Following up on an invitation by Juantorena, an educational tour took place to Cuba to study its sports system. More than two decades later, at the University of Brighton, this friendship was instrumental in helping to bring the 2011 World Congress of the International Sociology of Sport Association (ISSA) to Havana for a conference entitled *Sport and the Winds of Change*. The Cuban Minister of Sport, erstwhile 1988 Rhode Island jogging partner, Senor Alberto Juantorena, gave the opening address.
13 For a more detailed rendition of these arguments, see Michael B. Poliakof, *Combat Sports in the Ancient World* (New Haven: Yale University Press, 1987).
14 Eduardo Galeano, *Football in Sun and Shadow* (London: Fourth Estate, 1998): 15.
15 For further debate about this see Heather Reid, "Olympic sport and its lessons for peace", *Journal of the Philosophy of Sport*, 33/2, 2006: 205–214.
16 Leigh Montville, "Once upon a time", *Sports Illustrated*, 7 March 1994, reproduced in Roel Puijk ed., *Global Spotlights on Lillehammer: How the World Viewed Norway During the 1994 Winter Olympics* (Luton: University of Luton Press, 1997): 26.
17 Malcom Brown and Shirley Seaton, *Christmas Truce: The Western Front December 1914* (London: Pan, 2001): 149.
18 Iain Adams and Trevor Petney, "Germany 3-Scotland 2, No Man's Land, 25th December, 1914: Fact or fiction?", in *The Bountiful Game: Football Identities*

and Finances, eds. Jonathan Magee, Alan Bairner, and Alan Tomlinson (Oxford: Meyer & Meyer Sport, 2005): 39.
19 Exhibit in Towneley Hall Art Gallery & Museum (First World War Room), Towneley Park, Burnley, Lancashire, United Kingdom, viewed/accessed 15 March 2017.
20 For further accounts of such incidents see, Colin Vetch, "'Play up! Play up! and Win the War.' Football, the Nation and the First World War 1914–15", *Journal of Contemporary History*, 20/3, 1985: 363–378. See too Modris Eksteins, *Rites of Spring: The Great War and the Birth of the Modern Age* (London: Black Swan, 1990): Chapter 33, "In Flanders' Fields".
21 For a full account and interpretation of this episode, see Ryszard Kapuściński's *The Soccer War* (New York: Knopf, 199). See too Lindsey Barrett, Colby Leachman, Claire Lockerby, Steven McMullen, Matthew Schorr, and Yuriy Veytskin, "The Soccer War," at *Soccer Politics Pages*, http://sites.duke.edu/wcwp, accessed 16 April 2017. Kapuściński's biographer Artur Domoslawski, revealing that numerous vignettes in his subject's reporting were sheer inventions, writes that "Ryszard Kapuściński – the hero of Ryszard Kapuściński's books – is also a fictional character". This is quoted in Sigrid Rausing, "Introduction", *Granta 138 Journeys*, 8 February 2017, https://granta.com/journeys-introduction/, accessed 16 May 2017. A debunking of the Kapuściński legend is starkly achieved in Artur Domoslawski, *Ryszard Kapuściński: A Life* (London: Verso, 2012).
22 Elizabeth Longford, *Wellington: The Years of the Sword* (London: Harper & Row, 1969): 14.
23 Ibid., 15.
24 Ibid., 15–17, where Longford debunks the myth of the source and origin of the epigram.
25 Angela Partington ed., *The Oxford Dictionary of Quotations, Revised Fourth Edition* (Oxford: Oxford University Press, 1996): 727.
26 The poem was written in commemoration of an act of imagined heroism carried out during the British military campaign to restore control over the Sudan after the capital, Khartoum, had been sacked by Sudanese warriors led by the Mahdi in 1885. As pointed out in the introductory chapter to this book, John Sugden spent a year as a volunteer in the Sudan in 1975–1976 surrounded by the relics of Britain's colonial past, including its sports and games, and those experiences had a huge and lasting influence, without doubt a subliminal presence in the pages of this book. We are grateful to Lincoln Allison for conversations and clarification on the significance of the Newbolt and Kipling poems which, though not directly related in any way such as statement-response, do nevertheless represent oppositional stances on the values of sport.
27 See Samantha King, "Offensive lines: Sport and state synergy in an era of perpetual war", *Cultural Studies: Critical Methodologies*, 8/8, 2008: 527–539.
28 For more detail, see John Sugden, "Watched by the Games: Surveillance and security at the Olympics", *International Review for the Sociology of Sport*, 47/3, 2012: 414–429.
29 Orwell's most detailed memoir about the suffering he endured during his early school years can be found in the essay *Such, Such Were the Joys*, which focuses on his time at St Cyprian's preparatory school Eastbourne, the site of which is less than a mile from where we have spent many years at the University of Brighton's Eastbourne site discussing these questions. It was first published with some changes of names in *Partisan Review*, September–October 1952 (though written by May 1947). His most scathing attack on organised sport came in the essay *This Sporting Spirit*, published in *Tribune*, 14 December 1945. For *Such, Such Were the Joys* see pp. 379–422, and for *This Sporting Spirit* see pp. 61–64, in The

Collected Essays, Journalism and Letters of George Orwell, Volume IV, In Front of Your Nose 1945–1950, eds. Sonia Orwell and Ian Angus (Harmondsworth: Penguin Books in association with Martin Secker & Warburg, 1970).
30 *The Collected Essays*: 63 and 64.
31 Jules Boykoff, *Power Games: A Political History of the Olympics* (London: Verso, 2016) includes the water-polo encounter between Hungary and the USSR in his section on 'boycotts and dustups'. Quoting IOC president Avery Brundage's claim that international sporting encounters should not be halted as a response to the violation by politicians of "the laws of humanity" Boykoff wryly comments that such laws were hardly observed by the competitors in the pool. He quotes *Sports Illustrated*: "Like barracudas, the contestants flailed at one another underwater, sending up whirlpooled proof of titanic struggles beneath". The water ran with blood, Boykoff adds, emanating from a below-the-water punch-up (pp. 91–92). US movie director Joe Eszterhas was a 12-year old boy in the "strudel ghetto" of the Near West Side of Cleveland, Ohio at the time, "in love with the wonders with this new American world" of baseball, rock 'n roll and film. But the Hungarian water-polo victory he recalls with passion: we "beat the Russians bloody . . . we danced in the streets in Cleveland. We burned the Hungarian communist flag. The Americans in our neighbourhood looked at us like we were nuts. We didn't care. Maybe we were nuts. That polo match may have been a Pyrrhic victory, but it was victory nonetheless. Maybe one of the greatest victories in Hungarian history"; see Joe Eszterhas, "I hit Mikoyan with a rotten egg", *The Guardian*, 7 May 2008: 4. David Goldblatt, *The Games: A Global History of the Olympics* (London: Pan Macmillan, 2016) also provides rich detail on Olympic contradictions and excesses in a powerful blend of historical, sociological and political analysis of the Olympic phenomenon.
32 The classic, idealist statement of this position can be found in Philip Goodhart and Christopher Chataway, *War Without Weapons* (London: W. H. Allen, 1968). Their final chapter is entitled 'A kind of warfare', and opens with the provocative statement that the US sports writer Jimmy Breslin's description of the Notre Dame v. Michigan State University football match in 1966 "deserves a place in an anthology of war reporting" (p. 139). By the end of the chapter they are reconciled with Orwell though, as their reading of his "war minus the shooting" phrase is proffered as a form of advancement of sport's "ultimate justification"; sport is "a kind of warfare perhaps. But war *without* the weapons" (p. 158). For a more critical and contemporary take on the same theme see Mike Marqusee, *War Minus the Shooting: A Journey Through South Asia During Cricket's World Cup* (London: William Heinemann, 1996).
33 The Laureus Foundation, unsurprisingly, highlights and reprints this speech at any available opportunity, such as its Nelson Mandela International Day in July 2016, and takes such opportunities to remind the world that Mandela's vision "has become the philosophy of Laureus Sport for Good and the driving force behind its work", www.laureus.com/ . . . /mandela-day-laureus-academy-members-honour-our-first, accessed 17 May 2017. Unfortunately a cached address has blocked access to the source, entitled "On Mandela Day, Laureus Academy Members honour our first Patron".
34 See www.laureus.com/news/15-years-laureus-anniversary-very-special-speech, accessed 17 May 2017.
35 See Lincoln Allison and Alan Tomlinson, *Understanding International Sport Organisations: Principles, Power and Possibilities* (London and New York: Routledge, 2017): 218–219, on the messianic leader as a key figure in the contemporary history of the sport-related international non-governmental organisation (the SINGO).

36 This interview was conducted in Cairo's Grand Hyatt Hotel in 1997, see John Sugden and Alan Tomlinson, *FIFA and the Contest for World Football: Who Rules the Peoples' Game* (Cambridge: Polity Press, 1998): 232–241.
37 Norbert Elias's masterpiece, *The History of Manners: The Civilising Process 1* (Oxford: Basil Blackwell, 1978) was first published in 1939. It is a majestic study of "the pattern of affect control, of what must and must not be restrained, regulated and transformed" (p. 152) in social life, from eating habits to sleeping patterns, covering all aspects of everyday life. Uninhibited physicality would be curbed by new restraints on everyday conduct and relations as a more civilised, bourgeois life evolved. Sport – in its restrained, regulated forms – can be seen in this Eliasian framework as a sphere embodying these core features of the civilising process; but also in certain conditions and circumstances, threatening the newly established cultural order by returning to the impulses of a previous stage.
38 See Norbert Elias and Eric Dunning, *Quest for Excitement: Sport and Leisure in the Civilizing Process* (Oxford: Basil Blackwell, 1986).
39 There is a voluminous academic literature on all these subjects, compendia of which abound. Among the best of these remains Jay Coakley and Eric Dunning eds., *Handbook of Sport Studies* (London: Sage, 2000).
40 Bruce Kidd, "A new social movement: Sport for development and peace", *Sport in Society*, 11/4, 2008: 370–380.
41 Simon Darnell, *Sport for Development and Peace: A Critical Sociology* (London: Bloomsbury, 2011); Richard Giulianotti, "The sport, development and peace sector: A model of four social policy domains", *Journal of Social Policy*, 40, 2011, 757–776; Richard Giulianotti, "Sport, peace-making and conflict resolution: A contextual analysis and modeling of the sport, development and peace sector", *Ethnic and Racial Studies*, 34, 2010: 207–228; Roger Levermore, "Sport: A new engine of development?", *Progress in Development Studies*, 8, 2008: 183–190; Roger Levermore, "Sport-in-international development: Time to treat it seriously?", *Journal of World Affairs*, 14, 2008: 55–66. See too Lyndsay Hayhurst, "The power to shape policy: Charting sport for development and peace policy discourses", *International Journal of Sport Policy and Politics*, 1/2, 2009: 203–227.

Recent scholarship has focused in more closely on particular contexts and objectives rather than broad theoretical debate. See for instance Iain Lindsey and Tony Chapman, *Enhancing the Contribution of Sport to the Sustainable Development Goals* (London: Commonwealth Secretariat, 2017); and Iain Lindsey, Tess Kay, Ruth Jeanes, and Davies Banda, *Localizing Global Sport for Development* (Manchester: Manchester University Press, 2017), which is rooted in grounded research with young people and youth in Zambia.
42 Jacob Naish, "Sport for development and peace: Alignment, administration, power", in *Routledge Handbook of Sport and Politics*, eds. Alan Bairner, John Kelly, and Jung Woo Lee (London and New York: Routledge, 2017): 310.
43 Ibid.
44 Weber noted that there is an inbuilt tension between a formal type of rationality and a sort of rationality based upon some "absolute value . . . regardless of consequences"; see *Max Weber, Selections in Translation*, ed. W.G. Runciman (Cambridge: Cambridge University Press, 1978): 28, from *Economy and Society* first published 1922. Rationality and action based in such absolute value becomes, in modern life, increasingly subservient to or replaced by formal rationality whose dominance leads to "a suppression of value-oriented action", as Stephen Kalberg (p. 1174) put it in a classic, and usefully clear, discussion of Weber's types of rationality. See Stephen Kalberg, "Max Weber's types of rationality: Cornerstones for the analysis of rationalization processes in history", *The American Journal of Sociology*, 85/5, 1980: 1145–1179.

45 Frans J. Schuurman, "Critical development theory: Moving out of the twilight zone", *Third World Quarterly*, 30/5, 2009: 831–848.
46 C. Wright Mills, *The Sociological Imagination* (Harmondsworth: Penguin Books, 1970), see Chapter 2 on "Grand Theory" and Chapter 3 on "Abstracted Empiricism".
47 Toby Miller, *Greenwashing Sport* (London and New York: Routledge, 2017): Chapter 5 on the Olympic Games and its ecology agenda set by the organisation's "growth evangelism".
48 Aristophanes, *The Birds*, www.gutenberg.org/files/3013/3013-h/3013-h.htm, accessed 17 May 2017.

Chapter 6

SDP back down to earth – epistemological foundations of critical pragmatism[1]

Introduction

In the final two chapters, we return to answering the question posed by Dominic Malcolm, as related in Chapter 1. In this chapter we consider the epistemological foundations that have underpinned the evolution of the F4P work; in the final chapter we elaborate on the model that continues to evolve in our and related work on sport and its peace-building capacities. As Fred Coalter has pointed out, realistic and objective evaluation is a crucial element of successful sport-in-development programmes.[2] At every level of its articulation, applied research and evaluation have been essential features of the F4P work around which much of this book has revolved. The research has a complex, two-way dynamic: ongoing learning about the transcending social and political context that is used in the pragmatic design and development of the programme of intervention; and detailed evaluation of the impact of the project at each level, up to and including, where possible, tracking its influence on the transcending social and political context. This circular and inclusive approach to research and evaluation has helped the project to develop organically, from the bottom up, as the knowledge and viewpoints gleaned from all key actors and stakeholders have been used to refine and reform interventions year on year. It has also helped to facilitate growing local ownership and sustainability of the project as the communities themselves take increasing responsibility for the design and delivery of F4P events, as well as using ideas drawn from this experience in the development of programmes of cross-community cooperation outside of the F4P framework. But all of this has been framed in a theoretical and methodological framework, and here we pause for a sort of methodological interlude in order to contextualise more fully that framework.

Epistemology: the road to critical pragmatism

The argument has been made elsewhere that having a well-attuned sociological imagination can provide a compass for sport-activists to navigate a course between hope and expectation, or between idealism and fatalism.[3]

Whether articulated or inferred, social activism requires epistemological foundations. In this chapter we return to the example of C. Wright Mills in expanding our methodological rationale and epistemological position, initially in debate with a complementary adaptation of a Millsian framework. In his book *C. Wright Mills and the End of Violence*, examining peace processes in Northern Ireland, Israel and Palestine, and South Africa, John Brewer demonstrates the value of using Wright Mills's concept of the sociological imagination as a means through which to make sense of the extremely complex web of circumstances that have led very different societies down the roads of peace and reconciliation.[4] We considered the importance of Wright Mills's work in the opening chapters of this book, and have referenced his principles throughout. Our backgrounds in various branches of Marxism and neo-Marxism, critical and cultural theory, symbolic interactionism and interpretive phenomenological and ethnographic approaches to social science had equipped us for all levels of sociological debate. But we nevertheless found Wright Mills's empirically grounded critical sociological accounts of social structure and power in the post-war USA stayed refreshingly accessible and plausible. The sociological thrust was always his imperative, as opposed to performing the intellectual acrobatics of the social theorist. "Theorising about" a particular phenomenon, rather than theorising for theory's sake, or using theory as a form of framing epistèmology, has been a priority in our research and intellectual work.[5] Central to this chapter therefore is the conviction that Wright Mills's deep understanding of the relationships between biography, social structure and history not only helps us to understand deeply divided societies, but also provides us with arguments and a rationale as to how to develop strategies for civil society interventions in those societies.

Brewer argues that a sociology of peace process should not offer grand theory or a universal scheme to understand peace processes in general. He begins by observing that peace processes are exceedingly complex and unpredictable entities, making sense of which involves high levels of informed retrospection. "Between God and chance you find sociology" says Brewer, arguing that Wright Mills's work shows us that sociologists are amongst the best qualified to engage with and make sense of a world in flux and turmoil; but their work should be restricted in its applicability to specified cases that exist in real time and space.[6] In this regard context is everything and history is a critical feature of this context. Understanding peace processes must focus on the relationships between biography, social structure and the political process. This is no mere abstract formulation. On the contrary, it is important to show the interaction between the local and the societal by exploring how ordinary people experience conflict and its consequences, and to ascertain as to how those people's responses in turn affect the conflict and the peace process – the dynamic and dialectic at the heart of Wright Mills's vision, the relationship between 'personal troubles' and 'public issues'.

Finally, based upon this, it is our task to develop appropriate theoretical explanations and models for action through a dialogue between historical and contemporary experience and existing knowledge. In different ways the three case studies considered in the chapters above clearly exemplify this. Woe betide any peace activist who attempts to meddle in community affairs in South Africa, Northern Ireland or Israel/Palestine without having a deep understanding of the confluence of local, regional and national historical currents flowing into the conflicts that they are attempting to help resolve and "that have saturated the cultures of the parties that they are seeking to" reconcile. We also believe that a credible sociology must avoid tendentiousness, beware of slipping into a standpoint epistemology in which the analysis so often precedes the evidence-gathering.[7]

Wright Mills was no slave to theoretical dogma. Rather, guided by his mentor, Hans Gerth, he was a well-informed eclecticist.[8] He had a deep understanding of the classic tradition in sociology embodied largely by Marx, Weber and Durkheim, but in terms of his own ontological/epistemological positioning he was highly influenced by the subject of his doctoral studies, pragmatism. Based on the works of the American philosophers and educationalists, William James and John Dewy, pragmatism advocates the science of the possible whereby action and intervention are linked to outcomes that are themselves based upon a critical assessment of what can be achieved within a given set of situational circumstances: in its psycho-philosophical mode, it constituted a perceptive form of structure-agency theory.[9] There is of course a huge volume of work concerning the notion of 'critical' social science, and while we note this we do not seek to engage with all of the related issues. In our own work we have prioritised the sense of critique underlying a critical sociology.[10] Combining this sense of critique with the central concerns of James and Dewey, our approach is one that we label 'critical pragmatism'.[11] In this approach, utilising Dewey's notion of pragmatism, change and progress through intervention and development, emphasis is placed upon theoretical development and refinement through critical, practical, empirical engagement, rather than fixating upon abstract debate and unmoveable theoretical principles. This view recognises that the construction of society is not passively structural, but is an embodied process of individual and collective actions. As Alison Kadlec puts it, "much is missed when we impose artificial arrests on a world in flux, as not only does this impede our ability to perceive deeper and more nuanced relations of power that constrain and repress, this also stunts our ability to perceive and cultivate new possibilities for change".[12]

Relatedly, the emergence of left realism within critical criminology can in some ways be viewed as a branch of critical pragmatism. Disillusioned with conventional theories of crime and deviance emanating from the political right, and the failure of class struggle/revolution-fixated Marxists to provide the foundation for the development of an agenda for empirical investigation and intervention, scholars developed a new approach that became known as left realism. This new paradigm allowed for the mobilisation of a radical and critical sociological imagination in determining strategies for progressive and pragmatic engagement with social problems with a view to influencing local policies and interventions that could improve the conditions of society's most vulnerable groups. Space does not permit a full discussion on the merits or otherwise of left realism, but that can be found elsewhere.[13] Suffice it to say that for some radical thinkers and activists it can offer a way out of the inertia so often brought on by analytical or theoretical ossification, a sense for the critical scholar that one is always singing to oneself in an echoing cave occupied solely by the singer. Left realism reanimated critical criminology by taking the analysis and critique and raising questions of application and policy-informing critique. For instance, a rigorous discourse analysis of particular text-based discourse could be conceived as not negatively iconoclastic but rather as a form of critical renewal, reformulating and potentially shifting the discourse itself. In sport studies one variant of such a form of 'praxis' has been advocated in the context of sports activism by Marxist scholar, Ian McDonald, who argues that rather than being satisfied with armchair critique, "a radical sociology of sport should be seeking to assist the reconfiguration of the culture of sport by intervening against dominant relations of power", and by engaging with the challenge of what might be done or developed as an alternative to that which is critiqued.[14] This kind of critical left-realism can be applied equally to a range of sport for development programmes, including those that focus on fractured community relations and social conflict in divided societies.

Theory and method for peace-building

In addition to the adoption of a critically pragmatic sociological gaze it is important to account for and understand existing models of coexistence and peace. Many of these are based on the pioneering work of Paulo Freire and Adam Curle who drew on their fieldwork, respectively in South America and the former Yugoslavia, to advocate the notion of peace-building from below – a strategy whereby external forms of intervention and mediation concentrate on facilitating the organic empowerment and active participation of local actors and agencies in conflict-resolution and reconciliation.[15] Based on these approaches, Marie Dugan developed a "nested paradigm" which is a "sub-system" approach linking the challenges of conflict-resolution to the broader necessity of peace-building.[16] At a sub-system level, a peace-building strategy could be designed to address both the systemic concerns and the problematic issues and relationships. The sub-system approach allows one to both shape grassroots relationships, and contribute to wider systemic change; the 'conflict resolver' engaging with subjects in the matter of 'futures invention'. In concert with the thinking of Dugan, John Paul Lederach has also theorised a 'web approach' to peace-building.[17] He encourages interventions that explicitly focus on strategic networking or 'web-making', a term used to describe the building of a network of relationships and partnerships with significant local entities and actors, what he refers to as the "cultural modalities and resources" within the setting of conflict. The model he uses to help us envisage holistic and sustainable peace-building is a triangle or pyramid, the apex, Level One of which represents international and national political actors. The middle, second level comprises regional political leaders and constituency representatives, including religious, business and trades union leaders and so forth, who have connections with and access to Level One actors. Finally, at Level Three, the grassroots level, there is the vast majority made up of those who are most affected by the conflict on a day-to-day basis. Lederach argues that for a peace process to be successful and sustainable it must operate across and include all levels of the pyramid, especially Level Three where conflicts are played out in everyday life. We would also bring Galtung into the picture, as he identifies the interrelationship between visible and less visible violence.[18] In order to begin conflict transformation and achieve sustainable peace it is in many cases and contexts necessary to address less visible violence.

For Galtung, peace-building requires the '3 Rs': reconstruction of people and places, reconciliation of relationships, and resolution of issues and animosities. Sport interventions can help build positive social networks through relationships, a requirement central to many of the processes underpinning each of the '3 Rs'. Such relationships are central to Lederach's 'web approach'. He encourages interventions that explicitly focus on strategic networking or 'web-making', a term used to describe the building of relationships. Web-making is especially relevant for NGOs working in the field of sports. As they are middle-level actors, they are ideally located to bring people together and weave dialogue, ideas and programmes across boundaries. By capitalising on key social spaces, they are able to spin a web of sustainable relationships. As will be reiterated in the following, final chapter the web approach offers a useful approach to understanding the role that sport can play in the relationship between political and civil society which is key in understanding the role it can have in peace processes.

Schirch has pioneered the use of rituals as a process to transform identities in and among antagonistic people who have dehumanised each other through a protracted violent conflict.[19] It is essential in peace-building that conflicting groups are able to 're-humanise' their vision of each other as part of a reconciliation process that aims for sustainable co-existence. Rituals, Schirch argues, create spaces and opportunities for the 're-humanising' of the other. Rituals can take a variety of forms, from a shared meal, to dancing, to ceremony, to sport participation.[20] She emphasizes that success in the use of ritual is embedded in sensitivity towards and awareness of culture.

According to the theoretical frameworks mentioned above the extent to which sport can make a contribution to peace-building encompasses:

(1) helping people re-humanise each other through its rituals and ceremonies and ethics of 'fair play' and sportsmanship; (2) helping people (re)build relationships in the organisation and conduct of events; and (3) helping build webs and relationships at the sub-system level. These important theoretical and conceptual contributions have remained pertinent to the evolving SDP field and have fed into the development of the model that we discuss in the final chapter.

Human rights and social justice: whose side are we on?

When embarking on civil society interventions in divided societies, to quote the title of Howard Becker's influential 1967 article, the recurrent question in cycles of action and analysis is: 'Whose side are we on?'[21] That is to say what are and who sets the coordinates of the moral compass that guides our approach to critical intervention? Becker was one of the first sociologists to articulate what has since become a universally accepted tenet of sociological inquiry, that value-neutrality was neither achievable nor desirable. Becker favoured championing the underdog and the down-trodden, but as McDonald points out such an approach is in danger of sacrificing sociological integrity "on the altar of partisanship".[22] When working in the context of the 'perfect conflict' that is Israel/Palestine, wherein both sides have counter-balancing claims to righteousness and victimhood, this has been a particularly pressing problem.

One way forward is to draw upon higher-order principles of human rights and social justice. A starting point is the United Nations Charter for Human Rights first drawn up and approved in 1948. Article 26 states, "education shall be directed to the full development of the human personality and to the strengthening of respect for human rights and fundamental freedoms. It shall promote understanding, tolerance and friendship among all nations, racial or religious groups, and shall further the activities of the United Nations for the maintenance of peace".[23] While this clause provides some foundation to civil society activism, John Alt's articulation of how this can be realised through mobilising the emancipatory qualities of fair play suggests the elements of a central strategy for sports-based peace-building activities:

> Fair play in sport is related to social justice: individuals are free to consciously pursue the potential and limits of their interests, talents, and character while at the same time respecting the rights of others to do likewise. Justice in this sense implies reciprocal fairness in group life and relates to goodness or civility – being loyal, courteous, tolerant and beneficent as ends in themselves and as a means for furthering rightness.[24]

Of course appeals to such 'higher order' charters and moral principles can be criticised for being at best idealistic and at worst a form of neo-liberal Kantianism.[25] But Alt's sentiments fit well with the principles and the ideals that have fuelled pro-democracy movements across the globe in the modern era, including and especially in the wider Middle-East. Without them, when it comes to social and political activism one's hands are tied by the bonds of standpoint epistemology and cultural-relativism, which usually means the tyrants prevail.

Conclusion: on the right track – a paradigm for progress in SDP

Drawing from extensive experience in the field and on-going critical self-reflection on cycles of research, analysis and intervention, F4P and associated work have provided a way of thinking about, planning and doing sport for development work that is neither idealistic nor simplistic; the paradigm is justified from a humanitarian perspective, accounts fully for the local context, engages with and empowers local actors and partners, and connects with wider national and regional policy processes. The mobilisation of a fully informed 'sociological imagination', in combination with practical engagement and local contextual immersion, can work effectively together in strategic planning and project implementation.

It is now more than 15 years since 9/11 (an infamous date that needs no further qualification). That this event occurred the same year that F4P began its fieldwork is more than a coincidence in as much as at the root of both events is the strong belief that the 'situation' (as the conflict within Israel and between Israel and Palestine and the rest of the Arab world is referred to locally) sits at the heart of and provides the rationale for much of the conflict in the wider Middle East and further afield. That one interpretation led to mass murder while the other seeks to promote co-existence and reconciliation is testimony to the extremely complex and multi-faceted nature of the dynamic, dialectical and ultimately unpredictable machinery most commonly referred to as the 'Peace Process'. Looking back at South Africa and Northern Ireland it becomes clear that a multiplicity of factors – these include forms of violent resistance; state-sponsored responses to such violence; economic sanctions; international political pressure; passive forms of resistance; and inter-community civil society interventions – all played some part in energising what turned out to be a long-awaited, unforeseen, but no less welcome Peace Process in those theatres of conflict. These outcomes cannot be repeated formulaically in the Middle East, as each context is vastly different, but lessons can be learned, the chief one being that paradigmatic social and political change has multiple causes, with both negative and positive effects, all of which must always be counted and factored in to the final reckoning.

In the field, in Irbid, Jordan, ten years into the F4P work, one of us engaged in dialogue with the British Council's representative from Ammam. The setting was an F4P training camp for volunteers. The British Council man observed the activities and asked what was actually taking place, and we informed him what the work of F4P comprised, and what we hoped to achieve. He paused for thought before saying, "Well, this is admirable, what you are trying to do, but the situation here is so difficult that I fear that small interventions like this will not be able to make a difference". At that point, an analogy came to mind that might have helped him visualise the potential contribution of small-scale interventions. This was to think of the current peace-process in Israel/Palestine as an unfinished 10,000 piece, 3-dimensional jigsaw puzzle made additionally challenging because each piece is yet to be finished and no picture came with the box. F4P is one of the pieces that has a place in the jumble of pieces that fill that box. At an unspecified time in the future, as happened in South Africa and Northern Ireland, it is to be hoped that patterns will emerge and the pieces will come together to finish the puzzle. While interventions like F4P will of course never be so prominent or significant as seismic events such as the dismantling of the Berlin Wall that heralded the end of the Cold War, they have nevertheless formed and will continue to form a small part of the completed picture and as such they are invaluable. This conception of SDP work constitutes a critically pragmatic approach to social-science based interventions in the field. In the ensuing, concluding chapter of this book we present more fully the model that has evolved from and continues to inform and frame such work.

Notes

1. This chapter draws in parts upon John Sugden's address, September 15–17, 2011, to the conference *Sport as Mediator Between Cultures*, Wingate Institute, Israel.
2. Fred Coalter, *Sport-in-Development: A Monitoring and Evaluation Manual* (London: UK Sport/UNICEF, 2006).
3. John Sugden, "The sociology of sport and the quest for peace in societies in conflict: Between idealism and fatalism", in *Community and Inclusion in Leisure Research and Sport Development*, eds. Aarti Ratna and Brett D. Lashua (Eastbourne: LSA Publications, 2011).
4. John Brewer, *C. Wright Mills and the Ending of Violence* (Basingstoke: Palgrave Macmillan, 2003).
5. Alan Tomlinson, "Introduction: Analyzing Sport and Leisure Cultures", in Alan Tomlinson, *Sport and Leisure Cultures* (Minneapolis: University of Minnesota Press, 2005), xv–xix.
6. Brewer, *C. Wright Mills*: 152.
7. John Sugden and Alan Tomlinson, "Theory and method for a critical sociology of sport", in *Power Games: A Critical Sociology of Sport*, eds. John Sugden and Alan Tomlinson (London and New York: Routledge, 2002); and "Digging the dirt and staying clean: Retrieving the investigative tradition for a critical sociology of sport", *International Review for the Sociology of Sport*, 34/4, 1999: 385–397.
8. Hans Heinrich Gerth and C. Wright Mills, *Character and Social Structure: The Psychology of Institutions* (New York: Harcourt Brace and Company, 1953).

The title is a clear indication of the dual importance of the personal and the institutional in the work of Wright Mills, constituting a recognition of the importance of the structure-agency dynamic in social scientific work. As Robert K. Merton wrote in his Foreword to the book (p. vii), its chief objective was to "present a systematic statement" recognising that institutions "and historical transformations are connected with the character and personality, with the private as well as the public lives, of those living within the society".

9 William James, *Pragmatism: A New Name for Some Old Ways of Thinking* (Cambridge, MA: Harvard University Press, 1979), first published 1907; and John Dewey, *Liberalism and Social Action* (New York, NY: Putnam, 1935).

10 See the *Power Games* reference in Note 7 above.

11 Chris Gratton and Ian Jones, *Research Methods for Sports Studies* (London and New York: Routledge, 2010) have categorised the work of ourselves and of the Sport and Leisure Cultures researchers and scholars at Brighton as "critical interpretivism". Jim McKay, in his Introduction to a 'Special Issue: Sport Studies at the Chelsea School' edition of the *Journal of Sport & Social Issues*, observed that at that time "Brighton probably has the largest critical mass of critical scholars in the world", a "splendid example" of Wright Mills's sociological imagination, providing "a formidable alternative to positivistic orthodoxies in the social sciences". See Jim McKay, "The sociological imagination in practice at Brighton", *Journal of Sport & Social Issues*, 31/3, 2007: 205–207. It is out of that base of sustained and collective critical work that the critical pragmatism and critical pro-activism underpinning this book have been developed; see John Sugden, "Critical left-realism and sport interventions in divided societies", *International Review for the Sociology of Sport*, 45/3, 2010: 258–272.

12 Alison Kadlec, *Dewey's Critical Pragmatism* (Lanham: Rowan and Littlefield, 2007): 3.

13 We taught, together, several generations of undergraduates in a module on deviance at the University of Brighton in the early 2000s, and in that setting became convinced of the strength of the arguments made by proponents of left realism, and of the compatibility of these with our own evolving methodological position. At around the same time, we also taught final year undergraduates at the University of Sussex an option on the sociology of deviance, and their enthusiastic embrace of critical/left realist approaches reaffirmed for us the appropriateness of the approach. See David Downes and Paul Rock, *Understanding Deviance* (Oxford: Oxford University Press, 2003); Ian Taylor, *Crime in Context: A Critical Criminology of Market Societies* (Cambridge: Polity Press, 1999); John Lea, "Left realism: A defence", *Crime, Law and Social Change*, 11/4, 1987: 357–370; and Jock Young, "Left realist criminology", in *The Oxford Handbook of Criminology*, eds. Mike McGuire, Rod Morgan, and Robert Reiner (Oxford: Oxford University Press, 1997).

14 Ian McDonald, "Critical social research and political intervention: Moralistic versus radical approaches", in Sugden and Tomlinson eds., *Power Games*: 115.

15 Paolo Freire, *Pedagogy of the Oppressed* (New York, NY: Continuum, 1970); and Adam Curle, *To Tame the Hydra: Undermining the Culture of Violence* (London: John Carpenter Publishing, 1999).

16 Máire A. Dugan, "A nested theory of conflict", *A Leadership Journal: Women in Leadership – Sharing the Vision*, 1, 1996: 9–20.

17 John Paul Lederach, *The Moral Imagination: The Art and Soul of Building Peace* (New York: Oxford University Press, 2005).

18 Johan Galtung, *Peace by Peaceful Means: Peace and Conflict, Development and Civilization* (New York, NY: Sage, 1998).

19 Lisa Schirch, *Ritual and Symbol in Peacebuilding* (Boulder, Colorado: Lynne Rienner Publishers, 2005).

20 Lisa Schirch, "Ritual reconciliation: Transforming identity/reframing conflict", in *Reconciliation, Justice and Co-existence: Theory and Practice*, ed. Mohammed Abu-Nimer (New York: Lexington Books, 2001).
21 Howard Becker, "Whose side are we on?", *Social Problems*, 14, 1967: 239–247.
22 McDonald, "Critical social research": 106.
23 United Nations Declaration of Human Rights (1948). United Nations General Assembly, Paris.
24 John Alt, "Sport and cultural reification: From ritual to mass consumption", *Theory Culture and Society*, 1, 1983: 93–107; the quote is from p. 95.
25 See Christien van den Anker, "Global ethics and implications of globalization", in *Politics and Globalisation: Knowledge, Ethics and Agency*, ed. Martin Shaw (London and New York: Routledge, 1999), for some lucid discussion of the ethical (and deeply unsociological) implications of a Kantian commitment to the universalism of values cum ethics.

Chapter 7

Critical pro-activism and the ripple effect

Introduction

Based largely on personal journeys and the lived experience of others, and inter-related and accumulative case studies and contexts, Chapters 2, 3 and 4 featured empirical observations on the nature of the relationship between sport and peace processes. Those chapters represent the practice-based core of this sociological and interventionist project. The succeeding chapters outlined the key epistemological and theoretical issues and approaches brought to bear in the field in cycles of reflection and analysis. Together the practice and the theory have generated a way of thinking about and doing interventionist critical work in the areas of sport-related, civil society-based, peacebuilding initiatives. We related in the previous chapter our epistemological position of critical pragmatism. Informed by the fieldwork case studies and interventions, we present here a dynamic praxis-based version of critical pragmatism, formulated as 'critical pro-activism'.[1] This directly addresses the challenging problematic of practice itself; and we present in its fullest form the model that has been both fuelled by and generative of the interventionist practices in the deeply divided societies that have constituted the focus of the case studies – the Ripple Effect model. This model, we propose, depicts in comprehensive fashion how these theoretical and conceptual threads are woven together in articulation with the empirical evidence, to provide a template for planning and executing progressive, sport-based civil society projects in deeply divided societies.

We discussed Lederach's work in the previous chapter. Critical for the success of models such as his is the facilitation and management of the flow of communication between the three levels. Gavriel Salomon refers to such flows or processes as 'the ripple effect' through which the impact of peace education programmes spreads to wider social circles of society and eventually permeates overarching institutional and political frameworks.[2] The key values in this process are represented by those middle-level actors who have one foot in community cultures and the other in higher-level policy-making circles. It is through their input and output that lessons taken from work taking place at the grass-roots can be translated and transferred into constituencies that make use of it in the framing of broader public polices and political agendas. The ripple effect is most effectively created by identifying and building active partnerships with individuals representing organisations that have the proven capacities to operate between levels one, two and three as described by Lederach. As middle-level actors, as we argued in the previous chapter, they are ideally located to bring people together and weave dialogue, ideas and programmes across boundaries. By capitalising on access to and connections between key social spaces, they are able to spin what we call webs of sustainable relationships.

Critical to all of these approaches is the praxis element and through it the empowerment of subordinate actors and groups through their active participation in peace-building programmes and processes. This requires – again, embodying Wright Mills's distinct sociological mission – the creation of structures through which those experiencing the 'personal troubles' that attend those living in conflict zones can turn these into 'public issues', and so be part of creative programmes that allow them to contribute to progressive activities that can make a difference to their everyday lives. In this way grass-roots civil society activism can be seen to be influencing the thinking and manoeuvring of powerbrokers operating in civil society by creating a ripple effect that eventually washes over the shoes of those who walk in the corridors of power. We will conclude the study with a full presentation of the ripple effect in a model developed in part from Salomon's pioneering thinking. Before that, though, we consider the question of practice in a little more detail, including too reflections upon partnership relations essential for effective interventions.

Practice and praxis

In our book *Power Games: A Critical Sociology of Sport* (2002) we presented *critical* sociology as one of six overlapping elements characteristic of our sociological approach to researching sport: its importance is, of course, amplified in the subtitle of the book itself. At its simplest, we wrote in the opening chapter of that book, "to be critical is to be sceptical – that is, never take things at face value . . . seek out official statistics, but expecting them to be unreliable, in some cases even fraudulent; go in search of evidence that contradicts official wisdom . . . question authority".[3] It is this sense of the 'critical' that has consistently underpinned our research.[4] It is in an undeniable sense Gramscian, recognising the constructedness – and therefore the potential deconstruction – of 'common sense'; and carrying with it echoes of a Marxist commitment to praxis in both the sense that human agents are the architects of the world that they inhabit, and the sense that such agents can become the architects of renewal, reform and change. Some of that might be pie in the sky of course: to lay bare the features of commercial sport spectacle or the minutiae of the business economics of sport is hardly to threaten the media barons or the business opportunists (though it depends where, how and for whom one writes). But the point is to recognise the inherently critical nature of the analytical exercise. To engage in critical work with no or little sense of the potential impact of one's work in the world beyond the circuits of academic publication and communication, is to betray the second sense of praxis referred to above. This is not to say that critical work always has obvious repercussions and affects practices; too often it is too timid, not even seeking to reach out into the world of practices; too often it is undervalued when it does seek to reach out, elbowed aside by armchair theorists and dismissed as merely 'applied'. But critical work itself is by definition a form of cultural practice, potentially interventionist and imbued with an incipient agency of its own. Critique is indisputably practice.

Our developing framework of critical pro-activism has blended this critique with activist-inspired interventions, stimulated by the successive studies and cycles of analysis and research. Inevitably, this has required a principled commitment to collaboration and a pragmatic approach to partnership-building. We saw in Chapter 3 how in the context of Israel partners might represent perspectives far from our own social science-informed and academically anchored understandings of post-conflict situations, and the concomitant judgements we might make concerning the possibilities of change and inter-cultural understanding. There are undoubtedly significant advantages to be gained through forming partnerships with government organisations and related bodies, perhaps the most potent of which is access to funding, but to fall back on a well-worn cliché 'there is no such thing as a free lunch'. Perhaps the same can be said of all funding-driven partnerships forged in both the public and private sectors whereby the subservient client or organisation runs the risks of losing independence and endangering hard-earned reputations for neutrality and bottom-up community engagement. Such engagements can become tarnished with the broader geo-political positioning of the government agencies in question, and our interventions have run the recurring risk of being dragged into damaging institutional and interpersonal political quagmires not of our own choosing. Essentially, as sociologists who believe that the potential impact of our work belongs way beyond the comfort zone of the armchair theorist, we have had to be ready to make pragmatic decisions and accept varied outcomes, though we have been zealous in the transparency of our goals and ambitions, and in the commitment to a values-based approach to SDP that has informed the accumulative work.

Nevertheless, cross-sector engagement and partnerships are fraught with the potential for not mere misunderstandings but problems of potentially competing interests, and in not a few cases the problem of the breakdown of trust and the collapse of consensus. The F4P project has not been immune from such realities, and has experienced the damaging consequences of interpersonal and inter-institutional rivalries among key partners. We showed in Chapter 3 how we devolved our responsibility for the delivery of the projects to the Israel Ministry of Culture and Sport (IMCS), and always saw this as a positive phase in the dissemination and sustainability of the F4P initiative in Israel, but retrospectively it became clear that relations between key partners had begun to fracture. This was a consequence of the particular interests of agencies and their representatives, and the different visions for the future of the work that such agencies had. These agencies, at that point, included four primary partners: the University of Brighton; the British Council; the German Sports University; and the IMCS. Working relationships between these partners actually broke down. But, several years later a reconciliation took place when the IMCS's head of international relations met with the director of F4P and explained how F4P's legacy continued to be strong in Israel, and had shaped the country's ongoing sport-based community relations under a new title of 'Sport for Life'. Subsequent to this meeting the Israeli ministry sent a delegation of Sport for Life officials to Northern Ireland to observe F4P's work in Ireland in its partnerships with the Irish Football Association, Ulster Rugby, and Ulster GAA (Gaelic Athletic Association) – in doing so, leaving open the possibility of renewed collaboration between F4P and the Israeli ministry. While noting the perils of partnerships, these are outweighed by the positive outcomes of sustained and negotiated relationships, particularly when viewed in the long term.[5]

Overall, the peace-building work accomplished on the basis of the F4P model has been a form of values-based praxis, recognising culture – in the spheres of leisure, sport and popular culture – as a form of human agency with the capacity to contest and change cultural understanding, social relations and political orthodoxies. Sport could not be reduced to the Althusserian certainties of ideological apparatuses in the hands of the state, or Foucauldian frameworks depicting an omnipotent governmentality that seeped into the veins of the political, social and personal body.[6] Our presentations at NASSS in 1980 and 1981 and consequent publications have consistently embodied an engagement with the application of theory to sport in ways that deflects crude Marxist generalities, or sweeping grand theoretical accounts of sport's place in society.[7]

Critical pro-activism and peace-building: constraints, challenges and hope

As we have seen, peace processes are messy affairs: hugely complex enterprises that move forwards or backwards according to conditions prevalent in the transcending social and political order. Usually they are driven by activities and actors in political society. However, where there are major social and cultural impediments, 'road maps to peace' that take account of the political sphere alone are doomed to failure. Changes of heart and mind do not ordinarily take place because of political initiatives. Peace is only possible when significant proportions of ordinary people are ready for and open to conflict-resolution. By way of illustration, politicians may be in the driving seat but for the 'peace bus' to get anywhere meaningful along its road map there must be passengers willing to climb on board. This comes gradually through social and cultural engagement in everyday life. The challenge for peace activists is to discover ways to join up specific grass-roots, civil-society based, interventions with more broadly influential policy communities and those elements of political society that hold the keys to peace.

The giant jigsaw puzzle evoked at the end of the preceding chapter cannot, therefore, be solved without the benefit of having a picture on the box. There are political pieces, economic pieces, military pieces and cultural pieces. For the picture to be imagined and completed all of these pieces will have a part to play and while some – for instance the political corner pieces – may have more significance than others, all the pieces will be necessary for the picture of peace to fully emerge. In the specific contexts of peace processes in deeply divided societies, like South Africa and Northern Ireland, retrospectively we can see that, while not providing the most important pieces in each region's complex jigsaw of peace and reconciliation, sport does occupy a significant place in each completed picture. We began the work in Israel and Palestine a decade and a half before the completion of this book, yet still the picture of the jigsaw of peace is hard to visualise, not remotely complete. Those of us who choose to try to use sport as a civil society formation through which to influence broader agendas do so in the belief that when peace does come to this most troubled of regions and we look back at the events that contributed to that peace, we will at least be able to identify the positive role played there by inter-community sport.

A recurrent question for peace-building is: how and where to intervene? To begin with, the notion of 'peace' is itself an elusive and problematic concept embracing a variety of meanings from 'the absence of war' to 'a state of equilibrium and tranquillity', and many things in between. We have argued earlier in this study that sport in and of itself has no magical qualities, but is nevertheless a very flexible crucible into which we can pour ideas and ideals based on notions of human rights and social justice. As we have seen in the previous chapter, John Alt argued against structuralist theorists' reduction of sport to mere commodity or ideology, emphasising the emancipatory capacities of play and the connection of sport and fair play to models of social justice: fairness in life, loyalty, tolerance – the very principles that have been at the heart of the F4P work.[8] In the same year, Rick Gruneau's brilliant study *Class, Sports and Social Development* was published, and began with a sophisticated dissection of arguments concerning "problems of agency and freedom in play, games and sport", the title of its opening chapter.[9] There is too a strand within earlier neo-Marxist thought, best represented by the Frankfurt School, that acknowledges the dialectical potential of sport and related play forms within culture. Traces of this can be found in the works of Lukács, Marcuse and Adorno, but the preeminent voice on this theme is that of Ernst Bloch. In his magnum opus, *The Principle of Hope*, Bloch revives the utopianism present in many of the writings of the younger Marx and grounds it in a critique of the material conditions of everyday life. For Bloch, for progressive social change to occur, human actors must be able to construct a vision of a better future: in other words, to hope and then move beyond hope to purposive action or praxis.

Bloch's conceptualisation of hope combines elements of philosophy, theology, aesthetics and sociology in a running engagement with the works of Marxist and no-Marxist thinkers such as George Lukács and the doyen of the Frankfurt School of critical theory, Theodor Adorno. Bloch argued that art and culture must not be reduced to the "ideology of a particular ruling class", the mere "propagandist servant" of that class; rather, it should be recognised that there is a "utopian perspective of every great work of art".[10] Culture, for Bloch, therefore carries within it an innate potential for change, and his category of "hope" is central to his core proposition that in an age of enlightenment a sense of "more", that which is always "beyond" what already is, fuels a hope-filled consciousness. In an explicit attempt to combat resignation or defeatism, Bloch offers what he also calls a "plus-ultra of philosophy" which:

> need never capitulate before empirical method when the latter degenerates into a reified empiricism of fact; and of course it must never lose contact with process-empiricism, if its aspiration is not to become abstract eccentricity, and its ascent a descent.[11]

We see here an argument comparable to Wright Mills's critique of the excesses of the methodological and epistemological extremes of abstracted empiricism and grand theory, an argument that places a relatively optimistic world outlook at the heart of the critical method. One does not, in such an approach, critically analyse in order merely to condemn, but in order to identify and potentially launch alternative futures. Bloch's work posits a future achieved through critical interventions and hope-driven consciousness; critique and hope themselves are forms of agency, constantly in the making or remaking once the permanence of hope is recognised. "We are not here to eat but to cook; dining comes later and last", he wrote in his collection of aphorisms, anecdotes and reflections, *Spuren* (*Traces*).[12] For Bloch the "not-yet" feeds the here and now; our vision of the future must include a sense of how our societies and cultures are flawed and unfinished, but our consciousness and hope-oriented aspirations can be channelled into more humane or progressive forms of living and being. For Bloch, like Marx himself, this is a pragmatically realist rather than idealist project within which the possibilities that come with hope – most eloquently experienced through the daydream – are anchored in everyday experiences.[13] The critical issues become finding the out-of-structure space within which to experience the daydream and construct a ladder through the climbing of which that daydream can become reality. Drawing upon Bloch's core concepts and ideas – of the utopian future and the permanence of hope – we have used metaphors of utopian landscapes for the sub-titles of several of the foregoing chapters; in some cases, with a hint of irony. But we remain convinced that carefully constructed and executed SDP programmes can provide windows of opportunity through which visions of better futures can be imagined and appetites for progressive movement toward such futures cultivated.

Using Bloch's "principle of hope" framework to analyse one such sport-based intervention, the F4P work, John Doyle argues that

> utopia's great gift is to allow us the critical toolkit to imagine how the future might evolve. Sport as utopia therefore also provides us an opportunity to continue the journey, to glimpse into the future. It gives us a critical framework to assess the development and metamorphosis of sport institutions. . . . It provides a lens that refracts the future possibilities being created in the present.[14]

Critique, practice and hope, inter-related forms of agency – these are the motors of the peace-building/SDP work represented by the cases and interventions reported in this book, which concludes with the reaffirmation of the model whereby our framework of critical pro-activism can be seen to generate change, challenging the status quo and shifting discourse through informed interventionist practices.

SDP interventions: F4P and the ripple effect[15]

The different elements of thinking outlined so far in this study can be woven together to provide a theoretical and methodological reference point for practical engagement in SDP work. The "ripple effect" model represented in Figure 7.1 on the following page draws on critical left-realism to depict how this form of praxis can be achieved.

In this diagram the outer circle represents a human rights context, the locus of which is framed by the prevailing transcending social and political context, including the status of the peace process, represented by the next circle. Taken together they provide a framework upon which to make pragmatic and realistic judgements about the structure and content of any given project and its development goals. The two inner circles represent the actual programme itself. The bull's eye represents the core target participants, children and youth from different stakeholder communities. The second circle, surrounding the bull's eye, comprises adult volunteer coaches and significant others (relatives, teachers, community leaders, political figures etc.) from the local communities, and includes any international volunteers. The nature of the structure, organisation, management and delivery of activities and encounters taking place within these two inner circles is crucial in determining the outcome of any such sport intervention. In between,

130 Critical pro-activism

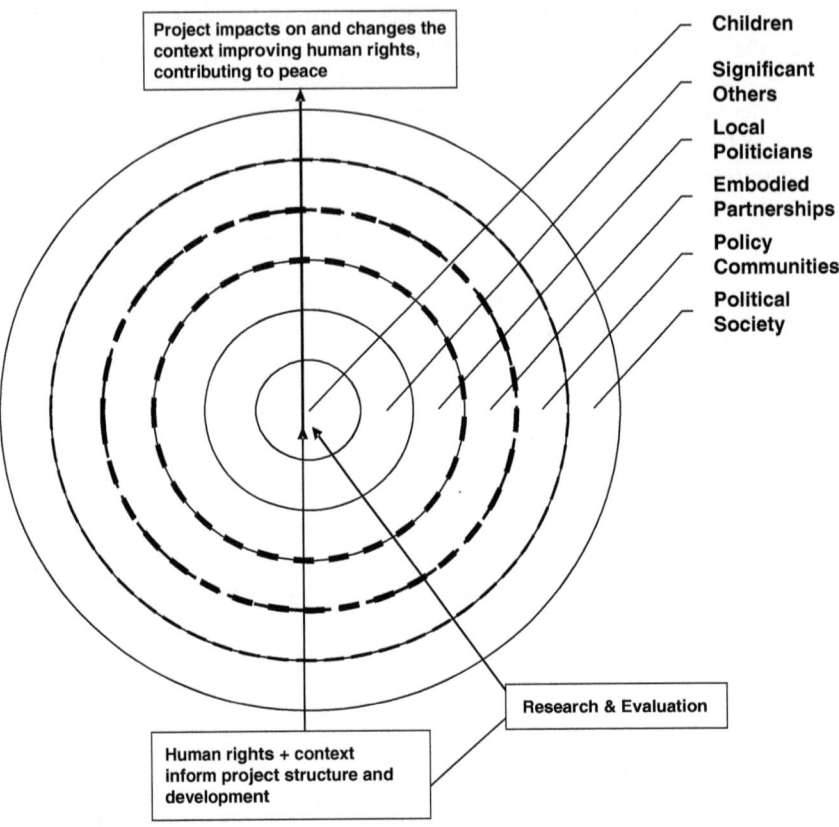

Figure 7.1 The Ripple Effect: Centres, Peripheries, Networks and Cycles of Feedback and Renewal

working from the middle outwards, the next circle represents the medium of knowledge transfer, comprising active representatives from a network of institutional partners through whom ideas and findings emanating from the project can be articulated within the wider policy community for sport. This in turn may act back upon and influence processes taking shape in the transcending social and political context and have an impact on the local human rights situation not only of those directly involved in the project but also further afield. Each level of the process is subject to research and evaluation and these findings are fed back to inform project modification, growth and redevelopment. The different thicknesses and permeability of the concentric circles is to indicate that, just like a stone dropped into a still pool of water, as the image in Figure 7.2 visualises, the ripple effect of an intervention like F4P dissipates as it moves further from the centre where the impact is more obviously felt and more easily measured.

Figure 7.2

In relation to the research and interventions reported throughout this book, children and youth have been absolutely central to the projects; they are the future and the carriers of hope. In our evaluations and research in Israel this was something recognised by parents themselves, who realised that whilst it was perhaps too late for them to make significant changes to the socio-political context and its conflict-ridden legacies, encouraging their children to participate in F4P could establish conditions and circumstances of potential change, progress in the direction of peaceful co-existence. Thus sport alone may not change the world but children playing with their enemies might.

We hope in this book to have demonstrated the underpinning dynamic of critical pro-activism as it has culminated in the development of the model presented in the diagram above. As we have shown, the deep roots of the F4P model are buried in Northern Ireland, where Belfast United created a snowball that rolled on to Israel, in so doing bringing with it the learning gleaned from the first-ever sport-based conflict-resolution and peace-building initiative to have been researched and published. Adapting the Belfast United design to the context of Israel generated new information and new learning that could be incorporated into the modified F4P model, which then could be further rolled out into new and different socio-cultural and political contexts such as South Africa, Gambia and South Korea. In the Korean case, for instance, the F4P model proved to be a ready-made implementation framework for the Korean Sharing Movement, enabling peace activists to access funding and political support. Such a snowballing process, that has underpinned the cross-cultural impacts and international expansion of F4P, produces knowledge that can be transferable, but always depending upon the context. This, we argue, is a prepotent and accumulative process, as the snowball metaphor implies. And in this continuing process, F4P has continued to be approached by potential partners, in Rwanda and Columbia most recently, for example. These snowballing effects are critical to the maximisation of the impact of the interventions, at all of the local, the national and the international levels. The scale of implementation can be modest, the model applied at club or community level. The FA (England) supported F4P from 2003 to 2008, some of its coaches and development personnel attending the project in Israel, and at complementary events. FA tutor Richard Astle, at the Derby County Football Club's Community Trust, tells how he "utilised the F4P model in a number of its programmes designed to be delivered in geographical areas where conflict resolution and equality are issues of particular significance", and in anti-racism projects in schools "much of which was based on the philosophy of co-operation and 'teaching moments' as utilised during the F4P delivery programme." Or the scale can be ambitiously framed, as in the Korea context, to wrestle with some of the highest-profile conflict situations in the world. The Ripple Effect model can illuminate interventions across this range of operation and aspiration.[16]

Of course, as Michael Mann reminds us societies "are much messier than our theories of them",[17] and the lived reality of any peace-building intervention is decidedly more fluid, complex and fickle than this perhaps simplistic-sounding, ripple-effect model might imply. In many ways the reality is more like Lederach's 'web approach' to peace-building as discussed in this and the previous chapter, whereby, starting with a small focus, the strategy is to build organic networks of relationships among individuals, communities and institutions around the delivery, development and expansion of that focus. Like a real spider's web, the more threads there are, the thicker they get; and the more anchor points they have, the more robust they will become, thus enabling them to better withstand potential damage, and be more amenable to repair should such damage occur. Finally, the above figure is a heuristic representation, a classically Weberian ideal-type, of what in reality is an embodied process.[18] The success and transferability of any such endeavour will depend on the animation and agency provided by key actors operating across and between each level of activity, set against the prevailing politics of the times. But we believe that this is a model that works. However incrementally, the effects of the interventions that feature centrally in this study have shifted perceptions, broadened experiences, challenged ethnocentrism, changed – and, in all likelihood also saved – lives. Playing with the enemy is more than just a catchphrase: it is a vital strategy for the survival of sport as a credible source of inter-cultural understanding in an increasingly volatile and troubled global order.

Notes

1 John Sugden, "Beyond *Power Games*: Critical pro-activism in Sport and Leisure Studies, the Brighton approach", in ICSSPE Bulletin Number 68 (Special Feature on *Critical Pro-Activism and the "Brighton Effect"*), 6 October 2015, online publication.

2 Gavriel Salomon, "The nature of peace education: Not all programs are created equal", in *Peace Education: The Concept, Principles and Practices Around the World*, eds. Gavriel Salomon and Baruch Nevo (Mahweh, NJ and London: Lawrence Erlbaum Associates, Publishers, 2002). Saloman's sense of 'peace education' complements our own view that the overall, transcending social and political context must be understood for effective work and interventions in the field: "the socio-political context in which peace education takes place supersedes" all other considerations (p. 5), he states, going on to offer a threefold classification of categories of contexts for peace education: "regions of intractable conflict … regions of interethnic tension … regions of experienced tranquility" (p. 6). He places Northern Ireland and Israel in the first of these categories. South Africa, in the post-apartheid era, would be an example of the second category. Salomon's first of four challenges for peace education is the creation of a "ripple effect" (which can be short-term or long-term in its effects) whereby programs can spread out to the wider society. See Gavriel Saloman, "Four major challenges facing peace education in regions of intractable conflict", *Peace and Conflict: Journal of Peace Psychology*, 17/1, 2011: 46–59. For the development of the model in the F4P context, see John Sugden, "The ripple effect: Critical pragmatism, conflict resolution and peace building through sport in deeply divided societies", in *Global Sport-for-Development: Critical Perspectives*, eds. Nico Schulenkorf and Daryl Adair (Basingstoke: Palgrave Macmillan, 2014).
3 John Sugden and Alan Tomlinson eds., *Power Games: A Critical Sociology of Sport* (London and New York: Routledge, 2002): 11.
4 This short discussion of critique as practice draws upon Alan Tomlinson, "Theorising a critical politics of sport", presentation at Political Studies Association Inaugural Meeting of Sport Group, University of Reading, April 6th 2006; oral text of presentation, see Alan Tomlinson typepad blog, 2 November 2006.
5 John Sugden with Graham Spacey, "SDP partnerships and the Government sector: Mana from heaven or Faustian pacts?", paper presented at University of Illinois Symposium, *Sport for Development and Peace*, 7–8 March 2017.
6 For the classic Althusserian take on sport, see Jean-Marie Brohm, *Sport: A Prison of Measured Time* (London: Ink Links, 1978). On the potential of a Foucauldian framework for illuminating how the mechanisms of power and the processes of governmentality work in the SDP world, see Jacob Naish, "Sport for development and peace: Alignment, administration, power", in *Routledge Handbook of Sport and Politics*, eds. Alan Bairner, John Kelly, and Jung Woo Lee (London and New York: Routledge, 2017).
7 John Sugden, "Sport and the dialectics of freedom in capitalist society", presented at NASSS, Denver, Colorado. November 1980; Alan Tomlinson, "The sociological imagination, the New Journalism, and sport", presented at NASSS, Fort Worth, TX, November 1981.
8 John Alt, "Sport and cultural reification: From ritual to mass consumption", *Theory, Culture and Society*, 1, 1983: 93–107, p. 95.
9 Richard Gruneau, *Class, Sports, and Social Development* (Amherst: The University of Massachusetts Press, 1983).
10 Ernst Bloch, *A Philosophy of the Future* (New York: Herder and Herder, 1970): 95.
11 Ibid., 10–11.
12 The quotation from Bloch's *Spuren* is cited in David Gross, "Ernst Bloch: The dialectics of hope", in *The Unknown Dimension: European Marxism Since Lenin*, eds. Dick Howard and Karl E. Klare (New York: Basic Books, 1972): 108.
13 Ernst Bloch, *The Principle of Hope: Volume 1* (Cambridge, MA: MIT Press, 1986) on "daydreams" and "everyday flights of fancy" as elements of anticipatory consciousness.

14 John Doyle, *Interventionist Sport as Mediatized Utopia: A Practice-Informed Critique of Football 4 Peace*, unpublished PhD thesis, University of Brighton, Brighton, 2012: 16.
15 The discussion of the "ripple effect" in this section draws upon the first publication on the emerging model in John Sugden, "Critical left-realism and sport interventions in divided societies", *International Review for the Sociology of Sport*, 45/3, 2010: 258–272, see pp. 268–270.
16 The Derby example was provided by Jane Bateman, Head of International Relations at The Football Association, in personal correspondence to the authors, 15 November 2013.
17 Michael Mann, *The Sources of Social Power: Vol. 1: A History of Power From the Beginning to A.D. 1760* (Cambridge: Cambridge University Press, 1986).
18 See Max Weber, *The Methodology of the Social Sciences* (New York: The Free Press, 1949) for discussion of the development of ideal-types as an heuristic method for what he labelled "a critique of concept-construction" that is central to advances in the social sciences that are "tied up with" shifts in "practical cultural problems" (p. 106).

Appendixes

Materials underpinning the Football 4 Peace (F4P) project

The Appendix comprises five documents, which are cross-referenced from appropriate chapters in the book, particularly Chapter 3 which covers the emergence and maturation of the Football 4 Peace research in Israel. The materials have been translated into Hebrew, Arabic and Korean and developed and adopted in an increasing number of theatres of conflict,

A   Football4Peace: The 2004 version of the values-based Coaching Manual
B   Excerpts from the Off-Pitch Activities Manual
C   A list of individuals who have contributed to the ongoing consolidation and adaptation of the manuals
D   Testimonials on the application and impact of Football4Peace in Ireland, Israel and South Africa
E   Excerpts from South Africa Coaching Manual

Appendix A

Football 4 Peace F4P
Coaching manual [early draft] 2004

Football 4 Peace (F4P) project: draft of coaching manual

Rationale

"Sport does have a meaningful and powerful role to play in the social transformation of society if care is taken to provide the necessary conditions for success." (Archbishop Desmond Tutu, South Africa, 1993).

In a world plagued with conflict, it is often claimed that sport can help to achieve what politics fails to do: provide otherwise warring parties with a neutral vehicle for communication and a medium for conflict prevention and resolution.

Soccer, 'the people's game', in particular, it is argued, provides a universal language through which those in dispute with one another can find common ground. No better example of this can be found than the impromptu truce and soccer games that took place on Christmas Day 1914 in which entrenched solders from rival British and German regiments left their positions to play football together and exchange gifts and cigarettes in the mud of no-mans-land. If this can happen during history's bloodiest and most brutal conflict, it can happen at any other time and anywhere else.

Let us not forget, however, that the fabled Christmas day truce came at the Great War's beginning, not its end. The antagonists returned to the trenches to once more take up arms, in some cases at the gunpoint of their own officers; simply playing a game in the midst of conflict is of course unlikely to have a long-lasting impact on peace. Meaningful sport-based peace projects need to be seen as part of a long game, a series of carefully structured sporting experiences that, alongside a wide variety of cultural, educational, economic and political interventions can make an important contribution to the peace process.

This is the starting point for F4P, but not the end. Unless carefully managed, history also tells us that bringing rival groups together in sporting competition can lead to more and not less conflict. We believe that it is not just playing the game that is important, but crucially how the game is played, what the spirit of the contest is, how long the game lasts, and what is learned and taken from the field of play.

The aims of most standard soccer training schedules is to enhance ball skills alongside the development of technical and tactical understanding. In most cases, an unintended but inevitable consequence of a good coaching programme is that players learn to work and play together in groups and teams.

The F4P coaching programme highlights the social and fraternal attributes of soccer in such a way that those who participate not only develop knowledge specific to soccer, but also consciously and unconsciously adopt, practise, and endorse the fundamental principles of fair play and good citizenship. In this regard, the F4P coaching programme is designed to be especially effective in areas where civil society is fragile and there are high levels of community division and social conflict.

Specifically, through participation in fair sport, F4P aims to:

- Provide opportunities for social contact across community boundaries;
- Promote mutual understanding;
- Engender in participants a desire for and commitment to peaceful coexistence;
- Enhance soccer skills and technical knowledge.

In addition to the enhancement of soccer skills and technical knowledge, the project emphasises the following principles and learning objectives:

1. Neutrality
2. Equity and Inclusion
3. Respect
4. Trust
5. Responsibility

F4P's Five Principles of Fair Play

1. Neutrality
   F4P is a politics-free zone. Those who participate in F4P – players, coaches, parents, administrators – leave their political views and ideological positions outside. This does not mean changing political and ideological standpoints – this is not our business – but we do require that such positions are not expressed in and around the F4P experience.
2. Equity and Inclusion
   Within F4P all participants are treated equally and the commitment to equality is recognised in the way that practices and games are organised

and run. Those who want to play can play regardless of ethnicity, race, religion, gender, or ability.

3   Respect
The appreciation of one's own individuality and the value of others in a context of social diversity calls for respect. Respect for oneself, respect for team mates and opponents, respect for coaches and parents, and respect for the laws of the game and those that administer them are essential features of F4P.

4   Trust
Players that trust one another play well together. Learning to have faith in the capacities of others to carry out their roles and responsibilities dutifully and mutually, in ways that also contribute to the wellbeing of team mates, is an essential ingredient of good sportsmanship.

5   Responsibility.
With trust comes responsibility, the understanding that individual behaviour in practice sessions and in games influences and has impact upon the performance and experience of others. Working with and for others are key aspects of F4P Projects. Success in sport, particularly team sport, relies upon mutual aid and self-sacrifice.

The programme

In the following section we outline a wide range of themed coaching sessions within which, alongside skills and technical understanding, the five principles of fair play are at various levels emphasised, learned, and revisited. In practice, it is expected that these five principles can be applied and will be apparent within a variety of coaching sessions. However, for the purpose of this project we have highlighted and emphasised one particular principle and coaching theme for each of the five coaching sessions.

Each session follows a similar pattern:

Introduction to the principle and the theme and warm-up activity

It is within this that the selected F4P Fair Play principle will be briefly explained and the coaching theme introduced. Particular focus upon the principle in question will be given during the warm-up session and practices have been designed to best facilitate this.

Main coaching period

This part of the session will be structured around the selected coaching theme (for instance heading or shooting) and skill development will be the main focus. However, as much as possible, practices have been designed to emphasise co-operation through working in pairs or small groups.

Small-sided conditioned games

At this point the children are introduced to a variety of small-sided games within which the identified coaching theme is given prominence. Alongside this the dynamics of team-building are practiced.

Warm-down

At the end of the session the children are engaged in some warm-down activities during which they are taught how to stretch and relax muscles and generally cool down. While they are doing this coaches briefly revisit some of the key points related to the coaching skill and selected F4P principle. It is during this period that coaches recall some of the best features of the day's session with a particular emphasis on good examples of the selected F4P principle working in practice.

Teachable moments

The examples of good practices alluded to above are known as 'teachable moments'. This refers to those incidents and events that happen during the flow of the practices that the coach can seize upon to illustrate the main points that he or she is trying to get over to the children. Once more this is especially important in terms of helping to translate some of the five F4P principles, which are concepts and abstractions, into practical examples. For instance, during a session dedicated to turning, while trying to get the group execute a particularly difficult turn, the coach sees one child who has mastered the skill help to teach one of the others who has not. The coach can then stop the practice and have the youngster demonstrate how he helped his colleague. This not only helps in the teaching of the coaching skill but also give the coach the opportunity to talk briefly about this as an example of taking responsibility.

The F4P contract

Football played and practised in the spirit of F4P's principles is highly satisfying and very enjoyable for everybody. Games that are most fair are also games that are most fun. F4P is a social activity requiring the development of physical and technical skills and the forming of relationships in fun-filled settings. As such F4P projects are designed to provide the basis for lasting friendships for all involved.

For this to be achieved it is important that all those who are involved in F4P, whether they are players, coaches, match officials, administrators, or parents must accept and act in accordance with the principles upon which F4P is based. It is particularly important that all coaches endorse and embody these principles as coaches serve as role models for the young people with whom they work.

The core themes and principles mentioned earlier are further emphasised and achieved by motivating the group through enthusiastic verbal and physical actions, physical contact such as high fives, hand shakes, team or individualised hand shakes, team cheer, group huddles, warm-up type activities, buddy systems, team talks, saying hello in each other's language, and learning someone else's physical greeting.

For group cohesion and bonding to be achieved it is essential to have some ground rules in place before the session starts such as no put downs, encouraging other team members when they make a mistake, giving praise to each other, listening to who is talking and not interrupting, getting to know everyone in your group, working with someone different as often as possible, and making collective decisions.

At the beginning of each session the theme of the day is stressed and a joint definition of each of the core values is the starting point. For example, the group may decide their own interpretation of what Respect, Trust, Responsibility, Neutrality, and Equity/Inclusion mean to them. This could be related to the game where children show respect for opponents, team mates, officials, understanding that everyone is trying their best and respecting their efforts. Discussion points can be built upon such as how you earn respect, what makes you respect another person. What do you think of disrespectful behaviour? All of these guidelines can be used for each of the other core values associated with the F4P project.

When planning for each session it is particularly important that the central focus is upon the core value highlighted on the day and that through the medium of football a series of individual, co-operative and competitive tasks is used such as ice-breakers, getting acquainted, building trust and cooling down.

Staffing and recruitment

The rationale and aims for the project are clearly established. Another crucial process that must be addressed is to recruit the right people to coach the young people in our care and train them to follow the F4P coaching guidelines.

The project will only be as good as the people that are staffing it. A team of coaches has been recruited that reflects the diverse nature of the communities that are represented on the project. These coaches are open-minded, adaptable, effective communicators, have experience of teaching football and are committed to conflict resolution/peaceful co-existence in their society. A coaching qualification is an advantage but not essential. It is to be expected that such people will vary in age, gender, background and vocation. Such diversity will be one of the strengths of the scheme.

This football coaching manual is designed as a tool to help cross-community tolerance and understanding. It has a set of clearly stated values that permeate through the programme from start to finish. The operation of these values will be critical to the success of the conflict prevention and reconciliation aims. We have identified the values which will underpin our project. The next step is to ensure all coaches have a grasp of each one and to convince the coaches and sports administrators of the importance of these values.

A planned programme of training that all the coaches attend prior to working with the players will be beneficial to the success of the project. This will have the purpose of establishing aims, setting out the shared values of the programme, developing teaching techniques that are effective in this context, and building positive working relationships between all those concerned.

Some of the coaches themselves may well be from the divided society that they are working in and may arrive with certain strong political, ideological and religious 'baggage'. Although nobody is asking these people not to hold certain views, the success of the scheme depends on the assumption that any views which run contrary to the aims and values on which the project is based are abandoned at least for the duration of the project. Anyone involved who feels that they cannot do this should withdraw from the project. Social cohesion between the coaches is essential and any possible areas of conflict should be avoided. Likewise any behaviour from the coaches that may undermine our stated values and serve as a bad example to those being coached must also be avoided.

For the July project a day is set aside in the training schedule of the coaches for an introduction to the project which will set out the aims and objectives followed by some team building, problem-solving and trust games. As far as possible these will be organised so that the coaches that will be working together at each venue are placed in the same social grouping. By the end of the training programme each cluster of coaches will know each other very well and should have established a sound working relationship. Education for mutual understanding through sport is a major theme running through the F4P project and this applies to the coaches as much as the players.

Once the aims and values are established and a positive relationship is cemented between each group of coaches they then need to be trained in the best methods of teaching these values to the young people in their care during the football project. We set out below some strategies for coaches to use when coaching football with an emphasis on peaceful co-existence and reconciliation. The success of the whole programme is based on accepting the F4P values as being of crucial importance to the project, understanding his/her role in modelling them at all times, having the ability to recognise these concepts in action.

The F4P values will be top of the coaching agenda throughout each session. Each session will focus on a certain value which will be introduced through a warm-up. This warm-up will not follow a traditional format of pulse-raiser and progressive stretching to prepare physically for the activity. It will include a trust game to introduce a theme based on the F4P values followed by an introductory physical activity which will follow the same theme. During the skill-learning and games elements of the session the coach will be observing for teachable moments where he/she can draw attention to situations when one of the F4P values is either violated or, even better, demonstrated in a positive way. These teachable moments can either be addressed at the time or later during the cool-down. The cool-down will consist of a combination of gentle physical activities based around the values theme of the day and some discussion of the teachable moments. It should be a plenary phase that consolidates the players' understanding of the notion that each abstract value can be attached to specific behaviours and attitudes that may be exhibited in the session. Ultimately, it is our aim that these behaviours and attitudes are transferred to life beyond the football field.

We are going to ask coaches to coach football using a format and a style that may be alien to them. In order that they can adapt from a traditional coaching approach (which has an emphasis on learning the skills and game principles) to a player-centred approach that emphasises personal and social development, certain issues need to be addressed. Any training of coaches that takes place, whether on or off the field, should cover the principles that are set out below.

Shared values

Each project may be different in terms of the issues that divide their community. However, we have identified a set of values that we believe are fundamental to any football project that aims at conflict prevention and reconciliation. It is not an exhaustive list of values that support our philosophy and can be added to. It is a set of values that we feel are important and generic to this type of football 4 peace programme.

Under the heading FAIR PLAY, to reiterate, we advocate the following values:

Respect, Trust, Responsibility, Neutrality and Inclusion/Equity.

Our aim is to develop these values in all the players through competition, learning, co-operation and friendship with an emphasis on fun and enjoyment.

The teaching that takes place will be based on players being able to recognise these concepts in action and learning to model them. Remember that by the end of the programme the young people involved should be able to attach each value to specific behaviours and attitudes. The main purpose of the project is that they transfer these behaviours to life beyond the football pitch.

Coaching principles

Organisation: Every coaching session needs to be discussed and planned in collaboration with the rest of your coaching cluster. It must follow the structure laid down in the F4P manual although there may be variations in the practices used within each section. Keep to the times allocated for warm-up, coaching phase and cool-down so that one aspect is not neglected. Ensure that the equipment needed for your sessions is always ready.

Communication: Working with three languages can be very challenging for a teacher. Use the coaches from each community to translate small chunks of information at any one time. Take time for this to be done properly. Try to explain certain points by gesture and body language. Use demonstration to explain practices and skills.

Manner: Every coach will need to look like a football coach. Wear football-related clothes and shoes. Always come across as upbeat and relaxed with fun being a priority. Young people learn most effectively when they are enjoying themselves so avoid conflict, boredom, inactivity and lectures in the sessions.

Observation: This underrated aspect of a coach's repertoire is particularly important in a programme with a focus on personal and social behaviour. Not only will the coach need to step back and check that the practice is running smoothly and the players are performing appropriately but he/she will be observing for those vital teachable moments. There will usually be three coaches with each group so one would hope that the majority of examples of behaviours relevant to the F4P values will be observed.

Evaluation/Reflection: These skills will be vital to the F4P coach. Apart from the usual evaluation of the effectiveness of the session, the coach will need to be able to use the cool-down to reflect on the teachable moments. He/she will need to articulate as simply as possible to the players, through the translators, the connection between the F4P values and their behaviour.

Learning principles

Modelling: People learn through observing and interacting with others. This has implications for the coach as a role model. Being a positive role model involves:

- Conducting yourself in the way that you would want your players to act

- Showing respect for the players
- Being positive about losing
- Being consistent with rules
- Not arguing with referees and other coaches
- Using only language that you want your players to use
- Admitting mistakes
- Showing the same standards that you are expecting of your players
- Understanding the needs of your players
- Taking responsibility for your group of players in terms of their behaviour and safety

Dialogue: As already stated, the handling of dialogue is not easy when in a trilingual situation. However, dialogue is an essential element of each phase of the coaching session. Good practice in promoting dialogue will be characterised by the coach:

- Being a facilitator of dialogue and not a lecturer
- Asking effective questions and giving people sufficient time to answer
- Allowing time for reflection
- Knowing how and when to incorporate dialogue
- Offering feedback

Dialogue is an interactive process between coach and players and between players themselves.

Rewards: The coach will have certain rules for the people involved in the session and these may be related to the F4P values. It may be that the equipment is set out each day by a different pair of players; this will emphasise responsibility. Rules, therefore, are connected to values. The reward for efficient assistance with the equipment may be recognition or first choice of position. Alternatively, a breach of a rule such as a put down showing disrespect may lead to a consequence, for example an apology or a substitution from a game.

Developing positive relationships: Personal and social development usually takes place within the context of a relationship. Healthy relationships provide people with a safe place where they can grow. To create positive relationships with young people a coach should follow the following principles:

- Give time to the players to think about the activities and give your time to players if they need encouragement or deserve praise
- Give attention to those who need it (who are not always those that demand it)

- Listening to the players will help to understand problems and allow them to articulate their views. Sometimes repeat the sentence back to the player without any subjective judgement as this type of active listening allows them to hear their own thoughts and maybe answer their own questions
- Empathy is the ability to understand their feelings, thoughts and issues. Young people are more likely to listen to guidance if they think that you understand them
- Show respect for them. Talk to them as you would an adult and listen to their opinions
- Give them direction and limits as they need boundaries to their behaviour just as they need them around their pitches. The rules and guidelines that you give them are their parameters. If these rules come with a set of consequences that are consistent they will feel more secure
- There are also times when children need to be independent, show responsibility and develop the confidence to make judgements for themselves

Creating an environment of physical and emotional safety is an important role for every coach involved in the F4P project.

Structure of coaching sessions

It is expected that there will be some autonomy for coaches in their choice of drills and practices within a theme. Each coach will have their own style of delivery. There is, however, a standard F4P structure for each session. It consists of three phases:

The warm up (approximately 20 minutes)
- This section will include a team-building or trust exercise
- The values theme for the day will be introduced. It may involve some simple goal-setting by the players or the coach eg. demonstrating respect by playing the whole game without questioning the referee's decision.
- The coach will set the agenda for group dialogue in this phase. It will be proactive and based around the chosen theme of the session
- Other football-related activities in the Warm Up will both connect to one of the F4P values, and prepare the players physically for the next phase

The technical and game phase (T&G) (approximately 80 minutes)

This phase will be made up of technical practices and small-sided games that place the players in learning situations where the five F4P values may be highlighted. Teachable moments will occur that the coach can pick up on either as they happen or during the cool-down. These will be concrete examples of the abstract concepts/values.

The cool down (approximately 20 minutes)

This phase directly follows the T&G phase. It consists of a closing physical activity that will consolidate learning and some group discussion of reactive topics based upon the teachable moments. These are based around the F4P values. The children can then easily see the connection between values and behaviour. The coach can use questions – What? So what? Now what? – on which to base his and the players' reflections on teachable moments.

Dealing with competition

Sport is, by its very nature, competitive. The challenge for the F4P coach is to present competition as part of the learning process, an opportunity to show improvement. He/she should take the emphasis away from winning and losing and place it on skill development and improvement. During the games section the coach will need to emphasise performance goals rather than focus on outcome goals. Young people should be taught to retain the F4P values in competitive pressure situations.

The training and education of coaches into the F4P methods and ethos is a crucial part of the project. They will then be prepared with the practical and theoretical knowledge to deliver the programme of coaching.

Authors: John Lambert, Gary Stidder, John Sugden and Andy Theodoloudes, 2003/04

Appendix B

Football 4 Peace: edited extracts from an off-pitch activity programme for conflict-prevention and peaceful co-existence

Team Building *Shared Decision-Making* *Problem-Solving*
Trust Games *Orienteering* *Life Saving* *Swimming*

The purpose of this manual is to highlight some of the germane issues that pertain to the teaching of Outdoor Education and swimming activities and to identify some principles and practices that can help community leaders provide Off-Pitch programmes within the F4P project. Furthermore, this manual aims to provide leaders with a rationale for the inclusion of Outdoor Education, and a potential activity programme – a blueprint of sorts – that may address some of the concerns amongst volunteers to the project. These suggestions intend to provide leaders with ideas of how to introduce Outdoor Education within safe and manageable environments without the need for specialist equipment, national governing body qualifications, or particular expertise.

A rationale for the inclusion of outdoor adventurous activities

The over-riding rationale for the inclusion of Outdoor Education within the off-pitch activity programme is based upon the notion that all children are entitled to a range of experiences that can enhance their personal, physical, and social education . . . For example, outdoor education can help to develop physical, personal and social skills which can have a positive effect on pupils' behaviour and attitudes. Proponents of outdoor education have also recognised that it can provide challenging endeavours for children and . . . can stimulate self-reliance, self-discipline, judgement, responsibility, relationships, and personal awareness. The acquisition of skills associated with journeying and exploring can also provide pupils with an environmental and ecological understanding of the outdoors.

Health education, citizenship and key skills

Education through Outdoor Education can lead to healthy and active lifestyles and develop positive personal and social qualities amongst young people. Well-taught leisure skills can also promote the moral, spiritual and cultural development of children and develop skilful body management techniques. Furthermore, Outdoor Education can promote creative and aesthetic experiences through movement, and provide competitive activities among individuals and groups based in challenging experiences in a variety of outdoor environments

All activities should be underpinned by the promotion of citizenship and key skills, achievable within the confines of a sports ground without the need to use off-site facilities. Through orienteering, leaders can promote the development of key skills whereby children can improve their own learning and performance, enhance their literacy and numeracy skills, and work with others to solve problems using communication skills.

Notions and principles of citizenship can be developed through Outdoor Education as it can promote communication skills (verbal and non-verbal); enhance interaction between pupils; build trust, co-operation and sharing; increase working relationships; develop leadership skills; encourage team work; allow joint decision-making and problem-solving; encourage individuals to work outside 'safe' friendship boundaries; and develop positive personal and social qualities. Outdoor Education can also potentially develop wider concepts and skills. In this context children can be encouraged to plan their own adventure activities and assess the types of problems they may encounter, using numerical skills, map reading techniques and scientific applications. Children can devise their own variations, develop their own original ideas, quite often devising more imaginative and taxing challenges than do adult leaders.

A developmental approach to teaching off-pitch activities

The focus of the activities is on the teaching and learning of citizenship and personal responsibility. This should involve children in a series of related activities including problem solving, physical challenges, team building, trust games, navigational exercises, orienteering activities, raft building and, if facilities permit, swimming and life-saving activities. A child-centred teaching approach through the processes of planning, performing and evaluating should be used to develop practical knowledge and understanding. This process-based approach focuses on learning from doing, ownership of learning and independent learning. Children's knowledge, skills and understanding of core skills and techniques should focus on children acquiring and developing skills, selecting and applying those skills and then evaluating and improving their own and others' performance. Through a developmental approach to teaching and learning the knowledge and understanding of fitness and health should permeate through every taught session so that children can monitor their own training, exercise and activity programmes.

Dr Gary Stidder, University of Brighton, 2005
Edited and excerpted by Alan Tomlinson, May 2017

Appendix C
Making the manuals

The following individuals have made contributions to the development of the F4P Coaching Manual, the manual for off-pitch activities, and to the adaptation of the original manual for use in other sports. UoB indicates University of Brighton; UJ indicates University of Johannesburg.

Coaching Manual for Football 4 Peace

John Lambert (UoB)
Dr. Gary Stidder (UoB)
Prof. John Sugden (UoB)
Dr. James Wallis (UoB)
Dr. Andy Theodoulides (UoB)
Joanna Gardiner (UoB) graduate
Joe Doherty (Irish FA)
Kevin Doherty (Irish FA)
Eli Fraktovnik (Israel Sports Authority)
Aunis Edris (Israel Sports Authority)
Dr. Jayne Caudwell (UoB); now Bournemouth University
Eamon Brennon (UoB) graduate
Nadine Brelstaff (UoB) graduate
Chris Howarth (UoB) graduate
Ghazi Nujeidat (Israel Sport Authority)

Off-pitch manual

Dr. Gary Stidder (UoB)
Graham Spacey (UoB)
Adrian Haasner (Deutsche Sporthochschule)

Rugby manual

Jessica Foster (UoB)
Graham Spacey (UoB)
Sion Hughes-Gage (Eastbourne Rugby Club)
George Ward (UoB) graduate

Neil Davies (UoB) graduate
Natalie Smith (UoB) graduate
Sean Torrance (UoB) graduate

South African manuals

Jack Sugden (Queen's University Belfast graduate); now Edge Hill University
Cassie Ogunniyi (UJ) graduate
Jurgen Rademan (UJ) graduate
Prof. Cora Burnett (UJ)
Prof. Charl Roux (UJ)

Appendix D

Testimonials on the Application and Impact of Football4Peace in Ireland, Israel and South Africa

On Israel

"Football4Peace has been a leading cross-community sports project in Israel recognised by the Ministry of Culture and Sport as their 'flagship project' in 2012. . . . There are many organisations bringing kids from different communities together by arranging sports activities. The difference in F4P is the methodology and manual of activities that leads to a positive outcome. These developments have been the direct result of the University of Brighton research. . . . the Brighton team instigated an approach which focused on values like respect and equality and led to a positive outcome, a change in the attitudes of participants, and a change in behaviour of the teams as a whole.

Football4Peace has also changed professional practices in Israel by bringing cross-community activities to the forefront and seeing an increase in allocation of budgets for such activities. The Israel Sports Authority (ISA) became official partners in F4P bringing in additional partner communities and increasing funding allocated to the project each year. F4P also captured the attention of the Ministry for Regional Cooperation as they aspire to forge partnerships and peaceful relations with Jordan and the Palestinian Territories and now see a well-designed sports programme as a vehicle for positive engagement with neighbours in the region.

In addition, the Brighton model of Football4Peace brought Child Protection issues to the forefront and . . . practices such as child protection training and police clearance for all coaches, became an integral part of the project. . . . The ISA F4P coordinator has become an advocate for child protection . . . now implementing child protection training and is a leader in changing child protection policies at the ISA. . . .

Engagement with the University of Brighton research team and the development of F4P has been a positive experience for the British Council and partner institutions in Israel which . . . left behind a sustainable model for continued cross-community sports activities in over 30 communities".

Jane Shurrush, Manager Nazareth,
British Council Israel, 22nd October 2013

On Ireland

i.

"Value Based Coaching is becoming a very important cornerstone of the IFA's new Football Development Department. I was honoured to be part of the Football 4 Peace team that went to Israel in 2005 and the experience opened my eyes up to the importance of the values of Inclusion, Trust, Respect and Responsibility. . . . my finest Grassroots Development Officers have participated in Football4Peace . . . embedding these values in their coaching reaching thousands of children throughout Northern Ireland.

I have added Value Based Coaching to the training menu for my Coaches. . . . Working in partnership with the University of Brighton's Football4Peace team we look forward to making value based coaching central to all we do in Football Development".

Michael Boyd, Director of Football Development,
Irish Football Association (Northern Ireland),
13th November 2013

ii.

"Brighton research on F4P has informed political debate in Ireland, concerning equality, peaceful co-existence and democratic participation. . . . Within the early phases of the Football4Peace programme in Ireland we have been funded by Peace 2 and the International Fund for Ireland. Without the Brighton-based links and international recognition of the credibility of the programme and model, we would not have been able to receive such strong support. We have been able, too, to influence the Peace 3 funding in Northern Ireland in sport, drama and the arts, as the then Chairperson, Senator Cecila Keaveny, attended several of the events and was able to see the potential for its wider adoption in the community. In the more recent stages of the Ireland project, advised by Professor John Sugden, we have gained access to networks of school and governing bodies, establishing and reaffirming partnerships to make plans for the programme to be fully sustainable in Ireland".

Damien McColgan, Project Manager,
Football4Peace Ireland, October 28th 2013

On South Africa

Collaboration with F4P has resulted in "developing two 'Life Skill Manuals' – one for primary school and one for secondary school . . . based on the F4P methodology with the utilization of indigenous games from

South Africa (primary school) and sports (secondary school) as the activity bases. Not only is this very novel, but these manuals will serve to educate students (during recreation camps) and in formal coursework of Life Orientation/Physical Education training (about 200 students) to implement in schools and recreation centres. The manuals will also be made available to 52 members of the Nike Sport for Social Change Network in Southern Africa, working in impoverished communities... Having worked with Prof John Sugden... contributing meaningfully to the existing body of knowledge [on sport-for-development and peace]... [it was confirmed that the] holistic and educational approach within the [F4P] methodology resonated with our Life Orientation Curriculum (Grades 10-12, the last three school years or FET). It has been integrated in the coursework and was particularly timely as South African schools are newly implementing material for teachers' training and school implementation".

Professor Cora Burnett and Professor Kobus Roux,
University of Johannesburg, Department of Sport and
Human Movement Science, 16th October 2013

Compiled by Professor Alan Tomlinson, June 21st 2017

Appendix E

Excerpts from "Life Skills", the South Africa Coaching Manual

LIFE GAMES

Value-based Life Skills Training
through Physical Activity for Youth

Secondary School

UNIVERSITY
OF
JOHANNESBURG

THE DEPARTMENT OF SPORT AND MOVEMENT STUDIES
UNIVERSITY OF JOHANNESBURG

©This draft copy of *Life Games* is copyright protected by the University of Johannesburg.

The Department of Sport and Movement Studies at the University of Johannesburg produced the "Life Games" manual for youth, and the "Play Life" manual for children, thereby straddling the primary and secondary sectors of the South African education system in a revitalization of the physical education curriculum. Here we reproduce, with the permission of the University of Johannesburg, the opening pages and the introductory overview of the "Life Games" edition.

1 Introduction

1.1 Overview

We are glad you are joining us to explore life skills and values through physical activities with youth of secondary school age. This adventure will use a variety of indigenous games, activities and modified sports to touch on twelve key values that are considered important in a youth's life.

Throughout the past century, physical education has had its ups and downs. There have been periods of growth and innovation and also of confusion and stagnation. Physical education has a unique, but not exclusive, role to play in the education of youth to enhance a holistic well-being. The focus should be not only to teach them a wide variety of motor skills, but also equip them for meaningful and successful living in a rapidly changing and transforming society.

Since the inception of outcomes-based education, physical education was phased out in the majority of the government schools. Hence the South African youth are increasingly becoming more inactive, with many illnesses such as obesity and diabetes emerging.

Contemporary education should focus on assisting learners in reaching their full potential. Due to South African schools changing to a multicultural establishment, and hence a heterogeneous society, they are more racially and culturally diverse than ever. With the inclusion of indigenous games, these manuals provide a meaningful approach for education to promote all developmental domains from a variety of familiar games and activities. These manuals can also develop a sense of community in the heterogeneous society and therefore demonstrate and provide acceptable values contributing not only to the cognitive, affective and psychomotor development of the individual, but also to the social domain contributing towards nation building. These manuals could also be utilized for the teaching of moral values in other settings such as church group, recreational facilities for facilitating social interaction, cultural sharing and team building.

Process

This manual was inspired by international and national innovative work in the NGO, private and public sectors. It was developed in a collaborative process under the guidance of the Department of Sport and Movement Studies from the University of Johannesburg, with the assistance of consultant Jack Sugden from the United Kingdom. Jack's prior experience as a youth leader, trainer and manual developer with the organization Football for Peace in Israel, Northern Ireland and Britain provided deep insight into the practical workings of how sports sessions should be designed to illicit candid discussions around important values. International journal articles related to life skills programs were used to develop a framework of values to work from. Other contributors from the University of Johannesburg included Prof Cora Burnett, Prof Charl J. Roux, Ms. Cassie Ogunniyi and Pastor Jurgen Rademan.

The indigenous games were selected from a more comprehensive indigenous games manual that was compiled utilizing research conducted throughout South Africa.

Early in the development of the manual focus group sessions with youth leaders from Altus Sport gave insight into the South African context and what activities and approaches were more effective in the locations around South Africa, as well as where the needs were greatest in the NGO sector. The Altus Sport Focus Group also assisted in highlighting the important values to be focused on. Sessions were piloted at the Orlando Children's Home in Soweto as well as at the Nike/Grassroot Soccer AIDS Day Event and feedback was incorporated into the design of the manual.

Manual layout

Like any resource, the end product is only as good as the people who are using it. This manual is meant as a guide to set you on a path in the right direction. The life skills are based on a holistic approach that follows value sets from trust and self-belief to decision making and leadership. In the following pages it will provide a more detailed overview of how the manual is set-up, keys to running an effective session, summaries of the key values, a detailed outline of the 30 sessions, followed by a set of annexures that include the more complete sets of rules and skills for the games used in the manual.

This manual is meant to be interactive and feedback on any new ideas that you have to improve the individual lessons or the overall structure of the program is appreciated. At the end of each session there is space to make notes on what worked and what can be improved for the next time you do the session. At various times during the program, it is advisable to conduct assessments and evaluations, both on what the participants are learning, as well as how the program is being run and received overall. We trust as we take this adventure together we will all learn something new and become better citizens able to give back to the community around us!

1.2 Session structure and content

All sessions and individual games are adaptable depending on the environment and context in which it takes place. The structure of the games and the timing of each section should only be used as a guide not to be followed to the letter. Throughout the sessions there is a progression of values starting with a more personal focus and finishing with a focus on leadership. The questions and 'Teachable moments' are designed to help link the games and activities with the value for the session and ensure transferability from the playing field to everyday life situations. Below is a general guide to how each session should be delivered. Each session should take anywhere between 1 – 1.5 hours and is divided into four sections: 'the introduction/warm up', 'the first game/technical phase', 'game 2' and 'the cool down'.

Each session description begins with an outline of the purpose of the session, the number of participants, the equipment needed and an approximate size of the playing area needed. The equipment needed can be adjusted according to the availability of equipment, number of participants. Games can also be adjusted according to the amount of equipment available. If store bought equipment is not available, recycled/found/home-made materials can also be used for the same results.

Introduction/Warm up – 10 minutes

- Greet your group enthusiastically/ playfully and depending on your goals for that session, either briefly outline the value(s) you will be working on to get them thinking about it and/or go straight into the introductory/warm up exercise.
- It is often the case that the children will arrive excited and full of energy so it is often useful to quickly greet them, go straight into the warm up and have a short discussion after the warm up.
- The warm up should be vigorous and short.
- When introducing a new game, make sure that you describe: a) what game will be played and b) how the game will be played.

Technical Phase – 15–20 minutes

- Consists of technical or practice games as participants are encouraged to work together to conquer a new skill, task or to solve a problem.
- Each game is designed to bring out certain values, these will be listed at the beginning of each session, and the coach should observe and remember what takes place to reflect on immediately or later on in the cool down phase.

Game Phase – 15–20 minutes

- This section is normally the longest and gives the children the chance to play! In this section a certain level of responsibility and independence is handed over to the participants as they take part in the game.
- Again the coach must observe and remember any behaviour for reflection later on, however he/she must allow the game to progress so any stoppages must be brief and to the point.

Cool Down/Reflection – 10 minutes

- The most important part of the session, the cool down should be about looking at the behaviour of the participants in relation to the values and then talking about these skills in relation to real life outside of a sporting context.
- The coach should guide the discussion and spend as little time talking as possible, allowing all the children time and space to talk and share their experiences.

Guide to reflection:

A short guide on how to facilitate the discussion linking experiences to values and real-life lessons:

- Begin by reflecting on self-experience of the participant: Ask 'Tell me about the game you played, was it easy/hard/fun?
- Then ask them how they felt during the game for example: How did you feel when you scored? Or stepped forward to bat on your own?
- Then you can ask about 'teachable moments' asking if they saw any good/poor examples of fair play, belief, courage, respect etc. Reinforce good suggestions with a high five or praise for speaking up.
- Discuss how the 'teachable moments' can relate to everyday life. For example: If a player was scared to step forward and bat but eventually overcame that fear and gave it a try, you can relate this to the importance of self-belief and courage which is important if you are to succeed in difficult situations.
- The coach should ensure that this discussion takes place in a relaxed and friendly environment so that the children feel comfortable discussing what could be a sensitive issue affecting them or their community. Feel free to break into smaller groups for these discussions.

Above is only a guide however, a coach should be adaptable and facilitate the discussion however he/she sees fit according to the environment in which it takes place.

1.3 Teachable moments

'Teachable moments' refer to those incidents and events that happen during the flow of the sessions that a coach may seize upon to illustrate the main points which they are trying to get across to the children. These should be highlighted and related to the core values.

For example, in a practice dedicated to 'throwing and catching' a coach may see a child who has mastered the technique, turn to a child who has not mastered the technique, to offer help and advice. The coach can then stop the practice and ask the child to show how they helped out their friend. This will assist in coaching the skill but will also allow the coach the chance to point out and praise a good example of positive behaviour such as responsibility reinforced with group applause. Alternatively the coach can let the session flow and bring up the teachable moment during a short discussion at a natural break in the session.

Positive examples of behaviour are often most powerful, however negative examples can also be useful. For instance, if there is violence during a game. Once the situation is diffused you can return to it later and ask the culprit(s) questions such as was that a useful way to deal with the problem? After you shook hands did it help? You can then open it up to a group discussion about experiences with violence and possible solutions and ways of avoiding violent situations. Once you have identified and discussed 'Teachable moments' (TMs) in the first one or two sessions you should encourage the participants to point out TMs for themselves, if they haven't already.

Most activities in the session plans are designed to bring about 'Teachable moments' and there are reference notes in each plan as to what values may be developed in each practice/game. You can then anticipate how players may react and/or take note of positive and negative behaviours to be discussed during the cool down. For example: if you have given the children the responsibility to referee their own game then conflict and indecision is likely to occur, followed by the realisation that some compromise and cooperation will have to take place. During this scenario the coach must not only take note of their behaviour but allow it to take place so it can be referred back to later.

1.4 The coach/facilitator

A key part of the method is the ability of the coach/facilitator to run the sessions effectively. A session is only as good as the person who is running it. He/she needs the confidence to use guided discovery in order to create opportunities for behaviour to take place which the group as a whole can learn from. Aside from all the regular attributes you would expect from a coach/facilitator such as organisation, clarity, care, responsibility, leadership etc. A coach/facilitator in these circumstances should be able to adequately carry out the following:

Facilitate – They should be able to plan and organise a well-structured session which flows well and creates a positive environment in which 'TMs' can take place.

Anticipate – They should anticipate what kinds of behaviours and issues are likely to arise during the session and be able to adjust the environment accordingly in order to maintain control.

Observe – This is key, as the coach/facilitator should allow behaviour to take place in order to see how the participants react to each situation.

Remember – The coach/facilitator should remember what they have seen, often several examples of good and bad behaviour should be remembered for discussion.

Reflect – Following the session the coach/facilitator should *always* allow adequate time for reflection on what has taken place. This is often the most important aspect of the session and should be managed correctly. The coach/facilitator should join the participants at their level, sitting in a circle in the shade for example, and talk in a relaxed manner about what has taken place and what can be learnt from the behaviour to make the participants feel more comfortable and reduce the power dynamics with being in a higher position physically.

Allowing the children the opportunity to talk is essential, ideally it should be them discussing with the coach/facilitator playing a passive role in steering the discussion in the right direction.

1.5 Session planning and organisation

Each session should be carefully planned and memorized prior to delivery. If you are unable to remember, then you can write a short version of the plan down and keep it handy to be glanced at during an activity.

Almost all of the sessions are designed to take place within a grid which varies in size according to the number and age of the participants. This grid should always be arranged carefully bearing in mind what games are to be played and how it will need to be adjusted.

> E.g. If you know that the end of your session will conclude in an game requiring an 'end zone' your grid should be set up at the beginning as normal, but with extra cones place so that the area can be transformed quickly.

Before: After:

Place extra cones at these two points

Planning ahead in this respect ensures that the session runs smoothly, making the most out of the time so that the children get the most out of the session.

John Sugden and Alan Tomlinson are grateful to the University of Johannesbug for permission to use these extracts from the *Life Skills* coaching manual (pp. i–ix in the original).

Index

Authors' note: This index covers the foreword, all of the chapters and their accompanying notes and references. We have not, though, indexed the numerous works of our own that have been cited within the book, and these can be located within the 'Notes' following each chapter.

Adair, Daryl 133n2
Adams, Gerry 27
Adams, Iain 108n18
Adar, S. 61n17
Adidas 104
Admirals All 97
Adorno, Theodor 127, 128
Africa, scramble for 12n7
African National Congress (ANC) 65, 81, 85
Alabarces, Pablo 14n21
Ali, Mohammed 105
Allison, Lincoln 88n1, 109n26, 110n35
Allport, Gordon 21, 31n5
Al Qaeda 98
Alt, John 118, 122n24, 133n8
AMANDLA 82, 84
Angus, Ian 110n29
Archer, Robert 88n1
Aristophanes 107, 112n48
Armour, Kathy M. 61n28
Asian Football Confederation (AFC) 40
Asmal, Kader 24
Astle, Richard 132
Ateek, Naim 58, 63n47

Bacher, Ali 69
Bairner, Alan 24, 31n8, 59n2, 109n18, 133n6
Balfour, Arthur James 60n6
Balfour Declaration of 1917 37
Banda, Davies 111n41
Ban Ki-Moon 82
Baskin, Gershin 62n41

Bass, Orli 90n21
Bateman, Jane 134n16
Becker, Howard 118, 122n21
Bedford, David 34, 44
Ben-Porat, Amir 40, 60–61n11, 61n14
Ben-Porat, Guy 61n14
Bethlehem, F4P programme in 53–56
Beyond Sport World 104
Birds, The 107
Black, David R. 89n16
Black September, 1972 97–98
Blatter, Sepp ix, x, 82, 89n19
Bloch, Ernst 128–129, 133n10, 133n13
Boer War 97
Bolsmann, Chris 90n26
Bonaparte, Napoleon 97
Booth, Douglas 88n1
Boxing and Society 9
Bouillon, Antoine 88n1
Boyd, Michael 29
Boykoff, Jules 110n31
Brennan, Deidre 29, 32n12
Brewer, John 114, 120n4, 120n6
British Empire 6–7, 38
British Sociological Association (BSA) Study Group 10, 13n17
Brohm, Jean-Marie 133n6
Brook, Norman 84, 86
Brown, Malcolm 108n17
Burke, Edmund 57
Burnett, Cora 59, 68–69, 81, 87, 89n9
Buttery, Jim 63n49
Bush, George W. 98

C. Wright Mills and the End of Violence 114
camaraderie 20
Campbell, Chris 83
Cantelon, Hart 10, 13n16, 14n19
Carter, Thomas F. 108n9
Caudwell, Jayne xi, 61n25
Chapman, Tony 111n41
Chataway, Christopher 110n32
Chicago School 17, 30n1
Christmas Day armistice, 1914 95–96, 108–109n18, 109n19, 109n20
Class, Sports and Social Development 11, 127
Coaching for Hope 84, 87, 104
Coakley, Jay 111n39
Coalter, Fred 103, 113, 120n2
Cohen, Greta L. 107n3
Cold War, the 93–94, 99, 120
Conibear, Tim 84
Coopoo, Yogo 68, 72, 89n6
Cornelissen, Scarlett 78, 90n26, 90n28
Corporate Social Responsibility (CSR) 104
Cottle, Eddie 73, 90n22
critical pragmatism, epistemology of 113–116
critical pro-activism 123, 125–126; peace-building and 126–129
critical sociology 124–125
Cry, the Beloved Country 5
Cuba 93–94
Curle, Adam 116, 121n15

Dalton, Eric 73–74, 90n24
Damon, Matt 66–67
Danjani, Munther 62n41
Darnell, Simon 103, 108n9, 111n41
Dart, Jon 42, 61n21
Davidson, Jimmy 25
Davies, Glynn 73, 90n22
de Coning, Christo 90n29
Derby County Football Club 132
Desai, Ashwin 64, 69, 75, 78, 88n2, 89n10
Dewey, John 115, 121n9
diasporas, Israeli and Palestinian 38–39
Dickens, Charles 5
Domoslawski, Artur 109n21
Donnelly, Peter 10, 13n18, 14n21
Downes, David 121n13
Dowty, Alan 38, 60n7
Doyle, Dan 30–31n3, 107n6

Doyle, John 129, 133n14
Dugan, Máire 116, 121n16
Dundee, Sean 70
Dunn, Seamus 31n9
Dunning, Eric 3, 12n3, 101–102, 11n38, 11n39
Durkheim, Emile 115

Eastwood, Clint 66
Economist, The 69
Edwards, Harry 8, 13n13
Eini, Ofer 42
Eksteins, Modris 109n20
Elias, Norbert 101–102, 111n37, 111n38
Elizabeth, Queen 27, 28
Elfrat, Elisha 62n33, 62n37
Elon, Amos 61n23
epistemology of critical pragmatism 113–116
Eszterhas, Joe 110n31

Fascism 38
Fédération International de Football Association (FIFA): ix–x, xiii, 33, 104; in Israel 40–42, 101; in South Africa 70–74, 76–77, 82, 89n17
Fenucane, Senan 28
FIFA: The Men, the Myths and the Money 3
FIFA and the Contest for World Football 65
Fish, Mark 71
Fitzgerald, Taoiseach Garret 27
Football 4 Peace (F4P) programme 29, 30, 34–35, 42–49, 58–59, 113, 120, 125–126; in Bethlehem 53–56; coaching experience 45, 46; coaching manual 136–146; complexities and challenges in implementing 49–53; edited extracts from off-pitch activity programme for conflict-prevention and peaceful co-existence 147–148; first project 43–44; international training camp 48–49; in Jerusalem 49–53; making the manuals for 149–150; materials underpinning 135; normalisation and 56–58; objectives 42–43; off-pitch activities 46–47; REF Impact Case Study 59n3; ripple effect and 129–132; second project 44; testimonials on application and impact of 151–153;

values-based training curriculum 44–48; *see also* Israel
Frankfurt School 127, 128
Freeman, Morgan 66
Freire, Paulo 116, 121n15

Galeano, Eduardo 95, 108n14
Galily, Yair 61n20
Galtung, Johan 117, 121n18
George, Mululeki 70
Gerth, Hans Heinrich 115, 120–121n8
Giulianotti, Richard 103, 111n41
Gilchrist, Paul xin3
Goffman, Erving ix, xin5
Goldblatt, David 110n31
Goodhart, Philip 110n32
Gore, Al 101
Gowdy, Brian 93, 107n4, 107n5
Grassroots Soccer 82
Gratton, Chris 121n11
Gruneau, Richard 10, 11, 13–14n19, 14n20, 88n1, 127, 133n9
Guelke, Adrian 88n1

Hahn, Kurt 47
Hargreaves, Jennifer 13n17
Hargreaves, John 13n17
Harris, H.A. 60n8
Harvey, Jean 14n19
Harvie, Scott 26, 31n10
Hassner, Adrian 47, 62n31
Havelange, João 101, 102
Hayhurst, Lyndsay 111n41
Hendricks, Denver 68, 69, 78, 79–80, 89n7, 89n11
Henley, William Ernest 67
Herzl, Theodor 36, 59n4
Hills, David 89n17
Hogan, Michael 28
Hollands, Robert 13n16
Holocaust, the 38
Holt, Richard 13n11
Houlihan, Barrie 31–32n11
Horne, John 13n17, 90n26
Howard, Dick 133n12
human rights and social justice 118–119
Huish, Robert 108n9

Infantino, Gianni 42
International Cricket Council (ICC) 66
international non-governmental organisations (INGOs) 81–85, 105
Invictus 66

ISIQUALO 83–84
Islanders, The 97
Israel 33–35, 58–59, 101; Bethlehem 53–56; complexities and challenges in implementing the F4P model 49–53; conflict between Palestine and 35–39; Israeli Defense Forces (IDF) 49–50, 52–54; Jerusalem 49–53; normalisation and F4P programme in 56–58; sport and football in 39–42; *see also* Football 4 Peace (F4P) programme
Israeli Defense Forces (IDF) 49–50, 52–54
Israeli Football Association (IFA) 41

Jackson, H. C. 7
James, C. L. R. 11
James, William 115, 121n9
Jarvie, Grant 88n1
Jary, David 13n17
Jeanes, Ruth 111n41
Jennings, Matt 31n6
Jerusalem, F4P programme in 49–53
Jerusalem Foundation (JF) 50–52
Johnson, Pat 43
Ian Jones 121n11
Jones, Richard 90n26
Juantorena, Alberto 93–94, 107n7
Juvenal vi, xin2

Kadlec, Alison 115, 121n12
Kalberg, Stephen 111n44
Kanin, David 94, 108n11
Kantianism 119
Kaufman, Neilsen N. 89n13
Kapuściński, Ryszard 96, 109n21
Kay, Tess 111n41
Keim, Marion 90n29
Kelly, John 133n6
Kelly, Maura 30
Kelso, Paul 89n17
Khor Taggart 5
Kidd, Bruce 102–103, 111n40
King, Samantha 109n27
Kipling, Rudyard 97, 109n26
Klare, Karl E. 133n12
Koemen, Katrin 63n48
Kollek, Teddy 51
Krotee, March L. 88n1

Lambert, John 34, 45, 59n3, 61–62n29
Lange, Vize-Feldwebel 96

Lashua, Brett 120n3
Laureus Foundation 100–101, 104, 110n33
Lawrence, T. E. 37, 59–60n5
Lea, John 121n13
Lederach, John Paul 116, 117, 123–124, 121n17
Lee, Jung Woo 133n6
Leisure Studies Association (LSA) 10, 13n15
Levermore, Roger 103, 111n41
Lewis, Eddie 70, 89n13
Lidor, Ronnie 63n48
Lindsey, Ian 111n41
Longford, Elizabeth 109n22, 109n23, 109n24
Lukács, George 127, 128
Lyras, Alex 30n2

Mac Brádaigh, Caoimhín 19
Macintyre, Donald 61n17
Maidement, Paul 16
Magee, Jonathan 109n18
Malcolm, Dominic 1, 12, 113
Mandela, Nelson 64–67, 71, 72, 75, 78, 85–87, 91n42, 100–101, 105, 110n33
Mangan, J. A. 6, 12–13n8
Mann, Michael 134n17
Manzenreiter, Wolfram 90n26
Marcotti, Gabriele 61n19
Marcuse, Herbert 127
Markgraaff, André 70
Marqsee, Mike 110n32
Marx, Karl 115
Marxism 9, 114, 115–116, 127–128
Mbeki, Thabo 24, 65, 81, 91n33
McCartan, Eamonn 28, 108n9
McKay, Jim 14n21, 121n11
McColgan, Damien 29
McCrum, Robert vii, xin4
McDonald, Ian 116, 118, 121n14, 122n22
McGuinness, Martin 27, 28
McGuire, Mike 121n13
McIntyre, Thomas D. 108n9
McLaughlin, Judith 31n5
Mead, George Herbert ix, xin5
Melnick, Merrill J. 108n9
Miller, Toby 107, 112n47
Mills, Lucy 84, 91n40
Mkhonto, Thokozil "Kelly" 80–81, 91n32

Montefiore, Simon Sebag 62n32
Montville, Leigh 95, 108n16
Mooney, Tom 107n6
Morgan, Liam 61n22
Morgan, Rod 121n13
Moynihan, Dave 28
Mulvaney, Katie 107n6

Nabbi, Zayn 69, 89n10
Naish, Jacob 103, 104, 111n42, 133n6
Nauright, John 88n1, 89n16
Nazism 38, 99
Nematandani, Kirsten 71, 89n17
neo-Marxism 127–128
Neubeck, Ken 9
Nevo, Baruch 132n2
Newbolt, Henry 97, 109n26
New Israel Fund (NIF) 41, 61n15
Nike 104
non-governmental organisations (NGOs) in South Africa 81–85, 104, 105
Northern Ireland 15–17, 26–30, 33, 92–93; Community Relations Council (CRC) 21, 26; as a living laboratory 17–24; peace process in 127; theory, practice and intervention and their influence on policy community for sport in 24–26; Troubles in 15–16, 17–18, 21
Ntini, Makhaya 67
Nye, Joseph S. 13n10

Oceania (Australasia and the South Pacific) Football Confederation (OFC) 40
Odendaal, André 88n1
Oliver Twist 5
Olympic Games, Munich, 1972 97–98
Orwell, George 11, 98–99, 101, 102, 109–110n29
Orwell, Sonia 110n29
Oslo Accord 43, 53

Paisley, Ian 27
Palestine and Israel, conflict between 35–39, 101; *see also* Football 4 Peace (F4P) programme; Israel
Paton, Alan 5
Peace and Understanding through Sport 93, 106
peace-building: critical pro-activism and 126–129; theory and method for 116–118

Peace Process 119–120
Pell, Claiborne 94, 100, 102
Perkin, Harold 13n11
Peters, Mary 93
Petney, Trevor 108n18
Pienaar, François 65, 67
Pietersen, Kevin 68
Pillay, Udash 90n21
Pino, Angel 94
Poliakoff, Michael B. 108n13
Power Games: A Critical Sociology of Sport 11, 124
Principle of Hope, The 128
Puijk, Roel 108n16

Quinn, Peter 25

Rajoub, Jibril 55
Ramsamy, Sam 62n42
Ratna, Aarti 120n3
Rausing, Sigrid 109n21
Reid, Heather 108n15
Reiner, Robert 121n13
Reinhart, Tanya 62n40
Riordan, Jim 24
ripple effect 4, 123, 129–132
rituals 117
Rock, Paul 121n13
Rogge, Jacques 55
Roux, Kobus 87
Rudolf, Eric Robert 98
Runciman, W.G. 111n44

Sacks, Oliver x, xin8
Said, Edward 58, 61n24, 63n46
Saladin of Egypt 36
Salomon, Gavriel 123, 132n2
Sampson, Anthony 89n5
Schirch, Lisa 117, 121n19, 122n20
Schulenkorf, Nico 133n2
Schuurman, Frans 112n45
Scott, Jack 8, 13n13
Schneider, Karl Heinz 63n48
SDP *see* Sport for Development and Peace (SDP)
Seaton, Shirley 108n17
September 11, 2001, terrorist attacks 98
Sharon, Ariel 41, 43, 54
Shaw, Martin 122n25
Sidzumo, Lunga 82, 91n37
Sinn Fein 27, 28
Skykes-Picto Agreement of 1916 37
Smith, David 89n4

Soccer War, The 96
social justice and human rights 118–119
Sociology of Sport Journal 10
Sorek, Tamir 60n10
South Africa 56–57, 59, 64–65, 85–88, 107; elite and professional sport in 66–76; "Life Skills" coaching manual 154–161; National Sport Plan 78–79; NGO initiatives in 81–85; peace process in 127; as Rainbow Nation 64–65, 85; state interests and governmental and education issues in 76–81; state of sport in 65–66
Soviet Union, the 95, 99
Spacey, Graham 12n2, 62n30, 63n49, 133n5
Sport, Sectarianism, and Society in a Divided Ireland 25
Sport and the Sociological Imagination 10
Sport Evangelism 100–102
Sport for Development and Peace (SDP) 1–4; debate over efficacy of 93–100; epistemology of critical pragmatism and 113–116; in Israel 33–59; literature of 97; NGO initiatives and 81–85, 104, 105; in Northern Ireland 15–30; paradigm for progress in 119–120; ripple effect and 123, 129–132; in South Africa 64–88; Sport Evangelism and 100–102; theory and method for peace-building and 116–118; war and 95–97
Sport in Divided Societies 33–34
"Sporting Spirit, The" 98–99
Sports Illustrated (SI) 92, 95
"Sports Saves the World" 92
Sport the Healer 25
Spuren (Traces) 128
Stead, Marcus 89n8
Stidder, Gary 34, 43, 45–46, 47, 62n31
Stone, Michael 19
Streetfootballworld 84, 104
Sudan 4–8
Sugden, John 1–2, 4, 94
Swart, Camilla 90n25

Thatcher, Margaret 27
The FA (The Football Association, England) 41, 61n16
Theberge, Nancy 10, 13n18
Theodoulides, Andy 34, 45, 61n28, 61n34

Thoughts on the Cause of the Present Discontents 57
Tamir, Ilan 61n20
Taylor, E. 61n13, 61n18
Taylor, Ian 121n13
Telfer, Hamish 61n29
Tinkler, Eric 71
Tomlinson, Alan ix, 3, 10, 11, 33
Tomlinson, Richard 90n21
Trump, Donald 42
Tshwete, Steve 77
Tutu, Desmond 91n42
Two Tribes Go to War 25

Ulster *see* Northern Ireland
United Nations Charter for Human Rights 118
utopianism 128

Vahed, Goolam 69–70, 89n13
van den Anker, Christian 122n25
Van Der Spuy, Bernardus 77–79
Van der Valt, Kobus 91n31
Varshaviak, Zivi 55
Vetch, Colin 109n20
Vitai Lampada (They Pass On The Torch of Life) 97
Voysey, Karl 83, 91n38

Wallis, James 34
Walt, Kobus van der 79
war and sport 95–97
Ward, Ian 7–8
war on terror 98
Weber, Max 63n45, 111n44, 115, 134n18
Wellesley, Arthur (Duke of Wellington) 97, 109n22, 109n23, 109n24
Whannel, 62n42
Whitehead, Jean 61n29
Whitfield, Geoffrey 33–34, 43, 44, 61n26
Wilde, Oscar 5
Williams, Chester 67
Wolff, Alexander 92, 95, 107n1
Woman of No Importance, A 5
Woodham, Jonathan 108n11
World Sports Peace Project (WSPP) 34, 43
Wright Mills, C. 1, 9–11, 12n1, 17, 106, 112n46, 114–115, 120–121n8, 124, 128

Yiannakis, Andrew 8, 108n9
Young, Jock 121n13

Zionism 36, 51
Zwanziger, Theo 50

Lightning Source UK Ltd.
Milton Keynes UK
UKHW022012190321
380673UK00004B/61